BrandSimple

BrandSimple

How the Best Brands Keep it Simple and Succeed

Allen P. Adamson

BRANDSIMPLE
Copyright © Allen P. Adamson, 2006.

First published in hardcover in 2006
PALGRAVE MACMILLAN™
175 Fifth Avenue, New York, N.Y. 10010 and
Houndmills, Basingstoke, Hampshire, England RG21 6XS.
Companies and representatives throughout the world.

PALGRAVE MACMILLAN is the global academic imprint of the Palgrave Macmillan division of St. Martin's Press, LLC and of Palgrave Macmillan Ltd. Macmillan® is a registered trademark in the United States, United Kingdom and other countries. Palgrave is a registered trademark in the European Union and other countries.

ISBN-13: 978-1-4039-8490-6 paperback
ISBN-10: 1-4039-8490-5 paperback

Library of Congress Cataloging-in-Publication Data
Adamson, Allen.
    Brandsimple : how the best brands keep it simple and succeed / Allen Adamson.
       p. cm.
    ISBN 1-4039-7405-5
    1. Brand name products—Philosophy. 2. Brand name products—Planning. 3. Business names—Philosophy. I. Title.
HD69.B7A24 2006
658.8'27—dc22

                                                                    2006043154

A catalogue record of the book is available from the British Library.

Design by Letra Libre, Inc.

First PALGRAVE MACMILLAN paperback edition: August 2007
10   9   8
Printed in the United States of America.

Contents

I would like to gratefully acknowledge my colleague, Betsy Karp, for her steadfast assistance in researching, writing, and editing this book. She kept me on topic and on schedule.

Acknowledgments

As with any endeavor of this sort, there are a great many people I would like to acknowledge and thank.

First, I'd like to thank Craig Branigan, Landor's chairman, for giving me the freedom, flexibility, and support to write this book.

I would also like to extend thanks to my colleagues and friends in Landor's offices worldwide for their encouragement and willingness to share their invaluable learning experiences. Their insights helped shape many of the concepts found within the book.

In addition, thanks to my Landor team in New York, including Mich Bergensen, Richard Brandt, Joan Bogin, Hayes Roth, Richard Ford, Ken Runkel, and Diane Ashley, who served as an objective sounding board, helping me broaden—or refine—my ideas.

I would like to offer both thanks and gratitude to my incredibly patient and persistent support team, Kristin James and Leonie Derry, who cheerfully undertook the seemingly impossible task of keeping me organized and coordinating the countless interviews and calls. A thank you, too, goes to Chuck Routhier, Lee Aldridge, and Sean King, for their collective design talents in marshalling the cover and exhibit designs.

As I mention in the book, one of the most gratifying and enjoyable aspects of writing *BrandSimple* was the opportunity it gave me to reconnect with current and former clients, colleagues, mentors, and friends. Without the contribution of their personal experiences, wisdom, and insight, this book would not have been possible. The following people graciously shared their time and expertise: Cindy Alston, Douglas Atkin, Matt Baressi, Julia Beardwood, Toni Belloni,

Jed Bernstein, Jim Blazer, Roy Bostock, Gary Briggs, Stacie Bright, Paul Burke, Michael Capiraso, Tom Carey, Clive Chajet, Gayle Christensen, Michael Colacino, Beth Comstock, Nick Copping, Leslie Crombie, Duncan Daines, Richard Edelman, Mark Fields, David Fowler, Belle Frank, Amy Frankel, Tom Friedman, Steve Gardner, Peter Georgescu, Cheryl Giovannoni, Jerry Grossman, Jane Gundell, Matt Harrington, Edgar Huber, Giovanna Imperia, Chuck Jayson, Paul Kalbfleish, Patrice Kavanaugh, Peter Kaye, Elyse Kazarinoff, Kevin Keller, Eric Kessler, David Knight, Abby Kohnstamm, Gary Kusumi, Larry Lubin, Sue Manber, Mark McNeilly, Bob Michaels, Tom Murano, Priscilla Natkins, Martha Nelson, Susan Nelson, Stewart Owen, Michael Patti, Bob Pittman, Joel Portugal, Martin Puris, Lulu Raghaven, Courtney Reeser, Buzz Richmond, Rob Rush, Ken Roman, Andrew Salzman, Lisa Sepulveda, George Sine, Bill Smith, Amy Stanton, Peter Stringham, Kay Stout, David Suliteanu, Sidney Swartz, Marshall Toplanski, Rashmi Turner, Carin van Vuuren, Trevor Wade, and Andrew Welch.

Finally, and without question, most important, I thank my wife, Madelyn, and our children, Josh and Elissa, for putting up with my constant conference calls, weekends and evenings at the computer, and dad talking about branding 24/7. I love you more than words can ever express.

Foreword, *Sir Martin Sorrell*

At some point early in my childhood my grandmother slipped me a Kit Kat bar and confided to me, as if it were a well-kept family secret, that it was a biscuit and a candy bar all in one. She then removed the now-familiar red and white wrapping and, advising me to watch carefully, demonstrated the real magic of this delightful confection. Each finger could be "snapped" off one at a time and savored individually, something I found truly amazing.

Today the Kit Kat bar is manufactured for markets all over the world in a multitude of flavors. Although the world has changed, and as much as chocolate manufacturing technology has changed, one important thing hasn't. Kit Kat is still known as the chocolate treat that can be "snapped" apart, one delicious wafer section at a time.

You may be wondering why I am telling you a story about my affinity for chocolate. I'm not actually. I'm telling you about my affinity and respect for brands that succeed—brands that demonstrate a remarkable difference in the marketplace and remain strong. Why do I keep buying Kit Kats when I could just as easily buy a Hershey bar? Today, brands have a tough battle to wage against those that have found a comfortable place in our heads. While it's doubtful a new brand will ever completely replace my preference for a tried and true one, if a brand can demonstrate to me that it will make a worthwhile difference in my life then I owe it to myself to give the brand a go. If, after trying it, the brand proves its difference to me, I may consider rearranging my beliefs about my current brand preferences.

How does a brand replace a trusted one? How does an old brand reposition itself to try and recapture our attention? Beyond the recommendations given to us by beloved and trusted family members and friends, it seems rather mysterious how certain brands push their way into our consciousness. Actually, it's not all that mysterious. And that's where this book comes in.

For more than twenty years, Allen Adamson has defined, nurtured, and launched powerful brands and re-launched existing brands through inspired branding. (Read the first chapter of this book and you'll learn the important distinction between these two terms.) He's worked on the agency side, at advertising and branding firms, and on what is known as the client side, for companies known for producing the world's leading brands. Allen will be the first to admit that he's been involved in brand launches that have caught on like wildfire, and others that have fizzled. All of these experiences have added to his impressive knowledge of what it takes to make a brand stand out in the world's increasingly crowded marketplace.

If you're wondering what it takes, a glance at this book's title will give you a clue. It's something simple. Allen suggests that the truth goes back to what made my favorite brand of chocolate such a hit with my grandmother. He refutes the idea that there's a secret to why certain brands succeed and others don't. His premise (which I wholly support) is that the most powerful brands stand for something different and relevant, of course. But more important, that what makes these brands different and relevant is made simple for us to understand.

Why is this important? Allen explains that there are two essential reasons brands based on simple ideas succeed. First, we live in an information-rich world. Make something too complicated to understand and we'll turn off the receptors. Second, he makes it clear that becoming a dominant brand in the market is no longer a matter of pumping more dollars into the advertising budget. Brand management has become the responsibility of everyone in an organization, from the people making the products, to the ones doing the packaging, to those tracking the shipments, to those who oversee the customer calls and the websites. An idea must be a simple one if there's any chance of achieving organizational understanding, acceptance, and implementation.

Allen starts with the basics, explaining the components that make up a brand, how simple ideas come to be, and how to bring them to market. But beyond Allen's expertise and his mastery at demystifying the branding process, one of the most compelling aspects of this book are the examples he provides. Throughout the book Allen uses stories of specific brands that have succeeded—and some that haven't—to make his points. Most of these stories are about brands you'll most certainly recognize and, in many instances, brands you use and trust.

In the end, you'll see why it is that brands based on simple ideas are among the most powerful and enduring brands in the world. You'll appreciate why simple ideas resonate, and why brands based on simple ideas maintain their prominent positions. A brand should be simple to understand. *BrandSimple* makes it simple to understand why this is true and how it's done. The creators of Kit Kat knew how to get and keep my grandmother's attention—and later, mine. Allen Adamson will get and keep yours. It's a readable and persuasive book.

Introduction

I've spent a lot of my life in supermarket aisles. More specifically, I've spent a lot of my working life perusing one supermarket aisle or another for a year or two at a time. I'm not weird. It's just that I started my career as an executive in packaged goods marketing and for about twenty years it was my job to find out what was going on in the aisles in which my clients' products were located.

When I made the decision to join Landor Associates in 1992, it was because I wanted to expand my view of the world. I wanted to see between the aisles, to see over and beyond them. Having spent time attaining an incredible knowledge of packaged goods brands, I wanted to take my skills, apply them more broadly, and enjoy the experience of working with brands in a greater number of categories. I had learned a great deal in the first part of my career. I wanted to learn more and do more with what I learned. I've had the opportunity to do just that.

When I arrived at Landor, it was in the process of transforming itself from a corporate and brand identity firm into a full-spectrum brand consultancy, dealing with how brands are developed and what makes one brand more successful than another. After working in the world of brands, it was something that fascinated me. How does a brand become a brand? Why do some attain leadership status while others can't seem to climb out of third or fourth place in their respective categories? I had a remarkable run in the business of selling brand-name products and working with some of the best brand companies and best advertising agencies in the world. It was figuring out and focusing on what makes a brand tick that was the part of the job I enjoyed most. I wanted to do more of it.

I've gotten what I wanted. Since joining Landor, the sheer number of brands I've been able to work with has been amazing. Few firms have the privilege of being able to interact with such a sizable, diverse, and well-regarded group of organizations. Perhaps what's excited me most about what goes on at Landor is that all of the brands we deal with are in a state of important transition. The companies Landor works with are being forced by a significant event or change in business to transform the fundamental nature of their brands in some way. It's Landor's responsibility to make the transformation successful—big time. It might be that a new Chief Executive Officer (CEO) has come in with a new vision for the company. Or it might be a change in the way the company will be doing business. The transition might be the result of an important new product launch or the launch of a substantial sub-brand or company division. Some companies are going through mergers and need to find a way to signal an entirely new brand name or image. A number of brands we deal with are leadership brands feeling the nip of competition at their heels for the first time and are in need of refreshing or repositioning. Some of the brands are newly autonomous and require a completely from-scratch brand strategy.

The company now named Genworth, for example, was spun off from GE after GE decided to divest itself of its multibillion-dollar insurance business. In doing so, GE generated one of the largest initial public offerings in recent history. The CEO of this newly created company, which employed seven thousand employees and generated in excess of $11 billion a year, came to Landor with a couple of very interesting questions. What happens if you wake up one morning and realize you've got ninety days to figure out a new way to go to market without GE? Can a newly autonomous company survive after losing its integral linkage to GE, one of the most coveted brand names in the world? It's this kind of brand transformation (which was executed successfully), that makes my job exciting and full of fresh opportunity for creative problem solving every day.

Not all of the brand challenges I've been involved with over the years have been as large as Genworth, but they've all been fascinating in some way or another and have all provided some great lessons learned. The one lesson common to all of the brands I've worked with is this: For a brand to be successful it must differentiate itself from the competition in the minds of consumers and this difference must be relevant. More important, however, whatever it is that makes it different and relevant must be simple to understand—to both the people inside the brand organization and the people outside. The most powerful brands in the world, whether they're big brands or small, are based on clear, gut-simple ideas. Although this has always been critical to success, it's even more critical today given the extraordinary proliferation of products and service worldwide. Getting to simple, and executing your simple idea is what this book is about.

When I joined Landor, it was one of the only firms dedicated exclusively to the business of brands and branding. (For the record, a brand is what your product or service stands for in people's minds; it might be an image or, perhaps, a feeling. Branding is the process of executing and managing the things that make people feel the way they do about your brand. Details to follow.) I became part of what was then a niche industry. In the early 1990s, there weren't many firms that helped clients gain an understanding of the intrinsic nature of their brands and assisted them with the building or rebuilding of the brands from the inside out. Hundreds of firms dealt with the marketing and advertising of brands, of course, but few focused on the internal workings of the brand—the brand's DNA—the stuff that gets people to think about your brand in a certain way.

Like many other things, it was only a matter of time before the business of brands and branding got hot. That's because, obviously, as the number of products and services on a global scale began to proliferate, so did the competition among them. This proliferation didn't necessarily result in products and services that were fundamentally different from each other across categories, so identifying how to get your brand to stand out in the crowd became paramount. The number of people and firms claiming that they had the answer to beating the competition by way of innovative branding techniques was growing almost as fast as the numbers of new brands. Over the last ten years or so, firms and consultants galore have jumped on the brand wagon, touting all sorts of modeling techniques and quantitative methodologies. It's definitely not a niche business anymore. I look at the bookcase across from my desk and can see at least fifty books on the subject, each taking a different spin on how to win at the brand game. (I'll get to why I'm writing this book in a minute.)

Although there are quite a few exceptional firms out there that deal with brands and with branding, almost as many have taken the business far from its original purpose and far from what it should be. Paradoxically they've transformed the brand business from the focused art and science it should be into something extremely complex and somewhat mysterious. What I've witnessed can literally boggle the mind. For example, when my Landor team is called in by a prospective client to assess a brand challenge, it never ceases to amaze me how many of these clients hand us 300-page documents that had been prepared by another brand organization. These process-laden tomes look more like academic papers on advanced economics than solutions to simple customer needs. It's no wonder these prospective clients are still in search of an answer when they call us in. In fact, looking at some of these documents brings to mind that hyperaware comedian, George Carlin, who could easily use the industry catch phrases of the moment for a stand-up routine. "Excuse me," he might say. "It seems my brand equity has been diluted by brand fragmentation and brand flankers along with a couple of line extensions complicating my brand footprint and my brand mosaic. Seems I might need to use some brand voltage to jump-start the attitudinal segmentation fueling my semiotics."

A brand should not be complex, confusing, or mysterious in any way. Business and especially the brand business should not inspire the genius of comedians like George Carlin. As I said before, a brand should be simple. People use brands as shortcuts to make purchase decisions. A shortcut, by definition, is simple. Understanding what a brand stands for should be simple, You don't walk into a supermarket and look for a carbonated, caramel-colored beverage. You look for the familiar red and white Coca-Cola can or bottle. You don't ask your kids if they'd like to watch a puppet-populated educational TV show about numbers and letters. You ask them if they'd like to watch *Sesame Street.* You don't go into a pharmacy looking for an easy-to-swallow, nonprescription pain remedy that doesn't contain aspirin to stop your headache. You look for Tylenol. And you don't ask your friends if they'd like to get together to discuss the latest hot movie over a finely brewed and customized cup of Ethiopian decaf coffee, you ask them if they'd like to meet you at Starbucks. These brand names have become shortcuts.

When your brand is based on a simple, clearly defined idea aligned with a clearly defined business strategy it makes it easier for your brand organization to effectively signal to consumers what makes it different and why this difference is worth caring about. Simple brand ideas result in powerful and memorable branding that people immediately connect with.

For example, JetBlue's business strategy is to make money selling airline tickets. That's the business it's in. Its brand strategy is to signal that the experience of flying JetBlue is more enjoyable than any other airline experience. JetBlue's simple brand idea is that flying can be fun. The branding signals it uses to convey this include its very pleasant employees, the in-flight entertainment, the user-friendly Web site, and even the interesting choice of snack food. Everyone on the JetBlue team understands the simple idea on which the brand is based and knows how to bring it to life.

Target's business strategy is to make money selling a wide range of consumer goods, from housewares to clothing, to packaged foods at a discounted price. Its brand strategy is to prove that less expensive goods can still be stylish. Target's simple brand idea is cheap chic. Its branding signals include promoting hip designers like Isaac Mizrahi and Liz Lange for clothing, and Michael Graves for housewares, as well as the use of terrific advertising with quirky characters and toe-tapping music. Consumers have gotten so hooked on the simple-to-understand idea that drives the Target brand that many pronounce it *Tarzhay,* as if it were a sophisticated French department store.

It has been proven time after time that the strongest brands are built on simple, compelling ideas that grab people by signaling that something is different from what they've heard and seen before and is relevant to their needs. Landor looks at a client's business strategy to help identify what it is that's genuinely unique and better about what they're selling and then ensures the company has what it takes to deliver on it. We distill this to a simple, persuasive idea and then create or suggest the branding signals that will most powerfully and authentically convey the idea. When the idea driving a brand is simple, the people in an organization will more readily get what their brand stands for and the branding signals they generate will demonstrate this understanding. Consumers will remember your brand and what it stands for and they'll tuck it away in their heads to use as a shortcut to their purchase decisions. Your brand will be successful.

That's what this book is about. With all the books on my bookcase, with all the tomes and documents on brand building, I have yet to see one that explains why brands built on simple ideas are the most successful brands and how these brands achieved their status in the market. I have yet to see a book or document that takes the mystery out of brands and branding—something that shouldn't be mysterious at all. A book on brands should be as simple and clear as the brands about which it is written. This book was written to be just that.

Lest you think what I'm talking about is simplistic, there is a vast difference between "simple" and "simplistic." It takes rigorous thinking, discipline, and focus to get to a simple idea. It takes vision and an ability to think in a less than obvious way. (Although some ideas are so obvious, a lot of potentially brilliant brand ideas often get overlooked. I'll tell you stories about companies that knew to look right under their noses.) The most ingenious people in the business taught me that simple ideas sell best and that getting to simple takes work. Which brings me to how I got into the business in the first place.

The fact of the matter is that Steven Spielberg wasn't waiting with a job offer when I graduated from college in the 1970s with a degree in communications and an interest in filmmaking. Although I had some talent, it became apparent to me—quick study that I was—that I didn't have what it takes to make it in the film industry. Suffice it to say *Jaws* was made without my help.

While Steve was playing with mechanical sharks, I went on to get my MBA and decided to try my hand in the advertising industry, figuring I'd at least have a chance to make thirty-second films. At the time, I didn't know any more about advertising than what I'd learned from watching Darren, who worked at the Tate agency on the television show *Bewitched*. I soon became aware that there was a lot to know and I was lucky enough to have started my career at Ogilvy & Mather, where I gained incredible insight into the world of brands and advertising these brands. While there I never once ran into anyone who resembled Darren in any way. The folks at Ogilvy were incredibly smart, creative people who were passionate about what they did, and they did it brilliantly. Their culture was infectious and the firm invested heavily in training to ensure we were all well grounded in everything we needed to know to serve our clients well, from research and media planning, to how to write effective client presentations. (I still use a book written by former Ogilvy president, Ken Roman, entitled *How to Write Better.*)

It was at Ogilvy that I first became aware of the power that simple, compelling ideas have to connect with consumers and change opinions. Ogilvy clients included some of the best-known marketing companies in the world, from American Express to General Foods (now part of Kraft). They all understood the influence of simple ideas. The folks at these companies knew how important it was to have a focused yet different idea if you wanted consumers to sit up, take notice, and take action. They could look at a brand or marketing challenge and think without over-thinking about how to meet the challenge. They had the ability to ask exactly the right questions and not get overwhelmed by process or to second-guess themselves. What consumer need are we trying to address? What can we communicate about the brand that no one else has thought to communicate? With whom are we trying to communicate?

My clients during these early days in the business with Ogilvy included Maxwell House coffee, Country Time lemonade, and Good Seasons salad dressing. I worked a twelve-hour day—minimum—and I loved it. Agencies did much more for clients than create advertising. For most clients they served as an extension of the marketing department, making recommendations for a wide range of questions from product distribution, to manufacturing and packaging. I had gotten my MBA, but my experience in the field turned theory into very valuable practice.

After a few years at Ogilvy, I was recruited to join Lever Brothers in brand management. I went to the client side, as people call it. I knew that working on the other side of the table would give me another perspective on the business. I'd been fascinated with all those meetings with Ogilvy clients, and I wanted to experience firsthand what actually went into product development, down to the chemistry that allowed Wisk to clean Ring around the Collar. I was exposed to the processes and operations, manufacturing and distribution, and how decisions were made internally with regard to retail and pricing strategies. I learned how to work with a national sales force, how public relations could be used to build brands, and the ins and outs of consumer and trade promotions. I also got the chance to work with powerful ad agencies such as BBDO, public relations and promotions agencies, medical advertising firms, packaging and industrial design firms.

At the time I joined Lever, its products generally lagged behind similar Procter & Gamble products in popularity and market share. The company always seemed to be in follow-the-leader mode. In retrospect, it was a great time to join Lever. The company brought in new leadership, as well as new technology and operational processes that gave it an edge in the European markets. I was part of the team that launched a barrage of new products in the United States including Snuggle fabric softener, Shield soap, and Surf detergent. Even though a number of products we introduced didn't make it, I can honestly say I learned as much from the failures as I did from the successes. I've found that in this business—in any business—it's as important to know what you shouldn't do as it is to know what you should do. Learning from your mistakes in the brand business is a great teaching tool. In this book, I'm going to share a number of the most important lessons I've learned.

After spending time at Lever, I realized my interests and skills were more suited to the conceptual and creative side of the business, so I returned to advertising. At Benton and Bowles, I finally had the opportunity to work with Procter & Gamble. I say "finally" because whenever I was assigned to work on a brand that competed with a P&G brand, I knew we had our work cut out for us. P&G was masterful at building and marketing brands.

I became a regular on the 6:15 A.M. flight to Cincinnati back in the days when airlines served breakfast. I started getting my P&G lessons with Dawn dishwashing detergent. Dawn was an example of P&G at its best. The marketing team at P&G had identified a consumer insight relative to washing dishes—greasy dishes are the worst—and a product was developed that could literally get rid of grease in dishwater. The agency and P&G teams worked together to create focused branding based on the simple, differentiated promise that "Dawn takes grease out of your way." Dawn went from being a new brand to category leader in a few short years.

Perhaps more important than the actual details I took away from any one P&G brand was the thinking process I acquired regarding what it takes to establish and grow a brand. Back then each brand team was required to present its annual marketing plan at the budget meeting. I'd watch and learn as senior P&G management would grill the teams about everything imaginable, including their understanding of the consumer, the market, and the competition. What new insights had the team come up with? What technologies had been developed that could support product performance? Was there any one factor that could enhance the product's point of differentiation? How effective was the media strategy, the advertising? How was P&G holding out in terms of margin and share of wallet? It was like getting a Master's degree in Brand Administration.

I was on an incredible learning curve, and soon I was given the opportunity to begin teaching what I was learning to others. Every Wednesday evening about twenty-five students from the New School in New York would join me for classes on advertising and marketing. These were kids eager to get into the business. I was an adjunct professor there for a number of years and then went on to teach at New York University's Stern Graduate Business School and later at Yale's Graduate School of Business, where I had a roomful of MBA students. I shared my teaching responsibilities with my good friend and colleague Jed Bernstein, who had worked at Ogilvy on the American Express account and went on to pursue his passion for theater by marketing Broadway. Together we would present case histories using our particular client expertise. We'd challenge students to reposition and market everything from salad dressing to credit cards, to their business school, to Broadway. Looking back, my teaching experience allowed me to better understand the subject matter and sharpen my own skills. Most important, it forced me to simplify—to take what I was doing at work and get it down to the basics. Actually, the most effective insight I took away from my teaching experience was to get everything down to a Letterman Top Ten.

I spent a few more years at Benton and Bowles, which eventually became D'Arcy, McManus, Benton & Bowles after its merger with

D'Arcy McManus Masius, and again had the chance to work on some great P&G brands along with brands from General Foods and Mars. I went on to spend time with Ammirati & Puris, an agency known for its inspired work on BMW, Club Med, and UPS, and then decided it was time to broaden my scope of experience. I joined Landor.

Broaden my scope I did. Over the past fourteen years I've had the privilege to work with such consumer product brands as Pepsi, Gatorade, Clairol, Pampers, Bayer, and Mountain Dew. I've worked with technology companies including IBM, Xerox, Compaq, Unisys, and BlackBerry, financial firms including Goldman Sachs and Morgan Stanley. My clients have come from the industrial sector, including GE, ITT, and Textron, and communications firms such as AT&T and Verizon. I worked with organizations including the New York Stock Exchange, the Bronx Zoo, and even the Federal Department of Homeland Security. (Yes, there was a branding program, and I learned a lot about the great seal.) From Titleist golf balls, to the NFL, to Broadway, to the state of Florida: name a category and I've most likely had experience in it.

Working with such a wide spectrum of brand categories has given me the ability to see what works and what doesn't when helping a brand find its center of gravity. To see what makes it unique no matter what category it's in. What I've discovered is that what once made for brand success still makes for brand success. If you want to win, you must know what you're selling, find a way to prove that what you're selling is different, and distill this difference into a focused and compelling idea that can drive and unite everything associated with your brand. This was important when I started my career almost thirty years ago, but it's even more important today. Competition has never been stiffer, and the consumer's attention span has never been more challenged. You've got to be able to have something meaningfully different to say and make it incredibly easy to understand. There is no mystery in this. It's been proven.

A year or two ago I began to think about the books on my bookcase, and I decided to take a fresh look at them. Doing so confirmed for me that, although most are well written, they don't get to the root of the challenges many potential clients call about. They are filled with terminology that runs the gamut from buzzword to academic. A number of the books provide pep-talk ideology; others, highly analytical strategies and methodologies. None provides a basic, straightforward explanation of what goes into establishing and supporting a brand and the steps required to do successful branding. Think about the smartest people you've worked with—your best teachers, for instance. They had the ability to take complex ideas and reduce them to simple notions. You remember these ideas and can apply them yourself. That's what this book is meant to do.

A lot of good brands became good brands because they saw a gap in the marketplace and found a relevant way to fill it. I wrote this book because I saw a gap in the brand book marketplace. I wrote this book to make the subject of brands simple yet comprehensive. There are no buzzwords and no academics. I wrote this book to get to the core of what makes a good brand, to give you the basic terms you need to know, the history you need to have, and the key steps required to make your brand and your branding successful.

As I said, I've had the opportunity to work with brands in a vast array of categories and have helped solve every brand challenge you can imagine. I've had the opportunity to apply lessons learned from one category to another. This broad view of the industry has given me a solid understanding of what it takes to connect with consumers, especially now that everything imaginable is branded, including such basic commodities as water, chicken, and even lettuce. My broad experience has also given me insight into what people do to make their brands and branding efforts complicated. Just because the market has become oversaturated with brands and hard to navigate, the subject of brands and branding doesn't have to be. In fact, it should be just the opposite.

It's time to go back and look at what has always made the best brands successful. The most powerful brands have always been based on simple, logical ideas. This book cuts to the core of what makes the best brands tick. It shows you how the best brands get to simple ideas and convey them through effective branding. This book provides the framework for what anyone involved in brands or branding needs to know to succeed in the business. This book is called *BrandSimple,* because that's what a brand should be: simple.

Part I: What the Best Brands Know

1

Start with the Basics

What's a Brand?

What is a "brand"? The word is bandied about in all sorts of ways. Every day I see another definition or spin on the concept. People seem to make them up as needed. For the purpose of this book (and actually, for *all* intents and purposes), a brand is something that lives in your head. It's a promise that links a product or a service to a consumer. Whether words, or images, or emotions, or any combination of the three, brands are mental associations that get stirred up when you think about or hear about a particular car or camera, watch, pair of jeans, bank, beverage, TV network, organization, celebrity, or even country.

A brand exists in your mind. By way of analogy, think of the inside of your head as a computer desktop. (If it's anything like my desktop, it's very cluttered.) When you know enough about a brand, you assign the brand a mental "file name" and put it on your desktop. The bigger the brand, or the more you know about it, the bigger the mental file.

When the brand name comes up in conversation, or you have an experience with the brand, you mentally "click" on the brand file name. When it opens, the associations you link with the brand are set free. You feel something. You react in some way—positively or negatively—as a result of how these associations make you feel. The positive reaction means good news for the brand owner, as it may (but not always) result in your purchase of the brand. If you feel ambivalent, it means the associations haven't really sunk in, or they're not important to you. If you react negatively, the brand managers have some work to do, specifically if you're one of the consumers they'd like to reach. If you don't react at all, it means the brand hasn't taken up residence in your head. You don't have a file name for it.

Here's an example of how a brand's file name works. Florida. It's a state, yes, but, as a brand, it's a state of mind. When someone says they're going to Florida, my mental file clicks open and the associations that pop up have to do with warm, blue skies, lush golf courses, palm trees, the Miami nightlife, the Fort Lauderdale Boat Show, and the University of Miami Hurricanes. My friend's mental brand file opens and tells him early bird specials, gated communities, planes full of noisy kids going to Disney World, sweet old ladies driving 30 miles per hour in a 60-mile-per-hour speed zone, and real hurricanes. A strong brand will do its best to guarantee that more people have associations similar to mine than those of my friend.

A Good Brand Says Something Different

The people behind the strongest brands, whether they are smart brand managers or visionary entrepreneurs, know that a mental brand file name is hard to establish and quickly deleted if it's not worth "saving as." To become a permanent mental file filled with positive associations, a brand has to establish that it's different in some way. A good brand establishes that it is worth "saving as."

To make a brand worth "saving as," you've got to come up with a different meaning for your brand relative to other brands in your category. This difference in meaning has to be simple to understand. It can't be a complicated concept in any way. The idea on which you establish your brand's meaning in people's minds has got to be both unique and simple to grasp. You must identify something to convey about the brand that's authentically different. This doesn't mean a different feature or benefit (features and benefits become obsolete far too quickly), but how your promise to the consumer is completely different from what other brands promise. The best brands are set apart from other brands on the same playing field by both communicating and delivering on this different promise. Perhaps the brand ideas are based on a different way of thinking about an existing product or service, or perhaps they are something people have never seen before.

4

A good brand can get across to consumers how it's different and why it's better. A good brand idea does both.

Establishing a simple and different brand idea used to be pretty easy. So was the ability to sell it, literally and figuratively. Ivory was soap. Hershey's was chocolate. Maxwell House was coffee. Proof of "baby-soft skin" was simple and different enough. "Deep, rich flavor" was simple and different enough. "Good to the last drop" was simple and different enough. Today, with so many brands on the market, establishing a simple, differentiated meaning for a brand, something that hasn't already been claimed, is a huge challenge. Any coffee company can develop the technology to be good to the last drop. What else can you promise that will get people to stop what they're doing, listen to what you're saying, and consider changing their brand allegiance?

Every good brand manager knows you have to establish and signal a simple, differentiated meaning to consumers and ensure that it's something people will care about. I'm not going to tell you how your specific brand should differentiate its meaning, but I am going to outline a few exercises you can undertake to help you pinpoint a different brand idea you can claim as your own and help you sharpen this idea once you have it. I will explain how to focus your idea clearly so people inside your organization and outside can grasp the idea you're trying to get across. I'll also explain the critical importance of ensuring that your business strategy is aligned with your brand idea and tell you what happens when it isn't. (Your business strategy is how your company makes money—what it sells. Obviously, if you don't align it with your brand idea, you won't be able to keep your brand promise.) Finally, I'll explain how to do powerful branding—how to generate the right brand associations—once you've identified a different idea. Making your idea ingenious and relevant to your particular brand is up to you.

The Best Brands: Different in a Way People Care About

Look at any of the best brands in the marketplace, old or new, and you can immediately tell what makes them different from the others in the category. It's also clear what makes this difference relevant to consumers. Whatever it is that makes your brand's idea different must also be relevant to people's needs. There is no long-term value in a brand if it's not something people will use or find important to their lives. Difference for the sake of being different won't get you anywhere but in a financial bind.

A lot of brands have developed products without assessing relevance. Engineers and chemists, research and development departments have been given the task of coming up with amazing things. Truckloads of dollars are poured into the enterprise. Bonuses are offered to those who come up with the next big thing. The problem in most of these cases is that it is innovation run amok. What good is the next big thing if it isn't something people need or can use in a big way? Philips, for example, came out with a flat-screen TV with a special light source that projects various colors of ambient light onto the wall behind the TV to add depth to a specific scene. Let's say you're watching a show that includes an underwater scene. The TV projects a blue light onto the wall behind the television, while green light is projected when a forest or jungle scene appears. While it sounds kind of cool, I'm not sure this technological difference is all that relevant to consumers who are considering the purchase of a flat-screen TV. I'd check consumer data on something like this carefully before I committed a lot of money to it.

The Segway scooter is another example of getting excited about what you've developed without assessing whether consumers will be equally excited. The Segway was released with unprecedented hype as a product that would revolutionize not only transportation but the world. Investors expected hundreds of thousands of these two-wheeled power scooters for adults to be sold, generating billions of dollars in sales in the first year. In reality, Segway sold only ten thousand units in its first few years and is still trying to overcome an identity crisis. High price, not enough power, bans in urban centers, and problems with being able to balance the vehicle properly made it the revolution that wasn't. What can we learn from the Segway experience? Don't let your own excitement about a product or service shortchange your assessment of how it will really play in the market. Coming up with a brand difference and determining if the audience will find it relevant means looking beyond your own delight. Myopia is not an option. You have to assess carefully what people tell you in focus groups and quantitative concept testing. Determine if they really will take an interest once the product is on the market.

H. J. Heinz, for example, had one miss and one great hit with a couple of food products for kids. "They're not what a potato is supposed to be." This is how Heinz pitched funky fries—the weird chocolate-flavored, blue-colored French fries—to the world in 2002. Kids never warmed up to these odd fries, and a year later Heinz pulled them off the shelves. Chocolate French fries? Kids already thought French fries were fun, so why jazz them up in any way? That's why, even after extensive investment in production and manufacturing, Heinz pulled the chocolate, cinnamon, sour cream, and blue-colored products off the shelves.

However, Heinz had a winner with another product that was different and extremely relevant to kids. As I know firsthand from sitting across from my own kids during meals, kids love to gross out their parents and friends. The people at Heinz knew this when they developed green, purple, and pink ketchup. Sales went up as kids delighted in squirting this stuff on everything. The relevance of this product hit the bulls' eye with its audience.

Here's one more example. Despite a huge marketing campaign launched during the Super Bowl in January 1993, Crystal Pepsi lasted only one year in the United States. It is considered by some to be the company's equivalent of the New Coke: a massive commercial failure. (Consumers didn't want a New Coke. They were happy with the traditional Coke.)

Healthy living had become a popular concept in the early 1990s with focus on the very vague notion of purity. As a result of this, Crystal Pepsi was marketed as the "clear alternative" to regular cola drinks, equating its clearness with purity. In addition to color—or lack thereof—the branding signal for the new cola was the tagline, "You've never seen a taste like this." The taste didn't turn out to be much different from that of other colas, though, and consumers expected it to have the lemon-lime flavor of other colorless drinks. More important, the difference of a cola taste without the cola color was not really relevant to most consumers. Crystal Pepsi tasted much like the original Pepsi. Except for a small audience who looked to purchase the product through internet sites, there wasn't enough of a market for a clear cola.

All good companies, like the companies mentioned above, do research. And while research may have indicated people might go for adult two-wheelers, chocolate fries, or colorless cola, consumers behave differently when facing a purchase decision than when they're in focus groups. Research isn't a panacea. Use it wisely and follow your intuition.

Relevance Is Relative

The preceding examples are cases of brands that found something unique to promote, but the uniqueness didn't really matter. The idea behind this difference was irrelevant. Before you spend time and money, do your homework. Make sure you've established a brand difference that people will find relevant. But, although it's critical to establish a point of brand difference, the *degree* of relevance is relative. Relevance depends on the consumers you want to talk to and the number of consumers you need to appeal to in order to make a profit. Some of the greatest brands have identified a differentiated idea that's relevant to a relatively small number of people. These brands become successful by narrowing their focus to appeal to a select group of consumers they know will really find them relevant. These brands are called niche brands. Luxury brands are niche brands. Louis Vuitton, Rolex, and Rolls-Royce are good examples of niche brands. Some electronics brands also are niche brands. The BlackBerry, for instance, has something incredibly different to say and is extremely useful, but until recently only to a small group of Type-A business consumers. Successful niche brands stay successful as a result of keeping their business strategy and their brand idea focused on a select group of consumers.

Brands that are meaningful to larger numbers of people are obviously big ones: Clorox, Crest, GE, Panasonic, Oprah, FedEx, KFC, and Google, for example. The ideas on which these brands are based have proven to be different, better, and relevant to a lot of people. People also quickly grasp the idea behind these brands because the ideas are simple to understand. Note that many big brands start as niche brands that then go on to capture the heads and hearts of larger and larger numbers of people. In doing so, they become big brands, whether it was their intention to do so or not. Apple's iPod was a niche brand that expanded its consumer base to include more than the early adopters. Nike was a niche brand, as was Starbucks, BMW, and, in the U.S. market, Mercedes-Benz. These brands saw an opportunity to expand the base of consumers to whom they might be interesting, and in doing so, captured a greater share of wallet. The key to the success of these brands as they expanded their user base was maintaining the difference, the relevance, and the simplicity of their brand ideas.

While I tell a couple of specific niche brand stories later in the book, here's what to consider if you'd like to expand your customer base. First, you must take into consideration whether the difference in meaning you've established for your brand idea will truly be relevant to a larger audience and if you've carefully assessed the needs of the other consumers you'd like to go after. It's essential to make sure you don't dilute your brand's authority with your primary audience. You also have to consider what financial resources will be required to expand. Sometimes it's better to be a niche brand and command hefty margins from an elite group of buyers than to be everything to everybody and put yourself in a commodity position fighting a price war for profit. A lot of brands have failed to thrive as large brands because they moved too quickly from niche-brand strategy to big-brand strategy. Make sure you keep an eye on why people were attracted to you in the first place. Then make sure the other consumers you're going after will find you attractive for the same reason without turning off your loyalists.

A Quick Overview: How Brands Are Built

If you ask most people how brands are built, they probably will give you an answer along these lines: You start with awareness. You create some great advertising or a big promotion to let people know you're out there. Once consumers are aware of you, you get them to consider using your brand and then convince them actually to purchase it.

In terms of building a brand, this is backward. To achieve success in brand building, the first thing you need to do is to establish a differentiated meaning for your brand. Identify something unique on which to build a brand idea. Then determine whether this difference actually will matter to anyone. Is it relevant, and to whom? Is there a large enough audience of people who will care? Only after you've established a different and relevant meaning for your brand should you begin to think about generating awareness. You cannot think about creating awareness—that's branding—until you have a brand idea. Consumers need a way to make a distinction between one brand and another. This distinction is how they form preferences and make choices. You must establish your brand's difference and make sure it's relevant before you do anything else.

One of the most respected proprietary tools in the industry proves this point. Named BrandAsset Valuator (BAV), it was created by Y&R, an agency that is part of the same communications family as Landor. BAV is an incredible diagnostic tool for figuring out how your brand is performing relative to all other brands in the market—not just the brands in your category. More important, however, unlike many other brand valuation tools in the industry that attempt to place a current dollar value on the brand, BAV indicates what you must do to keep your brand strong and healthy. BAV can gauge the current health of your brand, project its future health, and indicate prescriptive actions. Why is this important? Well, I have found that Wall Street doesn't necessarily care about the value of your brand today. It cares about whether you can increase its value. More than being just a report card, BAV can tell you how to get better grades.

In the early 1990s some of the smart thinkers at Y&R got together to answer some questions essential to building a successful brand. What is it that makes one brand stronger than another? What can we learn about how brands grow and decline? I spoke about these issues with Stewart Owen, who is currently chief strategic officer at the firm McGarry Bowen, but who helped create the BAV model while he was vice chairman at Y&R.

"BAV looks at brands from a logical perspective," he told me. "The key challenge a brand has is how to increase its dominance.

This model is a good indicator of that. The most interesting thing about BAV is that it's based on the fact that almost all successful brands begin by being very simple. A brand doesn't start out by saying 'I'm going to sell lots of things to lots of people in lots of ways in lots of places.' It begins by selling one thing to a few people and ensures that it's different and better in a meaningful way."

"If you look at the upper left quadrant of a BAV chart, you'll see it's filled with strong brands that have created some simple but highly differentiated offerings. Many of these are smaller brands, but some

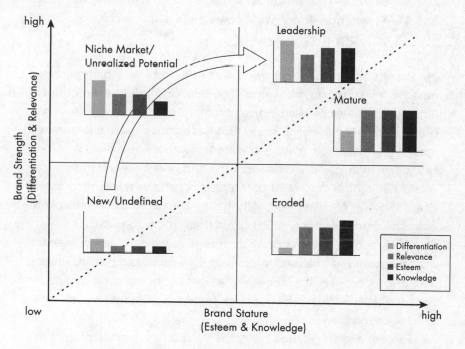

Source: Young & Rubicam Brands' BrandAsset™ Valuator

Y&R's Brand Asset Valuator plots brands according to four criteria: Differentiation, Relevance, Esteem, and Knowledge

11

are much larger. The reason brands stay in the upper left corner—an indication of strength—is because they've kept things simple but, more important, they've kept them different and relevant. Brands that lose sight of their different simple idea have a hard time growing."

The way BAV works is actually pretty simple. It's based on the interrelationships of four brand dimensions, or pillars:

1. Differentiation—what makes your brand unique
2. Relevance—how appropriate this difference is to the audience you want to reach
3. Esteem—how well regarded your brand is in the marketplace
4. Knowledge—how well consumers know and understand your brand

Brands should get built one pillar at a time, with differentiation being the first, most critical step. The relationship between differentiation and relevance is an indication of a brand's strength. A strong brand, as Stewart said, is a brand that has established a differentiated meaning in people's minds—a difference that's relevant. A strong brand has high levels of differentiation and relevance. A strong niche brand has a high degree of differentiation and is relevant to a very specific group of consumers. All healthy brands have greater differentiation than relevance, which gives them room to grow.

When a brand has a higher degree of relevance than differentiation, the brand has become a commodity—its uniqueness has faded and price becomes the dominant reason to buy. Kmart, Energizer, Bic, and Handi-Wrap are good examples of high-relevance, low-differentiation brands.

Esteem and knowledge, the other two pillars, make up a brand's stature. A brand with a higher level of esteem than level of knowledge is a brand that enjoys a good reputation, although people may not know a lot about it. This puts a brand in a great position to convince consumers to get to know it better. Brands in this position include Bang & Olufsen, Movado, Barilla, and Coach leatherware. In these cases, a consumer might say, "Hey, I've heard a lot of good things about you. I'd like to know more."

Too much knowledge and not enough esteem, on the other hand, can be a dangerous thing. In this case, consumers might say, "Hey, I know a lot about you and you're nothing special." The *National Enquirer* and Spam are good examples. One of the critical differences between BAV and other valuation tools is that BAV uses knowledge rather than simply awareness as a metric. A consumer may be aware of a brand. But having knowledge of a brand implies greater intimacy with the brand and is, therefore, a better indicator of consumer opinion.

In the case of leadership brands, all pillars are strong. Disney, IBM, and Coca-Cola are certainly examples of leadership brands. A successful new brand, or a successful relaunched brand, will demonstrate a desirable step-down pattern of pillars, the highest pillar being differentiation and the lowest, knowledge, indicating that the brand has found a meaningful way to differentiate itself in people's minds. It's ready to intensify its branding efforts in order to expand its knowledge base. WebMD, JetBlue, and IKEA were all in this situation and used it to their advantage.

BAV is a very useful tool for two fundamental reasons. The first, as I said, is that it's predictive and prescriptive. BAV indicates when a brand's differentiation in the market is starting to lag. This is an early indicator that there's big trouble on the horizon and a heads-up to get back to innovative thinking and to stop resting on your laurels. (Andy Grove of Intel once said, "In the world of business, only the paranoid survive." The same is true in the world of brands.)

Second, BAV prevents myopic thinking. It allows you to see where a brand resides within a broader range of categories, not just the category in which it lives. BAV lets you see which other brands occupy the same perceptual space in people's minds within the general universe of brands. Are the brands with which your brand exists perceived as innovative and hip, conservative and safe, or perhaps on the way out? Being able to see your brand within this context is critical to future strategic initiatives, not to mention a healthy reality check.

There's a lot more to learn about BAV, but for the sake of simplicity, I've kept it to the basics. Most basic of all, start your brand building with a simple, meaningfully different idea and, only after you've done this, figure out how to let people know about it.

Capture the Essence of the Brand Idea

Shakespeare said, "Brevity is the soul of wit." Adamson says, "Brevity is the soul of brand." If people don't get it, forget it.

As I've explained, a good brand is worth "saving as" because what it stands for is different and relevant to people. But the strongest brands are successful not merely because they've established a differentiated meaning for their brands and ensured that it's relevant. It's because they've reduced this meaningful difference to a simple, clear, and cohesive thought—an idea people can get in the split second they'll give you these days to explain your brand claim. You need to capture the complex nature of your brand's meaning in a clear and concise way. People are busy, they're inundated by messages, and there are too many brands for them to choose from. Make it easy for them to get the idea. Your goal is to become a shortcut for a consumer's decision about which brand to pick from the plethora of brand choices out there. My colleagues call these encapsulated brand ideas elevator ideas. In other words, see if you can communicate the comprehensive significance of your brand's meaning in the time it takes to get from the twelfth to the eighteenth floor. If you can't easily explain your brand idea to others in the organization and, importantly, to your agencies, don't expect your consumers to understand your brand idea clearly either. (Phineas T. Barnum of circus fame once told a businessperson trying to sell him on something to see if he could write it on the back of a business card—that's the same thing.)

Five Great Ideas Made Simple

Here are five super-quick examples of what I mean by elevator-simple ideas.

1. HBO's current business strategy is selling TV programming. That's how it makes money. The meaningful difference it has established in the television category is that it provides programming that can't be found on any other TV channel. This difference is relevant to a lot of people. Where else can you

find shows like *The Sopranos, Sex and the City,* or *Six Feet Under?* What's the elevator-simple idea behind the HBO brand? "It's not TV, it's HBO." It's an idea that needs no further explanation. (Just turn on the television and enjoy the experience.)

2. "We want every consumer, regardless of their skill level to think of Titleist, first and foremost, as the number one ball in golf. It's our mantra, our blueprint, our signature. The Acushnet Company places great value on the power of the Titleist brand," said George Sine, President of Golf Ball Marketing and Strategic Planning Worldwide for the Acushnet Company. Besides being its mantra, its blueprint, and signature, "the number one ball in golf" is also the Titleist brand's elevator-simple idea. Known worldwide for its exceptional golf equipment, it makes a good percentage of its money selling golf balls. In fact, the difference it has established relative to other brands in the category is that its golf balls are used by PGA tour champions, country club pros, serious amateurs, low- and mid-to-high-handicap weekend golfers—anyone seeking the highest level of performance from a golf ball. While Titleist manufactures and sells five different models, each with its own distinct playing performance and personality, it ensures that each golf ball model produced is authentic to the brand and consistent with the quality and performance that makes it deserving of the pedigree Titleist script. While there is lots of sophisticated technology behind each of these golf ball models, the idea behind the brand's meaningful difference is relative to all of them. It can be captured in six simple words that resonate with golfers from Pebble Beach, California, to Phuket, Thailand: "the number one ball in golf."

3. *Forbes* magazine is another example of a powerfully differentiated idea captured in a brilliantly simple way. Even though they may not always agree with the editorial content, there isn't a businessperson out there who doesn't find the magazine's idea relevant. It's the number-one business magazine in the world, and the tagline on the magazine's cover states the elevator simplicity of the brand's differentiated

meaning: "Capitalist Tool." Since its founding by Malcolm Forbes, this brand has never, ever veered from its promise of giving business people short and to-the-point insight about timely business matters. The authenticity of this brand idea is due to the fact that Malcolm Forbes was never embarrassed by his capitalist ethos: "working, winning and loving it."

4. Advil is "advanced medicine for pain." The brand established a completely different meaning for its pain-relieving abilities from others in the category. It owns "advanced medicine" and the simple idea is the ultimate promise. This brand idea has been able to evolve as pharmaceutical research and development has evolved—advanced is always ahead of anything else. Advil's simple, differentiated idea has served it well for more than twenty-five years.

5. Visa wanted to take on American Express, which was interesting because they're technically different types of payment vehicles. Visa is a credit card, meaning they extend you credit—you can make minimum payments over time. American Express is a charge card requiring payment in full each month. But consumers perceive the two as being in the same category. Tom Carey, former executive vice president of the Omnicom Group, told me the story of how Visa established its elevator-simple idea. "Actually, the beauty of the simplicity wasn't just in the idea of universal acceptance—its business strategy. Rather it was in making this acceptance, 'everywhere you want to be' the kicker, the real point of difference. Making places you want to be desirable and letting you know that Visa would be accepted in these places, while American Express wouldn't. It was brilliant. It immediately kicked up Visa's frame of reference and it enjoyed a double benefit. Usage of Visa at more upscale restaurants increased significantly, and as a result, the dollar amount of the check increased, as well. It was such a simple idea that it was easy to get the message across." "Everywhere you want to be" has played out consistently over the years and has proven a powerful expression of a simple brand idea.

Making your brand's differentiated meaning simple to understand is critical to communicating your brand idea, both inside your organization and out. If the people responsible for delivering on the brand promise don't understand what the brand stands for, there's no way your audience will understand it. Later on, in chapter 5, I'll go into detail about how to capture the essence of your brand idea in a single phrase that can drive all brand activity by ensuring clarity, consistency, and cohesiveness of meaning.

Deliver on the Brand Idea

In order for a brand to succeed, you must align your business strategy with your brand idea. Then develop a strategy to convey and deliver the brand idea—the brand strategy. I can't emphasize this enough. Your business strategy is what it is you do to make money—the product you sell or the service you provide. Your brand can only be as good as your business strategy enables it to be. The fact that you've established a meaningful different idea for your brand is irrelevant if you can't fulfill the promise behind the brand idea. You must be able to deliver what your brand idea says you are going to deliver. At the end of the day a brand can be only as good as the *experience* of the brand.

If your brand idea promises that flying will be fun, don't just give me a smile as I board the plane. Don't lose my luggage! Make sure your business is prepared to make this possible. If your brand idea communicates that your television programming is worth paying for every month, put in the effort required to make my staying home on a Saturday night to watch TV worthwhile. If your brand idea tells me that your movie studio creates movies both kids and parents can enjoy, make sure the story lines and the technology add up to something I won't mind putting in the DVD player when I'm home alone with the kids. If your brand idea is based on the promise that your dishwashing liquid will make the job of washing dishes faster and more efficient, make sure you have the technology to back it up. If you tell me my credit card will be accepted everywhere I want to use it, make sure it will be.

Simple, differentiated ideas are part of the equation for brand success. Making sure your brand organization has the resources, service, and people to support these ideas is another. Your brand idea must be linked to what you actually can deliver. Before you establish a simple and differentiated brand idea, before you develop a strategy to convey this brand idea, make sure you have what it takes to bring the idea to life.

What's Brand*ing*?

I mentioned earlier that there is a huge difference between a brand and branding, just as there is a huge difference between branding and advertising. I usually have to clarify this difference with potential clients, because people use the terms interchangeably.

Clients will tell me they want to relaunch their brands. Can Landor design a new logo, a new typeface, or a new package design? I explain that these activities are branding activities, and that you can't do branding until you have a meaningfully different *brand idea* on which to base the activities. Branding is how you go about establishing your brand's differentiated meaning in people's minds. A brand strategy is the plan you develop to convey your brand idea. Branding is about signals—the signals people use to determine what you stand for as a brand. Signals create associations. A great brand is the result of great branding. The simpler and more focused your brand idea, the more brilliant the branding will be, and the more powerful the associations.

The first thing I ask a client is what problem they're trying to solve. For example, have they been able to establish a differentiated meaning for the brand? What makes their brand unique? Is it a difference people care about? Do enough people care about the brand difference that the brand can turn a profit? Can the business strategy support the brand's difference? It's not until you solve fundamental brand issues that you can go on to branding. That "ing" is huge. Branding is the creation of signals that convey what your brand stands for and establishes its difference in people's minds. A brand is the idea. Branding is the transmission of the idea.

To sum up, a brand is a set of mental associations that reside in people's heads. We keep them in mental file folders. For consumers to find these associations worth "saving as," they must be based on an idea that's different and relevant to them and simple to grasp. Branding is the tangible process of creating and managing the signals that transmit a brand idea. Branding signals generate associations. A simple and sharply focused brand idea in alignment with a business strategy allows for the creation and management of inspired and inspiring branding signals—signals that transmit exactly what they should be transmitting with no question regarding their intent. Establishing a simple, differentiated, and relevant meaning for your brand with the power to inspire effective branding signals makes for brand success. That's the premise of this book.

Branding Signals: Everything You Think They Are and More

Branding signals are external and obvious things like logos and names, colors, signage, typefaces, images and promotions, package designs, and distribution channels. They also are things of a more experiential nature. The way a product functions can be a branding signal. For example, think about the fuel efficiency of the Toyota Prius. We associate this brand with its functionality. The way a product feels in your hand is a branding signal. The OXO Good Grips can opener is a good example. You like the shape of the Dove hair conditioner bottle and associate it with the way it doesn't fall over in the shower. It signals something about the brand. The manner in which the L.L. Bean customer service representatives answer the phone is a branding signal. It's something you associate with the L.L. Bean brand in your mind. Sound effects can be branding signals. Think about the four-tone audio sound to signal Intel inside. The Budweiser Clydesdale horses are branding signals, as are the Charmin squeeze, the Nike swoosh, the Coca-Cola contour bottle and red disc icon. The rich, deep, sophisticated voice-over for all the Lexus ads is a strong signal of this luxury automobile. The choice of Philip Bosco for this campaign was inspiring.

Retail personnel can be branding signals. For example, the relevant differentiation that Nordstrom's makes clear in both its business strategy and its brand idea is its special level of customer care. Its branding signals bring this idea to life. A branding signal can be a simple evocative color. Pepperidge Farm put great thought into its white packaging, one of its most powerful branding signals. Consumers talk about how Pepperidge Farm breads and cookies appear to come from a real bakery. Even though they rationally know better, they think of Pepperidge Farm products as being lovingly baked by hand. The pretty white cookie bags, the fresh white packaging for Pepperidge Farm breads and crackers take smart advantage of the emotional connection people have to the brand. Pepperidge Farm owns the color white as a powerful branding signal and has made it all its own.

Just as you shouldn't confuse the words "brand" and "branding," you shouldn't confuse the words "advertising" and "branding." It's something I learned from my many years working in both arenas. Advertising is just one of the many branding signals a brand can use to get its idea across. Some brands use their advertising as their primary branding signals. Beer brands are well known for this branding signal and do it quite well. So well we often pay more attention to the beer ads during a Super Bowl game than to the game itself. Advertising is often used as a branding signal by automobile manufacturers as it can be an incredibly effective way to signal difference in this very competitive category. More often than not, however, advertising is just one branding signal in an arsenal of signals. Advertising may be used to keep a brand top of mind—much as Lunesta sleep medication does or as IBM does. Brands like these know their most powerful branding signals lie in other areas. Lunesta's most powerful signal is in the efficacy of its sleep-inducing chemistry, and IBM's is in the enterprise computing solutions it offers its customers. Brand organizations that know which branding signals in which to make the greatest investment is something I'll cover in chapter 8.

Some brands, by dint of their business category, use a lot of branding signals to transmit their idea. Other brands use only a few. The two or three branding signals that have the greatest influence on what a consumer associates with a brand are called power signals. Power signals are the branding signals that have the power to generate a disproportionate impact for the brand. The Google name is a power signal. While it's a sort of made up name, it's been imbued with all the right associations. FedEx trucks and the people who work for

FedEx are power signals. The sweaty bolt on the Gatorade bottle is a power signal that indicates the difference this energy drink will make to your athletic performance. The squeak of a finger on a newly washed wineglass is a power signal for Dawn detergent. The eBay website is a power signal. KFC's Colonel is a power signal. There are many different types of power signals.

Washington Mutual's retail banking environment is a power signal. It has designed its banks to look like friendly stores, with no high, barrier-like counters and no teller windows. Although other banks encourage you to do your banking outside through ATMs, Washington Mutual has a concierge to usher you inside. (It also has lots of ATMs.) Washington Mutual uses as its power signal an environment that welcomes people. This power signal has created an enjoyable customer experience while differentiating Washington Mutual from other banks.

The Staples "Easy Button" is a power signal. The leader in office supplies, Staples has developed a brand campaign that's in sync with its brand signals. The Easy Button is a perfect signal for the brand's meaningful point of difference. Staples makes it easy for you to get the stuff you need and get out of the store fast. The brand's other branding signals support this idea. The store layout makes it easy to find what you need and get back to work and the store personnel always know exactly where to find the specific laser cartridge to fit your printer. You can even download an "Easy" search engine from staples.com to your PC desktop, allowing you to even more easily find office supplies. If so inclined, you can buy an "Easy" novelty button at Staples for about $4.99.

Another great branding signal is convenience, which Netflix has employed to great advantage. It has capitalized on the internet boom to create a service any movie lover can appreciate. Members can rent four DVDs at a time for $19.95 a month without schlepping to the video store, and there is never a late fee. Members receive and then return the DVDs by mail and either order new movies to be delivered, or have them automatically sent from a wish list they keep and update online.

Netflix.com currently serves over 500,000 subscribers and adds 15,000 new subscribers every month. It has surpassed Blockbuster as the number-one bulk buyer of DVDs from distributors. The convenience it affords, enabled by its operations, is a power branding signal. Yes, operations can definitely be a power signal, especially when they differentiate one brand from its major competitor. Netflix.com is one of the best business models online. It has built a brand on the idea of convenience.

This book will tell you how to assess the right power branding signals for your brand as a function of your brand idea. You'll see that it has to do with how and where your customers interact with your brand and which branding signals most effectively and efficiently convey the right associations. This book will also teach you how to ensure that your branding signals are in sync with both your brand idea and your business strategy. Lose the linkage between any two and you're in trouble. A brand that is not strategically aligned with branding signals spells trouble. Later I give you examples of brands that had incredible branding signals but lost sight of the idea on which the signals were based. I also give you examples of brands in which the brand idea was not aligned with the business strategy. Bigger trouble.

At the end of the day, a brand idea has to be simple and sharply focused for the people who will be creating and transmitting the branding signals—your employees. If this doesn't happen, you've got more than a transmission problem.

The Job of Branding Signals Belongs to Everyone

Over the years, branding signals have evolved in shape, size, and dimension. Most consumers form their opinion about a brand based on exposure to any number of different branding signals. This is another critical reason to make sure you get your relevant differentiation distilled to an elevator-simple idea. Just as you need to be sure the consumers you want to reach can connect with your brand idea, it's equally important to make sure your brand idea can be easily understood by the people inside your organization. Given the fact that in today's world, advertising is only one of several ways consumers pick up messages about a brand, branding signals are now the responsibility of every functional area of a corporate organization. Branding isn't just for marketing anymore. The people who do the branding—those who determine what the branding signals should communicate—need to know exactly what it is they're trying to communicate about the brand and why. If your brand idea is meant to communicate ease of use as a differentiator, the people manufacturing the packaging must understand this, as must the copywriters responsible for writing the operating instructions. If your brand idea is based on the difference of a no-questions-asked guarantee, you've got to make sure your phone representatives are aware of this fact and understand what it means relative to interactions with customers. You might also want to make sure your manufacturing partners look for ways to make your products as durable as possible.

It's essential to make your brand idea an organizational rallying cry. Doing so will ensure that it drives all brand behavior and activity in a consistent way. Comprehension and consistency lead to credibility and trust. When everyone in the organization gets the idea on which the brand is based, they can genuinely "be the brand." Beyond the all-important customer-facing implications this has, it can also easily extend to the human resources department, enabling better recruitment of the right people with shared values, and allows the finance department to better represent the brand in the business community. Engaging the organization in the brand idea is a critical component to brand—and branding—success.

What a Good Branding Signal Communicates

A good branding signal communicates something that seems almost intuitively right for the brand. It's almost as if you couldn't image the brand without it. Think about the Colonel and KFC, for example, or the lightning quick speed with which Google turns up the answer to your query. Good branding signals are not only appropriate to the brand idea, but bring it to life in almost magical ways. A good branding signal communicates something proprietary—something that could only be associated with or owned by your brand. A good branding signal communicates that the consumer won't be fooled and should trust what the brand is promising to deliver.

23

A good branding signal conveys the promise of the brand idea. It communicates that the brand is fun or easy or will provide security or peace of mind, that the brand will give you more energy, protect your investments, is accessible or approachable, will make your kids smarter, is a cinch to operate, or is mild on the hands. A good branding signal communicates something that is authentic to the brand idea and ultimately that is believable and memorable.

When I'm on a subway, laden down with newspaper and briefcase, hanging on with one hand, it's still incredibly easy for me to scroll through my iPod tunes with a single finger. This is a good branding signal because it communicates to me that my lifestyle was factored into the product design of the iPod. The product design signals exactly what it is about iPod that makes it meaningfully different and so popular to so many people. Functional, friendly design is an iPod power signal.

When I go into a Starbucks with my BlackBerry and settle down for a few moments, I know it will be uninterrupted time. No one is going to come over and ask me if I'd like some pasta to go with the latte. No one is going to rush me or tell me they need the table for the next reservation. I can sit there with my $3.85 latte and read my e-mail. The Starbucks environment is a good branding signal because it beautifully communicates what makes the Starbucks brand unique. It's a branding signal linked to both the Starbucks business strategy—sell coffee—and brand strategy—make the coffee experience seem like a relaxing European café. It's a personal public place that's more than just about coffee. The Starbucks environment is familiar and welcoming no matter where in the world it may be. It's a good branding signal because it wonderfully expresses the simple, different idea behind the Starbucks brand.

For that matter, the name BlackBerry is a good branding signal, as are the names ThinkPad, Leap Frog, and Google. All these products are based on pretty complex technology, but none of these names is intimidating or scary in any way. BlackBerry sounds kind of whimsical, in fact. Google, despite its phenomenal force as a search engine, actually sounds childlike. Leap Frog is a line of kids' electronics whose brand idea is to give your bright youngster a chance to leapfrog over the other bright youngsters in the class. It captures its brand difference in its name. And the ThinkPad name signals the simple idea of a more intelligent PC. A name is one of the most critical of all branding signals. These names are good branding signals because they intuitively signal that the experience of the product will be fun and easy.

When people make the decision to make their teeth whiter and brighter and they walk down the dental products aisle at the pharmacy, Crest Whitestrips jumps out at them. This name is a good branding signal because it signals, without a doubt, the difference inherent in the brand idea. These easy strips will make your teeth white. Business-wise, the product stunningly delivers on the idea. Need I tell you why Baby Einstein as a name is a good branding signal for educational infant products? In chapter 7 I give you more information on names and naming, especially names as branding signals.

Identify something that establishes that your product or service is different and relevant and make it simple to understand, and you've got a brand idea. Think about the best way to express this idea and you've got a brand strategy. Create good signals, and you've got branding. Align it all with your business strategy and deliver on it, and you've got a winner.

The Simplest Ideas Are "Genius in Hindsight"

One of the most gratifying aspects of writing this book was the opportunity it gave me to talk to a number of very interesting people. Some of these folks are former clients, some former bosses and mentors, and some colleagues from advertising agencies and brand organizations. Every conversation taught me something different and gave me something important to share.

Peter Georgescu, with whom I worked when he was CEO of Y&R, agreed with my premise that the best brands have always been based on simple ideas and that the success of these brands is the result of the enduring branding signals these ideas inspired. In fact, Peter said that "The best brands are often based on such simple ideas it somehow seems they can't be right. These ideas seem almost too obvious but, in the end, were proven to be genius in hindsight. Creativity is almost never logical prospectively. Thank goodness creativity isn't logical.

"Lots of simple ideas were so simple, they were hard to sell," Peter told me. "I remember a story about aspirin that involved lots of research. Weeks and weeks of focus groups on aspirin formulas, and the like, that yielded boxes and boxes of studies. Oddly, one theme that kept coming through wasn't contained in any of the formal research findings. It was the repetitive, off-the-cuff remarks made by many of the people we talked to. It came through by way of observational research. 'When I have a headache, I take two aspirin and a Dr Pepper. Two aspirin and a Dr Pepper' is what these people kept saying. It seems that for a lot of folks, aspirin and caffeine was a great remedy for headache pain. We were curious and Bristol-Myers listened and a sensational brand was born—Excedrin. By God, it worked, and Bristol-Myers captured and executed the idea brilliantly. The brand and its signals were the result of something as simple and now obvious as two aspirin and a Dr Pepper.

"Or go back to Marlboro Country," Peter continued. "It's a *cowboy* story, for goodness sake! It's almost silly, and seems too simple. It can't possibly work or be right. But it was. Leo Burnett was a genius, and the branding signals he created were genius and have become legend."

Another powerhouse brand Peter talked about was McDonald's. He told me that Keith Reinhard, currently CEO and chairman of the agency DDB Needham, made an observation about the brand and the category that was completely different and very meaningful to a large segment of the population: mothers. The observation he made? It's okay to take your kids out to lunch. You have permission to do so. What was the branding signal created to communicate this? The still-famous line, "You deserve a break today." It was revolutionary for its time, but the simple message endured and the brand has become a powerhouse. The golden arches, another of McDonald's power signals, reach out to hungry kids, moms, and everyone else. As Peter said, you couldn't look ahead and see the logic in any of the ideas. Only in retrospect do they seem brilliant.

Although many brand ideas have become brilliant in retrospect, the people responsible for these ideas didn't just pull them out of the air. As Peter said, these ideas often were the result of simple observations made about everyday things that other brand management teams may have overlooked. It wasn't serendipity but rather a matter of reading between the lines (or the aisles).

Some of the stories in this book relate to brands that looked beyond the obvious for their ideas and others that looked at the obvious from a delightfully different perspective. People who are responsible for the best brands know where to look for insights. They look either deep inside or far outside of what's been done before, and they take totally different perspectives. In doing so, they take risks. Safe ideas are boring, most likely undifferentiated, and definitely not worth "saving as."

I'm going to show you where and how to go about looking for insights that will lead you to a simple brand idea. I'm going to tell you how to sharpen your idea so that your organization can create and manage the branding signals that will most effectively communicate your brand idea. This book will help you understand what makes a good branding signal good and why some branding signals are simply more powerful than others at embedding the associations you want consumers to file in their mental file folders. You'll discover why some signals have far greater impact than others and which ones will save your organization time and money. This book explains why even the best branding signals fail if they don't live up to what consumers expect. Your branding signals must deliver on what your brand idea promises.

2

A Short History of the World of Brands—Really Short

Before we move on to how the best brands do what they do, I want to make sure we're not operating in a vacuum. That wouldn't be any more helpful than over-complicating issues. Here's some basic historical background on brands and branding so you can make sense of where we do go from here, and why.

In the beginning there was light. No, it wasn't GE. Actually, it was fire. The word "brand" comes from the Old Norse word *brandr*, which means "to burn." The Vikings branded their animals to identify them. In ancient China, Greece, and Rome, artisans marked—or branded—their wares to signal identity and also to help villagers establish preferences. In the twelfth and thirteenth centuries, various craft guilds required artisans to "brand" their goods as a means of legal protection. In the case of gold and silversmiths, it was also to guarantee the quality of the materials.

Real brand names as we know them today first appeared in the sixteenth century. Whiskey distillers burned the name of the producer of the potent potables into the top of each barrel. In the eighteenth century, brand names were chosen to make products easier to remember and to differentiate one from another. Competition was born and along with it the need to establish differentiation and relevance.

By the nineteenth century, brands had kicked in big time. Brand names were used to enhance a product's perceived value. "Old Smuggler. Scotch with a History" was one of the first. Among all the other things they brought with them, Europeans brought branding to America.

In the United States, tobacco and patent medicine manufacturers were among the branding pioneers. The signals they created—the packaging, posters, ads, and more—have become collectors' items. Individual manufacturers used this early branding to promote their wares to customers. Prior to this, local general stores sold bulk goods out of crates and barrels.

Railroads became the primary distribution channels as the country expanded, making products available nationwide. National brands emerged. Mass production made it possible for almost anyone who wanted something to have it. Communication channels, specifically newspapers and magazines, increased in number. Advertising became a significant means of funding these publications. The job of media buyer was created.

Companies like Procter & Gamble, Colgate Palmolive, General Foods, and H. J. Heinz improved on the art and science of individual packaging as well as print advertising. They discovered early on how powerful and even magical the right signals could be as a means of influencing consumers with regard to purchase decisions. Along with media buyer, industrial design became a good career choice. Long before we even knew what a computer file folder was, brands began to find residence in those of the mental variety.

The country grew. The population grew. Prosperity grew. The number of consumer choices grew, in both the number of products and the number of brands. And today, as we all know, you can apply branding to just about anything: a product, a company, an organization, a service, a retail experience, a place, a blog, or even a person.

Early Signals Were a Piece of Cake (or Chocolate)

Branding in early modern times, let's say the 1930s or 1940s, was relatively easy. As now, branding started with a simple idea that was different in meaning from similar brands yet relevant to the people you wanted to reach. Branding signals generally took the form of advertising, packaging, and promotions. Branding trademark symbols, popularized earlier as a way to distinguish one brand from another, were used even more extensively and very effectively. The Land O' Lakes™ Indian maiden and the Jolly Green Giant™ joined the little Uneeda™ biscuit boy, Tony the Tiger™, and the snappy Mr. Peanut™ on grocery store shelves. Symbols like these signaled freshness. They signaled quality. They signaled authenticity and grrrrreatness. These were easy signals to remember and they represented very good brands. At this time, marketing and advertising departments were mostly responsible for creating branding signals. Talented copywriters and graphic designers were in great demand.

Back in those days, the number of brands was far smaller than today. For that reason, branding signals had a better chance of reaching and registering with consumers. There wasn't too much competition—mental desktops were a lot less cluttered. You could safely assume without too much worry that your brand would find a place to reside in the consumer's head.

Just as there weren't as many brands as there are today, there weren't too many choices when it came to the size, shape, or dimension these signals took. In developing a branding strategy, your choices were generally newspapers and magazines, billboards, and radio. A great many radio broadcasts were totally funded by one brand, and the stars of the programs became associated with those brands. Not too many people today remember that Jack Benny's show was responsible for selling a lot of Jell-O. Afternoon drives in the country were brought to you by the Barbasol, Esso, and Coca-Cola signs that dotted the roadsides. Fast food hadn't been invented, nor had backseat arguments about where to stop for lunch. As always, word of mouth played a big role in spreading news of brands. Families still lived in the same three-block radius and shared Sunday supper. Mothers told mothers about the best new baby products. Branding at this time—the creation and management of signals—was one part art, one part understanding what people listened to on the radio, and one part family values.

Then Things Got More Complicated

Now let's fast forward a couple of decades, to the 1960s, 1970s, and 1980s. During this period, brands by the dozens started to crop up. This was the result of more efficient manufacturing and delivery capabilities and the financial strength of industry giants like Procter & Gamble, Colgate Palmolive, and Johnson & Johnson. A new playing field was taking shape and along with it a whole new set of branding rules. The need to find a different yet relevant point of view for a brand became increasingly challenging. Globalization was also becoming a critical factor in the brand and branding business. How will a brand play from one country to another? Can it, given all the diversity and cultural implications?

Beyond the proliferation of material goods and services, this era also ushered in new ways and means to signal a brand. As mental desktops began to fill up, attention to branding strategy became more critical. Whom do you want to talk to? Where are they? What are they reading, watching, or doing? Branding signals began to take on different dimensions. Radio gave way to television and a nation of couch potatoes. Although there were fewer newspapers, magazines took up three times more room on the corner newsstands. You could find publications for ladies, gentlemen, and children of all ages, not to mention gardeners, sports enthusiasts, runners, cooks, and news junkies, to name a few. Audience segmentation became a key consideration when determining to whom, how, and where to signal your brand idea.

The signals over which brands had immediate control were still more or less of the traditional media and media channel variety: TV ads, print ads, direct mail, radio spots, the emergence of telemarketing, promotions that involved movies, and the plastic toys inside McDonald's Happy Meal boxes. Word of mouth was, of course, still powerful, but the Internet had yet to exert its power.

Just as the competition among brands for space in people's heads was starting to heat up, so was the competition for space on the airwaves and on the page. Advertising agencies were hotter and cooler than they'd ever been. The quest for sensational creative minds took on even greater importance than before. Touting a basic feature or benefit no longer was enough. Anything of a commodity nature was simply cost of entry. Innovative thinkers were needed. Agencies like Ogilvy & Mather, BBDO, Ammirati & Puris, J. Walter Thomas, and McCann Erikson competed for clients and talent.

Brand*ing* took on greater importance as the contest to set a brand apart became more heated. The challenge to establish a different meaning on which to base a brand idea and determine how to best express this difference became harder. The ability to capture a message cohesively and coherently—make it shorthand—was the Holy Grail. Brand was the battle. Branding was the war. It became the niftiest game in town.

What I Learned From the 1970s

As I said earlier, I was fortunate to start my career at Ogilvy & Mather in the late 1970s. Advertising was at the top of its game. David Ogilvy, although retired, popped in once or twice a year from his chateau in France and randomly dropped by the offices of young account executives, as I was. He'd ask what you were up to. I can only hope I was up to something good when he dropped in on me.

I learned many things in those early days, but there was one thing that stuck with me more than anything else—the need to identify a simple but meaningfully different idea on which to base your brand and then to create and transmit the branding signals necessary to bring the idea to life. At the time, advertising was among the most powerful branding signals a brand could use to communicate what it stood for.

Ogilvy and a number of other agencies used advertising with a degree of expertise that continues to set standards for excellence and effectiveness. This ability has led to some very long-standing brand relationships. Although I didn't work on the American Express account, my colleague and teaching partner Jed Bernstein did and provided me with great insight on the idea behind the brand, and some of the branding signals from the 1970s that expressed the idea.

"Think about the number-one concern travelers had back then," Jed said. "I'm going to lose my cash or my traveler's checks. American Express not only had a product that addressed this concern, but they had an incredibly effective way of differentiating the idea. It was the idea of the security provided by American Express Travelers Cheques and an incredibly effective and powerful signal with which to communicate its idea: Karl Malden.

"Karl Malden, a well-respected actor, played a detective on a show called *The Streets of San Francisco*. He was a stern, nononsense character. Although we all knew that Karl Malden wasn't really a detective, it was suggested in the way the ad campaign was written that we could trust this man when he admonished us not to leave home without them, referring to American Express Travelers Cheques. The point was that if your Travelers Cheques were stolen, they would be replaced."

Malden was a branding signal—a simple, forceful, and emotionally persuasive image of the security provided by American Express. Dressed in his trench coat, he looked exactly like a detective, or even an agent from the U.S. Embassy who'd come to your hotel to help you out in an emergency. American Express was able to make Karl Malden, the ultimate detective, a powerful branding signal of its "Don't leave home without it" brand idea. Karl Malden was the voice of authority. He communicated the security associated with carrying American Express Travelers Cheques. Protection and security are pillars of the brand.

Another American Express branding signal was associated with the prestige of carrying the Card. The famous line "Do you know me?" accompanied a sensational advertising campaign. The brand idea and this long-running signal (used for over twenty years) came as a result of the wonderful insight had by American Express that all businesspeople share a similar fear—the fear of being embarrassed at an important client dinner meeting as the result of not having their credit card accepted. The business strategy behind the American Express Card is that it's a charge card, which means there is no preset spending limit. You pay as you go. The brand idea linked to this strategy is that you can have the confidence that you (the Card) will always be accepted.

I talked to Jed about the advertising campaign. "Yes, everyone does have a fear of having their credit card rejected—even the most well-known people," he said. "This campaign employed people who were all famous in some way, but not in obvious ways. You knew their faces but didn't know their names, or you knew their names but didn't know their faces: William Miller, who was a vice presidential candidate, the authors James Michener and Stephen King, the musicians James Galway and Itzhak Perlman, even Tom Landry was in the campaign.

"The way the ads were constructed was almost game-like. Each ad opened with the line 'Do you know me?' While the person in the ad talked to you about his or her accomplishments, it was a race to the finish to see if you could remember the name of the person before the name clicked its way across the bottom of an American Express Card in the last frame of the commercial. The campaign never got boring. There was always someone relevant to use in the ads, which were both in print and on television. The simple premise was that if shopkeepers and restaurant owners might not recognize names and faces—even famous names and faces—they'd always recognize and accept the American Express Card. It was the ultimate signal of prestige and acceptance for anyone who carried it."

Another of the people I spoke to was Ken Roman, who ran Ogilvy when I joined it. My job interview with him all those years ago has stayed in my memory. I was ready for some very tough analytical questions about segmentation models and subjects of that nature. Instead, Ken asked me about the last book I had read, the last museum exhibition I had seen. He knew that others in the firm with whom I had interviewed with earlier would have covered the business stuff. He wanted to know if I was creatively aware, because a good account person must be aware of contemporary trends and social issues in order to serve clients well.

Ken talked to me about American Express and a number of other Ogilvy clients. "American Express came out of the gate with a simple philosophy," Ken said. "They called it PSS: Prestige. Service. Security. They've stayed on message—this very simple idea—since the beginning. They've changed branding tactics to keep up with the times, of course, but American Express has never wavered from its philosophy: American Express will be there for you."

Although advertising and branding had evolved considerably by the late 1980s, Americans remained a nation of believers when it came to brands. Despite the fact that we were beginning to see an increase in the number of brands and the number of brand claims and promises, we weren't yet a nation of cynics. We weren't yet bombarded by the unsolicited messages made possible through the Internet. We were only just beginning to feel the effects of being overly stimulated by communications channels. We paid attention to Karl Malden, and we believed him when he told us what to do to protect our vacation money.

We paid attention when Tip O'Neill, Robert Ludlum, Red Adair, and Beverly Sills asked us if we knew them. What they were trying to tell us validated our most basic concerns. They, like us, worry about being embarrassed. American Express ads gave us permission to feel the same concern—and to enjoy the same security provided by the American Express Card. Advertising as a branding signal transmitted exactly the associations American Express wanted us to file in our mental file folders about its brand idea. It was an idea worth "saving as."

"One-Quarter Cleansing Cream"

The Dove soap story is another success story Ken Roman shared with me. "Dove soap is a beautiful example of establishing a simple proposition, or idea, and staying with it," he said. "David Ogilvy's original proposition for Dove soap has become legend. It was an idea conveyed by the simple image of velvety cream being poured gently into a bar of soap."

This image was used in all types of advertising, from television to print and billboards, and became an indelible branding signal. In fact, this signal, like other memorable signals, became the foundation for Dove's unsurpassed success as a brand. "Dove soap doesn't dry your skin because it's one-quarter cleansing cream." An undeniably simple idea transmitted by a persuasive image—an unassailable signal for its message.

As the soap category started to diversify in brand names and claims, Dove was able to identify something different to say, something that was extremely relevant to a huge percentage of the population. Ask a woman fearful of drying skin and wrinkles, and you can understand the power of the image of moisturizing cream as a branding signal. To this day, I can walk down a supermarket aisle, scan the incredible number of soap brands, catch sight of a Dove package, and think, "one-quarter cleansing cream." No matter what type of Dove product it is, the simple idea behind the brand has evolved beautifully.

Time for a Little Snuggle

I got my first inkling of just how powerful the right branding signals could be—and how exacting the process to identify them—when I was a brand manager at Lever Brothers. At the time, Lever was playing catch-up with Procter & Gamble in a lot of product categories. Most of the time it was able to develop products as well as P&G, but rarely better. Lever was in a slow-follower mode. With the exception of a few brands, such as Wisk, which pioneered the liquid laundry detergent segment, and Dove, which was superior to Ivory, Lever's products often were in the number-three or -four spot. For those unfamiliar with the business of packaged goods, it's harder and harder to make real money if your brand doesn't occupy the first- or second-place position. In fact, today many big retailers such as Wal-Mart and Costco distribute only the number-one or -two brands. Winning is not only a question of relative profitability but of survival.

At the time, I was working with the team on Final Touch fabric softener. Final Touch had long been taking a beating from P&G's Downy brand. No matter what we did, we couldn't come up with an idea for the brand that could contend with Downy. We couldn't get consumers to believe that Final Touch made clothes softer. We tried facts and we tried figures, and we even tried customer testimonials. Despite the fact that Downy and Final Touch were virtual parity products, nothing we did worked. Why?

First of all, P&G has always been masterful at understanding brands, how to connect with consumers, and how to transmit the right branding signals to get its ideas across. The name powerfully signaled the differentiated, relevant idea: Downy made your clothes soft. It was an emotional idea and made for visceral associations consumers could tuck away in their mental file folders. Besides its name, another of its branding signals is the trademarked symbol on its packaging: the picture of a sweet little girl with a soft, fluffy towel wrapped around her head.

The second reason Lever was taking a clobbering was that consumers don't connect with facts and figures. P&G knows that the best brands connect on an emotional level, not on a rational level, and that these ideas are signaled accordingly. It's a rare brand that can use mathematical equations to its advantage. Obviously, to succeed on any measure, the Lever team needed to find a way to approach people on a more emotional level. It needed an idea as simple and as compelling as Downy's, but something that established its own meaningfully different fabric softening idea. It was a challenge and Lever had a challenger brand. What could possibly say "soft clothes your family will appreciate" better than a brand named Downy?

The team in Europe, where Lever held a stronger category position, helped with the answer. A French brand of Lever fabric softener had come up with the simple idea to use a teddy bear to signal its softening ability. Its advertising showed a teddy bear being dropped onto a basket of freshly washed clothing. Both the idea—teddy bear softness—and the branding signals were connecting with consumers, and the French brand was proving a huge success. Lever decided to add another fabric softener brand to its line of American products and to use the idea of a teddy bear to sell it.

This is not the end of the story. Although it might have seemed that all Lever needed to do to succeed with its new product was bring the teddy bear back to America, it turned out to be more challenging than that. I received not only a lesson on brands and branding, but a lesson in the challenges of global branding.

To begin with, Lever wanted to make more of the teddy bear as a signal than the French were doing. Research told Lever that American consumers wouldn't connect with an inanimate bear. American audiences, it seemed, required a little more life in their brand icons—a personality. Choosing a bear with a personality didn't prove as easy an assignment as you might think. I would pass the firm's largest conference room and see zillions of teddy bears on the conference table surrounded by fifteen adults discussing how many fingers the bear should have, the texture of the fur, the size of the tummy, and on and on. One of Jim Henson's original puppeteers—a real "Muppet" guy—was brought in to assist. The Lever bear team debated attributes of teddy bears I didn't know existed. The process the team went through sounds amusing in retrospect, but it was serious business. For a branding signal to be a good one, it has to generate exactly the associations you want it to. The Lever team wanted a lovable, animated little bear consumers would associate with the softening ability of its brand. It finally succeeded in finding one—the current little fellow who was found to embody all the right emotional attributes the team members were looking for. They found something that could compete with Downy.

In the course of the teddy bear assessment, the decision was made to name the American version of the fabric softener Snuggle. This evocative name provided greater focus in the search for the bear. Remember, the more focused a brand idea is, the more effective your branding signals will be. The simple idea behind a fabric softener named Snuggle gave the team more clearly defined parameters for the choice of spokesbear (although it wasn't until just recently that the bear actually said anything). After some very interesting discussions, Lever finally found its Snuggle bear and gave Downy a run for its softness. (As a footnote, Final Touch was one of a number of household brands, including Rit and Niagara, sold by Unilever to Phoenix Brands.)

A Simple Idea Turned Sour

One client assignment taught me two lessons: the importance of a simple idea based on something of an emotional nature, rather than on facts and figures, even when functionality is a critical cost of entry, and what can happen when consumer faith in your idea is undermined. (In other words, what happens when consumers feel hoodwinked?) In this case, the product category was powdered lemonade mixes. The brand I was assigned to was Country Time Lemonade.

Country Time was created back in the early 1970s through the marketing power of General Foods and Ogilvy & Mather. At the time, General Foods was doing extremely well with another brand they'd created, Kool-Aid—a powdered mix to which you added water to make a variety of flavored drinks. The problem with Kool-Aid (besides associations with the horrific Jonestown story) was that it was hard to convince someone over ten years old to drink it. It was a kids' drink. The challenge for General Foods and Ogilvy became how to sell Kool-Aid to grown-ups.

The team began by examining the soft drink market, specifically the powdered drink market, and it came upon a brand called Wyler's powdered lemonade mix sitting on the shelf. Wyler's was marketed by Borden's and was sold in a canister. The Wyler's brand idea was based on functionality: its taste, which happened to be like real lemonade. The food technicians at General Foods went to work and in fairly short order developed a lemon-flavored powdered mix that tasted much better than Wyler's.

But that wasn't the answer. I'd learned (or been taught) that a brand idea based on a functional claim rarely wins. Here's a tip: Look for a category that is all about facts and figures and functionality, and see if you can go in with an emotional brand idea. Emotion almost always wins over function, even in the most commonly used or ubiquitous products. For example, we never used to care about the claims made by distributors of fresh chicken products until a man by the name of Frank Perdue came along. All of a sudden we cared. Here was a "tough man" offering us "tender chicken." I'd never met a poultry farmer in my life, but if I could have imagined what one would look like, he would be Frank Perdue. I wanted Frank's chickens.

But back to the lemonade. Our General Foods lemonade mix tasted as good, if not better, than Wyler's, but what emotionally differentiated idea could we use to win in the category? The brand teams at Ogilvy and General Foods did their homework, talking to consumers about how they felt about lemonade. In doing so they came upon what's known as the gold standard in branding—the one thing you can say to communicate that your brand is the best. The gold standard for a lemonade brand was the simple promise that it could taste like good, old-fashioned lemonade.

With this bit of information in mind, the first thing the team did was create one of the most powerful branding signals a brand can own—and transmit—to express an idea: the *name* of the brand. The right name can go a long way in transmitting and embedding the right brand associations. The name developed by the team was Country Time. With the idea and the name, the idea was very well focused. What other signals could be created to communicate the idea? Because advertising was still incredibly effective in those days, the team chose to use a story as a branding signal. A story by way of an ad campaign that featured a lovable, white-haired grandfather, suspenders and all, sitting on a sun-drenched porch on a sizzling summer day mixing up a pitcher of ice-cold lemonade. The pitcher was dripping with those little beads of sweat that captured the authenticity the brand hoped to convey. It was the sort of picture consumers talked about when they were asked about the idea of old-fashioned lemonade.

Once the name of the brand and the lovable grandpa sent out the powerful branding signals, the brand found its way onto mental desktops. Consumers craving good, old-fashioned lemonade ran to the grocery store shelves and left Wyler's high and dry. General Foods and Ogilvy had solved the problem of how to go about selling lemon Kool-Aid to adults. By the time I joined the account team, the brand was already being expanded into ready-to-drink cans and the diet drink market. Grandpa was rocking and rolling. He stayed rocking until the day Minute Maid introduced an ad for a new lemonade mix. That ad was the beginning of the end of the mix-it-yourself lemonade category.

The TV spokesperson in the ad had three canisters in front of him: Country Time, Wyler's, and Minute Maid. He announced with authority that Minute Maid was made from the juice of twenty lemons, Wyler's was made from the juice of two lemons, and Country Time was made from the juice of—uh-oh—no lemons. Which lemonade would you buy, ladies and gentleman, no-lemon lemonade, or twenty-lemon lemonade?

After seeing the spots, we knew it would not be business as usual for Country Time. Our team went back into the field to see how consumers were reacting to this new player in the category. Turns out facts and figures had people stumped. No one could remember which brand had two lemons and, while some folks did recall that Minute Maid had twenty, it wasn't enough to motivate them to try it. What people did remember, unfortunately, was that Country Time had zero lemons. How could you sell lemonade without lemons?

We thought about the idea of reformulating Country Time and reintroducing it as the lemonade with twenty-one lemons. In testing, however, that idea only brought attention to the initial negative response of having started out with no lemons. We toyed with telling consumers that Country Time still tasted better than Minute Maid (which it did), but we still heard the refrain, "No lemons!" We thought about talking about how Country Time got its tart and tangy flavor from lemon peels, but few consumers were interested in a chemistry lesson.

The first lesson I learned from all of this was that you can't sell lemonade with facts. Emotion sells. The second, more important, lesson I learned was that you should never, ever break your bond of trust with consumers. When people found out there were no lemons in Country Time, they felt hoodwinked and cheated. They felt the brand had broken its promise to them. Although Country Time ads never said anything about the composition of the lemonade, the brand seemed to have lost its authenticity. When I saw Grandpa, I believed in Country Time. Now, I don't trust the brand—or the lemonade mix category. Good lessons, frustrating story.

"Simple Trumps Everything"

I spoke with Bob Pittman, former CEO of AOL, who was responsible for inventing many powerful brands, including MTV and Nickelodeon. In fact, he revolutionized the television category with those brands. When I explained the "simple" premise of this book, he intuitively understood what I was talking about. He's put the premise into practice with great success countless times. "I got to AOL in the mid-1990s," he said. "It was a fabulous brand, but it was starting to get complicated. It was losing its focus. The good news was that AOL could do many things—and it could do them all well. The reality is that it was getting complicated for us to tell potential users what AOL was all about. We needed to boil things down to a simple idea. What do we have permission to be? Let's get to the core of what our brand stands for. What is our relationship with the customer? I've learned that before you can do anything, you must understand the brand's relationship with the customer.

"Now, these were ordinary mass-market customers we were dealing with. They made it clear they didn't want any mumbo-jumbo. They didn't want to spend their days configuring things. They wanted the benefits of e-mail and the Internet made easy. They let us know through focus groups that they didn't find any joy in the technological end of it. They just wanted things to be easy and to work. We needed to find a differentiated idea that would communicate we understood what they were telling us. And we had to make it credible."

I asked Bob how AOL made it happen. He told me the company came up with a line that it used to both drive internal branding activities, from engineering improvements to customer service, and as the tagline: "So easy to use, no wonder we're number one." It summed up exactly what AOL wanted to be known for. "If you're a number-one brand, I like to say it," Bob said. "The fact that we said 'easy' was okay. It was reinforcement for the promise we were making, so it wasn't seen as bragging. This simple idea became the powerful force that drove everyone and everything inside the company. Everyone from our engineers to our manufacturing reps understood what this brand idea had to do with them, and they understood the effect it would have on our consumers. For example, the engineers knew that what they created meant no extra clicks or fancy technology. With the AOL brand—actually with any brand—I've found simple trumps everything."

About four years ago Landor had the opportunity to pitch AOL for a chance to do some rebranding work. We talked to the company about the idea of going back to its roots, to what had differentiated it in the beginning: Bob's idea of simplicity. The brand's idea had gotten a bit muddled after he left the company. We presented AOL with the idea of using its well-known yellow "running man" icon as a more powerful signal, as he represents both friendliness and accessibility, both indications of simplicity. We suggested that AOL "tip" the little fellow into all sorts of online and off-line ads and promotions to inject energy and hipness into the brand. BBDO picked up the charge and launched a wonderful new campaign signaling AOL's message of accessible simplicity.

The point is that simple does trump everything. If your brand idea is simple and focused, you can execute it more easily, with greater clarity and creativity—and in a consistent manner—at all the points that a customer comes into contact with the brand. Your branding signals will express exactly what you'd like to get across. The essence of a great brand, Ken Roman emphasized, is "sacrifice." "What's the one thing you can say, the single, simple message you can send about your brand you know people will care about? Is it dry happy babies, security away from home, soft skin, a car that will keep your family safe? Sacrifice everything else and tell *this* simple story."

3

What's Changed Since 1970 and What It Means to Brands

We all know a lot has changed in the past thirty-odd years. Life in general has certainly changed since Dove, American Express, Snuggle, and Country Time first signaled their way into our psyches. The general business climate has changed, too, with regard to trust and credibility and questions of ethics.

More germane, however, is the incredible change in the number of products and services on the global market. There's been a mind-boggling proliferation of brands and brand categories. This includes everything from water to fruit drinks, tooth whiteners to floor polishers, technology to pharmaceuticals, and even branded celebrities: Oprah, Martha, The Donald, Madonna, JLo, and SpongeBob.

Then, of course, there's the proliferation of communication channels, distribution channels, and the variety of branding signals. More traditional branding signals still play a significant part in communication of a brand's idea. These signals include the name of the brand; its logo, colors, trademarks, packaging, and product design; and of course its advertising and promotions. Advertising is still part of the branding mix, although as a smaller percentage. Branding signals are also expressed through direct mail and telemarketing, online and toll-free customer service, online and toll-free ordering, in-store and kiosk experiences. In the years since I first entered the business, our mental files have been inundated with brands and branding signals. Our desktops have gotten cluttered. Suffice it to say, these days it takes a lot more to get a consumer to know you exist, let alone know what makes you worth "saving as."

The Internet and all things technological now play a major role in branding signals. The Internet itself is the source of different types of branding signals, from e-mail, to streaming video messages and pop-ups, to sponsored content links. Major books and papers have been written about branding *on* the Internet, as well as branding *and* the Internet. Ten years ago—five years ago, for goodness sake—who knew what a blog was? Now it's one of the most potent and influential means of shaping belief and opinion. We're just starting to learn how to harness its impact (and its credibility) as a transmitter of brand associations. By the end of 2004, blogs had established themselves as a key part of online culture. Two surveys by the Pew Internet and American Life Project in 2005 established new contours for the blogosphere: 8 million people say they have created blogs; blog readership jumped 58 percent in 2004 and now accounts for 27 percent of Internet users; a strong percentage of Internet users say they get news and other information from blogs and content-rich websites as it is posted online; and 12 percent of Internet users have posted comments or other material on blogs. One article I read stated there would soon be more content in the blogosphere than in the Library of Congress! Talk about new signals to take into consideration.

A lot more changes have taken place in the cultural and commercial worlds over the past years than I'm qualified to comment on. However, at least five major changes have taken place that have had a great impact on brands and branding. Here's what I take into consideration when considering a brand challenge:

1. It's about the individual.
2. The world is moving faster.
3. Consumers are in charge of how they consume marketing and media.
4. We operate on a global scale.
5. America is aging.

It's About the Individual

It used to be that people trusted the institutions they dealt with—banks, government, Congress, and even the family physician. We used to go to the doctor and unhesitatingly trust everything we were told. Now we can go to the Internet and get the medical answers we need and use them to challenge our doctors' recommendations. According to the Yankelovitch Monitor, a respected research resource, today trust in institutions is at an all-time low. Who are people more likely to trust than any institution? Themselves.

We've developed finely tuned credibility sensors. We can find holes in a story from a hundred miles away. The more complicated the story, the more holes we'll find in its fabric. And because people don't have time to listen, we'll chalk up a brand as a fake in the split second it takes to push "delete." It was once said that a great actor can fake authenticity. I'm not sure about that. In any event, don't risk faking anything. Make sure that the branding signals you transmit meet consumer expectations by genuinely delivering on your business strategy and that the brand idea you choose to deliver on is credible and authentic.

The World Is Moving Faster

Without question, the world has sped up. Information comes at us faster and faster and in shorter versions than ever before. I'm not sure if the globe is actually turning faster, but it feels like it is, and it's disconcerting. Technology and engineering, including the Internet, overnight delivery, cell phones, and instant messaging, have given us a sense (if not the reality) of compressed time. There is no time to think. We are forced to process and respond very, very quickly. Multitasking has become a way of life. Go to the gym, any gym in the country, and you'll see someone walking on the treadmill, alternately checking e-mail on a BlackBerry, reading the *Wall Street Journal,* and glancing up at CNN.

We used to send things by mail and, if critical, by overnight mail. If something was really critical, we'd send a telegram by Western Union. Now we send it e-mail. If it's critical, we send an instant message. The messages we send are getting shorter, more brusque, and often include annoying little hieroglyphics. ☺ Memos used to be two pages; then they were one page, then six bullets. Forget grammar and spelling. BlackBerries aren't even fast enough for some people. And talk about opposable thumbs. These digits are now deal breakers.

In addition to this, the world is going wireless. More than one-quarter of Americans use wireless devices—either laptop computers with wireless modems or cellphones—that enable them to go online to surf the web or check e-mail. The Pew Center for Internet Life reports that 18 percent of Internet users said they had used a wireless-enabled laptop, and 29 percent of cell phone users said they'd used a cell phone that can send and receive e-mails.

Bottom line: We get it fast. We listen fast. We process fast. Our brains have to be compensating for this in some physical way, but I'll leave that to the neurologists. I know our nerves are decompensating. What does this mean for a brand? With today's pace of change and information exchange, it's not practical to spend endless hours in a state of analysis paralysis. Trust your research, but trust your intuition even more. Take into consideration all of the new ways people are picking up information and assess them relative to your business and brand strategies. Determine how you make your money, how you can maintain leadership in relevant differentiation, and what branding signals will be most effective.

Consumers Are in Charge of How They Consume Marketing and Media

Because the pace of life around us is speeding up, we want everything condensed into bites—condensed chunks of information that give us a CliffsNotes version of life. We don't have the time or the patience to hear or see the whole story. It's a coping mechanism. The fast influx of information demands fast cerebral processing. We've learned to cut to the chase with everything in life. And we're ready to push the "delete" button at a moment's notice.

Sesame Street and MTV played, and contine to play, a significant role in this dynamic. *Sesame Street* perfected the art of the two-minute spelling lesson, followed by the two-miunte counting lesson, followed by the two-minute morality lesson, followed by the two-minute science lesson. Anything on the screen for more than two minutes and we start to squirm. MTV picked up on instant sensory gratification by feeding us music in quick cuts, pulsing video and visual cues, and a wild display of graphics. "I want my MTV"—and I want it now.

We get our news in sight and sound bites. CNN has perfected this tactic. It gives us just enough information to be able to carry on a conversation at a cocktail party. Heaven forbid if we're seated next to an academician at a dinner party. *USA Today* followed suit and then was made to appear almost archaic by the three-page daily newspapers handed out on metropolitan streetcorners. Our movie reviews, our stock reports, our celeb reports—short and sweet. It's all we can handle, because there's so much stuff out there, and because we have no patience for anything that takes time to think about. We think in shorthand and read in a way that would even make Evelyn Wood dizzy. *Variety* used to be a master at the abbreviated, attention-grabbing headline. Now every supermarket register newsstand is filled with instant eye candy about the latest celebrity breakup, makeup, or diet. A simple brand idea was necessary thirty years ago. Making the idea and the branding signals even quicker to connect with is even more critical today.

More than half of consumers (55 percent) would be willing to pay a little extra to get only the kinds of marketing messages they prefer, but marketers aren't listening, according to the 2005 Yankelovich Marketing Receptivity Survey. The study demonstrates that marketers mistakenly believe that the advent of new media will reengage the resistant consumers, but consumers continue to rebel.

More than 70 percent of consumers say they want technology to block out advertisng. At the same time, 55 percent say they enjoy advertising, up from 47 percent in 2004. The fundamental issue is how to tap in to the positive feelings. Well, 42 percent of consumers say they want marketing that is short and to the point. And more than 33 percent of consumers want marketing when it's convenient to them.

The lesson? It's obvious consumers will be engaged in new media technology, but not for technolgy's sake. J. Walter Smith, president of Yankelovich, says, "Improvements in marketing are more important to consumers than the greater dissemination of new media. Consumers expect marketers to use technology to improve how to appeal to them." The onus is on the people behind the brands and the branding signals to commmunicate messages in a way that best connects to consumers.

We Operate on a Global Scale

Some call it a global village. The writer Tom Friedman refers to it as the "flattening of the world." However you refer to it, the world of business and the world of brands now operate on a truly global scale. Whether it's outsourcing labor, relying on parts manufactured overseas, or achieving a competitive customer base, operating on a global scale is a cost of marketplace entry for some brands. With this global scope, there are any number of issues to take into consideration. Will your brand idea be understood and can it be supported by consistent branding signals throughout the world? Will your brand difference be relevant from one market to the next? Will you have to create a different brand idea for the same product on a country-by-country basis due to cultural differences? What's the cost of doing this? What's the cost of not doing this?

A fundamental question that often arises in the desire to create global brands: should we use the same name globally? The upside of efficiencies in global branding efforts may be significant. A consistent brand name may more easily allow for cross-country sharing of all types of branding signals, including packaging and signage. Nevertheless, it's important to check the prospective name of a new brand for cultural correctness.

Although there have always been matters of global importance to consider when managing a brand, the twenty-first-century global landscape poses a new set of challenges. There are new channels of communications, new political agendas, and new governmental regulations and trade agreements. As you go about thinking about your brand idea, if you believe you'd like to go global, make sure you know where you're going.

America Is Aging

We all think of ourselves as being at least ten years younger than we really are. This has gotten me into trouble on the ski slopes a couple of times, but I'm still skiing. Healthcare and financial service marketers have focused on the Baby Boom market for years, but many brand managers are still chasing the eighteen-to-forty-nine-year-old target. Today, more than half of the Baby Boom generation has crossed into the fifty-plus segment.

According to U.S. census figures, today there are about 76 million people in the United States over the age of fifty. By 2050, there will be over 80 million over age sixty-five (that's one in four). For the first time in history, America is moving away from being a youth oriented culture. Baby Boomers will spend more time retired from a career than they spent becoming educated. Women will spend more time helping their aging parents than they spent raising their own children. Housing, advertising, healthcare, marriage and family life, politics, and religion will all experience a wave of change generated by an aging society. (My eighty-three-year-old father is online. I can only imagine what I'll be doing when I'm eighty.)

As you look at your business strategy and your brand strategy, consider how these population changes will affect your brand.

"Whatever"

While not technically a sociological or economic change similar in degree to the preceding five, I'd also like to tell you to beware of something I call brand attention deficit disorder as you approach whatever brand challenges you face. One of the first symptoms of this disorder is "Whatever."

"Whatever" is a word you hear everywhere in response to all types of questions. "You want to go to the movies?" "Whatever." "You want to have pizza tonight?" "Whatever." "You want to get married?" "Whatever." It's become an all-purpose, generic response to, well, whatever. This ambivalent reaction, dispassionately voiced and accompanied by a Seinfeld-like shrug, is an overt symptom of our world on overload. More specifically, it's a symptom of a numbingly cluttered commercial world. From restaurants to movie channels, airlines to reality shows, SUVs to VCRs, there are too many choices and far too few distinctions between them. We all suffer from brand attention deficit disorder in some form or another. Richard Edelman, the CEO of Edelman Public Relations, a firm involved with a number of major brands, told me that his Microsoft client referred to this state of mind as "continuous partial attention."

As an example, try shopping for a PC from your home. You will quickly be overwhelmed with options, options, options. Desktop or laptop? Microsoft or Apple operating system? What type of processor? How much RAM? How big do you want your hard drive? What screen size? All of this before you even consider what software to purchase. In contrast, how about a simple machine that lets you do e-mail, surf the Internet, do some basic word processing, maybe organize your family photos? Whoever can simplify this for the average person will create differentation and break through the brand attention deficit disorder.

The number-one objective of those responsible for brands is to get people to stop and recognize—in an instant—that they're privvy to something they've never seen before and that it meets a justifiable and relevant need. Doing this is harder now than it ever was, for whatever reason and all of the reasons I talked about. In spite of all of the changes in the world and in the marketplace, the brands that succeed do so because they know that in some fundamental ways, things have never changed at all. While life has gotten faster, while attention spans have shrunk to accommodate more information coming in at a faster rate, today's strongest brands know that the rules for success are still the same. There is no mystery and there should be no complexity.

The not-so-secret sauce of brands and branding is to find something different to say about your brand, make your brand idea as simple and focused as possible, and align it with a business strategy. Doing this will allow your organization to execute and transmit brilliantly effective branding signals. The next section of this book will show you how these brands do it, what you can learn from what they know, and how you can do it, too.

Part II: How the Best Brands Succeed

I talked earlier about my conversation with Stewart Owen, who helped develop the BrandAsset Valuator tool. Stewart knows brands inside and out and, more specifically, the business side of brands. When I talked to him about the importance of getting to a simple, differentiated idea in order to do great branding, he offered some great comments. One of the first things he said was that if you look at any successful business, in any category, you'll notice that it's different in a way people value. Then, he said that before you can start any brand or branding project, you've got to ask yourself three basic questions:

1. What's your business strategy?
2. What does your brand stand for in the minds of your customers (or prospective customers)?
3. Can you align your business strategy with what you'd like your brand to stand for? In other words, can you deliver on the promise of the brand idea?

Although these questions may seem obvious, he told me, it's amazing how many of even the smartest businesspeople don't bother to ask them. It's something I've wondered myself when I think about the many potentially good brand ideas that have either failed entirely or failed to reach their full potential. The number-one reason brands get into trouble is because there's some sort of disconnect between the business strategy and the brand idea. Either there was never a connection to begin with, or the business strategy has changed and the image people have of the brand hasn't. If it's a new company, it's simply a lack of understanding that the two are inextricably linked. You must know what business you're in before you brand it, and you must ensure that you have what it takes to deliver it.

I want to take a minute to tell a story that illustrates Stewart's point. It's a point that's been proven incontrovertibly, and something you must fully understand before you can launch a brand. The story is about IBM. And while the story of IBM's rebound is well known within the business community, I'd like to tell it within the context of the point I'm making.

In 1993, the once-dominant computer company was on the verge of a breakup. Its stock price had hit a twenty-year low. It had posted an $8.1 billion loss and more than 100,000 employees had been let go—from a company that had always maintained a lifetime employment policy. Worst, IBM's whole way of computing and of working with its customers was viewed as antiquated. The company struggled under the weight of a management structure that created independent business units with redundant processes and disconnected information systems. Because of years during which it had no meaningful competition, IBM had become insular, siloed, and slow to react to changes, from the advent of new personal computers and computing platforms, to the rise of many small software and computer companies created by nimble entrepreneurs who were more customer-focused and could react more quickly to changes in the market.

Enter Lou Gerstner, former president of American Express and Chairman and CEO of RJR Nabisco. Some industry pundits thought he had been brought in primarily to accelerate a breakup of the company into smaller, autonomous businesses that could move faster and better compete with the nimble entrepreneurs.

They didn't think IBM could exist in its current state. Lou also decided it couldn't, but took a completely different approach to solving the problem. Instead of pulling the company apart, he pushed it together, creating a much more streamlined and integrated company. He recognized that there was a need to integrate the proliferation of technology piece-parts and systems, along with the services to support them. Lou understood that IBM's inherent strength was in its ability to put everything together for customers in combination with

IBM's tremendous understanding of business and business problems to create new value through total solutions.

To help begin executing this new business strategy, Lou brought in Abby Kohnstamm, who had held a number of senior marketing positions at American Express. To begin the alignment process between business strategy and brand idea, Abby took a brand "inventory" to assess how people felt about the brand, both its fact-based and aspirational attributes. She wanted to see what customers perceived that IBM stood for and what aspects of the IBM brand could be utilized as a base to build on.

Through this work, it became clear that the brand name was a powerful asset—but what it stood for needed to be more clearly articulated and made relevant to the information technology marketplace emerging in the 1990s. In the research, it was discovered that, despite IBM's problems, people had strong, positive emotions about the brand. People not only understood IBM's latent strengths, but also gave IBM permission to go into new spaces because of the company's legacy of excellence, innovation, and trust.

According to Abby, "IBM was a global icon. Many people were rooting for it to come back, both inside and outside the company. There was a high level of emotion about IBM. If you're in the business of brand building, or brand revival, you'd prefer that. It gives you something to work with. It's much harder to create emotional attachment from scratch. The worst thing is to have a well-recognized brand about which people no longer care.

"Our job became to reinforce the feelings and associations of those people with positive emotional attachment to the brand while neutralizing any negative feelings. In addition, we had to clearly communicate, on a rational level, some of IBM's existing and emerging strengths that weren't fully understood in order to help make IBM more relevant to the existing market, and to set the stage for the future. Lou's business strategy became the foundation for the brand strategy, driven in part by integration."

To support the promise of integration, Abby explained, it was essential to be able to speak with one voice. The bigger a company is, the harder this is. After doing an audit to assess how the brand was presenting itself visually, what it was saying about itself both in content as well as voice, tone, and manner, Abby and the IBM team made a bold move that rocked and shocked the advertising industry. They consolidated all of their brand and marketing business with one agency, Ogilvy. It was putting all of its chips on one number. But to communicate an integrated story—to speak with one co-ordinated voice—they had to operate in a more collaborative way internally and have an agency partner that mirrored IBM's strategies and objectives.

This was a radically different way of doing business, especially for a company that had, at one time, more than seventy agencies working across its many divisions. But this was an action that sent a strong message. IBM wanted to achieve consistency, to take its knowledge and present it in a coherent way. IBM wanted to assure integration at every level. With one agency it could do this, as well as dramatically simplify its marketing efforts. And those efforts had to be aligned globally. IBM's clients were increasingly operating in multiple countries, and IBM was itself a global brand. Having branding signals that were consistent worldwide, that expressed a unified idea, was just a smart strategy.

"If you want to present your brand to the outside world in a clear and coordinated manner, it's essential to have fewer marketing partners," Abby said. "Before making this decision, each of our partners had a tiny slice of the story and we couldn't project the coherent 'one IBM' message we needed to. Our resources were also fragmented, limiting the impact IBM could have from its investments. In addition, having one agency gave both IBM and Ogilvy the critical mass to attract and retain top talent, retain intellectual capital, and optimize our media leverage."

With Ogilvy on board, Abby and her team started to explore ideas that would shape the new IBM brand meaning in people's minds. "Ogilvy presented a number of great ideas to us, including one they described as 'off the wall,'" Abby told me. "We looked at it and intuitively loved it. The core idea evolved into the worldwide campaign, 'Solutions for a Small Planet.' It conveyed that we were a really different IBM—innovative, accessible, on the move. The word 'solutions' expressed what was in our DNA, but the way it was captured was completely different from how we'd presented ourselves in the past." The "Solutions" idea became one of the underpinnings for where IBM stands today, which is very much the market leader in integrated enterprise solutions.

The agency consolidation and its manifestation in "Solutions for a Small Planet" were stage one in the rebranding of IBM. Abby was using advertising as a branding signal to reintroduce the company to the world—to give it a different voice, a different emotional tonality based on humor, storytelling, and accessibility. It said, "IBM is up to something new here. Maybe you should pay attention."

Stage two was introduced a couple of years later as a key part of IBM's business strategy, crystallized around the idea "of e-business." With e-business, IBM and Ogilvy now had even more to work with. They had a comprehensive vision of how the Internet was transforming business and institutions of all types—and a unifying business strategy to turn that vision into customer value.

As a visual branding signal, the most immediately noticeable difference was a branding element introduced in the television ads—a format called "letterbox," wherein the ads are presented as stories across the middle of the screen, with IBM blue shown above and below as horizontal margins. But the introduction of e-business represented a lot more than a new visual branding design.

"A new voice and personality had been established with 'Solutions,'" Abby said. "Now we were able to add into our marketing a lot more specific content that made e-business come alive and helped people understand what we meant by this new idea. And we extended that voice and that content into many more branding arenas, far beyond advertising."

Advertising, as I said, is one powerful means—but only one—to signal what your brand stands for. With e-business, the rebranding of IBM was extended beyond advertising to all of the company's touch points—its presence at events (such as trade shows), its product and industrial design, its building signage, its direct marketing, its sales collateral, its public Web sites, and new offerings and capabilities.

In our conversation, Abby confirmed what we know to be a universal truth about brands. "The larger the company, the greater the importance there is to get to a clear, simple brand idea. Ours became a rallying point for the entire organization. It shapes the culture, it shapes business decisions, and it shapes behaviors. You see this in industry, in universities, and in non-profit organizations. People need to see what it is about you that makes you better and different and it's extremely important to make this simple."

IBM captured something simple. Its "Solutions" idea was about as simple as an idea can get. More than that, coming from IBM it was believable. Only IBM had the credibility to deliver on it. IBM had always been in the business of providing solutions to its customers. The idea of "Solutions for a Small Planet" encapsulated what the brand had always stood for. More than that, it put a global spin on it. IBM made it even more relevant and entirely ownable. Beyond this, IBM branded e-business. While everyone had always talked about it, IBM did something about it. And, with all the dot-com hoopla, it was, again, a wholly credible claim. You could trust IBM with e-business.

There are, of course, many reasons beyond marketing why IBM has today regained a leadership position in the industry—including new technologies and an enormous service business that provides new ways to acquire and manage them more effectively and efficiently. But, there's no doubt that the alignment of the company's DNA with marketplace opportunity and the management of its brand have played a pivotal role in the revival and return to leadership of a legendary company. The story of how it happened suggests some of the obvious questions you need to ask yourself before you start looking for a brand idea.

Are you clear on your business strategy, and is it—or, can it be—inextricably linked to your brand idea? Also, have you taken an inventory of your brand assets, the things that give your brand meaning? IBM had a couple of big advantages. First, Abby and her team were able to take an inventory with fresh eyes and ears. Also, they found something in the brand's DNA, its equity and history, which they could use. The brilliance was in knowing how to use it and to ensure it provided a solid platform for IBM's future growth. Whether you are considering the creation of a new brand, or assessing an existing brand, the IBM story demonstrates the importance of integrating your business strategy with your brand idea before you set out to build your brand.

4

Step One: Establish Your Brand Idea

The first step to BrandSimple—and brand success—(after you're sure of your business strategy) is to establish a simple and meaningful point of difference for your brand that you'll be able to embed in people's minds. This is your brand idea. I've already mentioned that starting the process of creating branding signals before you have a brand idea can be a costly mistake, not to mention wholly ineffective. You cannot create branding signals until you have a sharply focused idea to communicate. Don't think about the advertising, the signage, the telemarketing script, or the store design until you clearly understand what associations with your brand you'd like people to file away. Without a strong and clear brand idea, your branding signals will be irrelevant. Those responsible for managing the strongest of brands know this. You can't make consumers aware of something if you're not 100 percent aware of it yourself.

Many potential clients call and ask for a new logo, a new package design, a new graphic identity, or typeface treatment. I tell them no. We can't do anything until we determine what brand problem they are trying to solve. Are they looking to differentiate their brand from the growing list of competitors? It must be done from the inside out, not superficially. Consider how the competitors have been successful at differentiating their brands. You must understand what brand ideas your brand will be competing against.

Are you looking to appeal to a different audience—a younger audience, perhaps? What can you offer them, and why is it different from what you currently offer? Have you changed the way your product functions? What benefit lies at the core of this functionality change? Answer these questions before you determine what color packaging you want. Are you trying to unite several newly acquired companies under a common identity? What would you like this identity to say about your new brand? Brochures and press kits, office space, or delivery trucks can't be designed until we know this. When I take the time to ask prospective clients questions like these and listen to their answers, I generally end up with very satisfied clients.

Generating awareness or creating knowledge by way of any sort of branding signals is the second part of the brand equation. It's a critical part, but making sure you have a different and relevant idea worth signaling comes first. The BrandAsset Valuator I spoke about earlier is one of the most important studies on this subject. It proves that when you begin with a genuinely different and relevant idea that people care about, you've started down the road to brand success. Every well-known study of brands proves that difference and relevance are the foundation of brand strength.

How Do You Hit On an Idea?

Martin Puris, founder of the agency Ammirati & Puris, was famous for saying that "80 percent of advertising fails before pen is put to paper because it's not based on a powerful idea." I worked for Martin and agree with him 100 percent—whether we're talking about advertising or the brands advertised. As I've said, I'm not here to hand you an idea. That's your job. But I can provide a few rules of thumb for getting to a core difference on which to build your brand idea:

1. Don't get bogged down in research that simply asks consumers for the answer.
2. In the right hands, quantitative research can be a tool for the right idea.
3. Diverse minds attacking a problem from different angles always yield better solutions.
4. Listen!
5. Get out of your office.

Don't Get Bogged Down in Research

No consumer could have told you she wanted a graphical user interface before she saw the first Apple computer. None could have told you he wanted an iPod or a plasma screen TV. It's not that you can't get powerful answers from consumers; it's that asking them directly won't get you the answer. I don't mean that research doesn't work; you just have to do *creative* research to get meaningful insights.

Frankly, consumers either won't or can't tell you what they really feel. One of the best ways to find out what people really feel about something emotionally, which is where the strongest brands connect, is to take away their rational tool kit: take away their words. Projective exercises—in which people project the feelings they'd have in a certain situation—allow them to use their imaginations to answer the questions you have and are far more effective at uncovering a powerful brand idea. Let me give you an example.

One powerful projective exercise is to have people in focus groups draw pictures or to have the moderator share a simple hand-drawn picture to get participants to tell a story. When I worked on Dawn detergent, which faced stiff competition from Ivory, Palmolive, and Joy, we used a projective drawing exercise to try to uncover a differentiated idea for Dawn. The moderator presented the focus group with a stick-figure drawing of a woman standing at a sink doing dishes. We asked the participants to tell us about the picture. We were surprised by the answers. While some advertising signals in the marketplace show images of husbands and wives bantering casually while cleaning up after dinner, kids smiling up from the table, our group told entirely different stories of how the beleaguered woman is stuck alone in the kitchen doing dishes while everyone else in the family is off having a good time. The woman looks at the pile of dishes, which never seems to get smaller, and at the dishwater, which gets greasier and greasier. She's resentful and frustrated. She wants to get out of the kitchen, but the greasy water means she has to keep washing and rinsing and rinsing and washing until the dishes are clean.

This projective exercise confirmed that washing greasy dishes wasn't fun and was a thankless, lonely job. Advertising that depicted people cheerfully washing dishes didn't ring true with consumers.

Our research forced the Dawn team to identify a no-nonsense, gets-the-job-done attitude. The advertising that came out of this research ended with the phrase "because you've got better things to do." Consumers could connect emotionally with this. The empathy demonstrated proved incredibly successful for the brand.

Getting the insights you want out of research is a function of the stimuli you put into the research. Give your participants stimuli that they can connect with in meaningful ways. Here's another quick example from Dawn.

We did qualitative research on Dawn continuously (one-to-one dialogs with consumers and with small and large focus groups). During this ongoing research, consumers confirmed that greasy dishes and pans posed the greatest challenge and that they appreciated the advertising that demonstrated how Dawn "took grease out of their way." They agreed that grease was the worst offender, nodding yes when we asked them, until one day when we placed a plastic food storage container stained red from tomato sauce on the table in front of them. At the sight of the stained plastic, a new insight emerged. People didn't fry food much anymore, for reasons both dietary and due to time constraints. But people did microwave, and nuking food in plastic containers created a whole new set of cleanup challenges. Microwaved foods stain plastic, especially greasy, tomato-based foods. "When those greasy stains get into plastic storage containers, forget about it," consumers told us. Suddenly the focus groups stopped playing back what we already knew and gave us a new insight to work from. That's because we had provided the right stimuli to unlock it.

P&G took this insight, used quantitative data to confirm changes in cooking habits, and sent its R&D (research and development) teams to work. A few months later, Dawn was modified to better remove grease from plastic ware and the brand enjoyed another gain in market share. Consumers can give you answers, but you have to ask the right questions or use the right stimuli to get inside their head

Quantitative Research Can Be a Tool for Finding the Right Idea

A lot of people will tell you that quantitative research can't get you to the big idea. My former colleague Susan Manber, a director of strategic planning, says it's a matter of whether you start with "raisins or grapes." "Dry, boring questions will get you nowhere," she told me. "But if you put rich, juicy ideas into your research drawn from qualitative and ethnographic exploration and link it to the most profitable segment in your business, you're more likely to get rich juicy responses.

"While working with Dell," she told me, "we asked questions that allowed us to identify a key attitude shared by Dell customers that drove their decision to customize with Dell rather than buy an off-the-shelf, generic box. The attitude they shared: Dell 'helps me get the most out of my PC.'

"The key to the insight was this: Our analysis showed that while 90 percent of computers configured for the Dell consumer market were essentially the same three configurations, Dell customers felt that they had built their PCs precisely to their own unique needs, even if all they did was change to a larger monitor. We realized that while customization was Dell's claim to fame, the benefit to consumers was that they felt they were getting the most for their own personal use."

Sue and her team had taken the time to develop questions they felt would yield the most significant and insightful responses from research participants. They got what they were looking for.

Diverse Minds Attacking a Problem from Different Angles Always Yields Better Solutions

I don't mean decision by committee. I mean asking questions and getting input on the problem from every angle, and from different parts of an organization. Good organizations know how to work collaboratively. Too often in a big organization, the head of sales is so busy running the sales force he doesn't have time to talk to marketing, information technology, or customer service. Drawing on data and experiences from participants across the company can help you get answers you might not otherwise have gotten. Handing off ideas in a linear, conveyor-belt fashion won't get you where you want to be. An example of this is the story of an observant member of the Dove soap team who made an off-hand comment that his mother always bought soap to match the bathroom tiles. Further research proved that this was a trend and that the number of bathrooms being tiled in white was growing. Dove did not manufacture white soap at the time, but began to do so, and its brand grew nicely as a result. When a brand team consists of members from diverse disciplines who can offer up different perspectives, you are much more likely to hit upon an opportunity.

At Landor, we have an open office configuration with professionals from creative, research, strategy, and program management departments all sitting in the same area. When someone wants to bounce off an idea with a creative team member, she doesn't need to get on an elevator for an appointment in the creative department. Instead, she walks two feet and says, "Hey, Bill, what do you think of this?" Even more effective, we have a number of open, informal meeting places around the office where teams can sit in comfortable chairs and share their thoughts and ideas.

I do my best to encourage frequent, informal team meetings. If I see a chain of e-mails being passed from one team to another, I tell the team to bag e-mails, get in a room together and work the issue. Getting people to brainstorm and work face-to-face delivers the best work—constantly.

Listen to Everyone

- To the heads of departments
- To the "feet on the street"—the customer representatives who talk to customers every day
- To customer praise and complaints
- To what customers are saying to each other
- To founders of the business and others who have experience with it
- To your family and friends, who often have simple insights unclouded from day-to-day involvement with the brand

Get Out of Your Office

Go shopping with customers. Sit in their homes and watch them use your website. Get their permission to open their kitchen cabinets, file cabinets, and refrigerators. Look at the DVDs they have, what's in their living room, where the computers are in their house. Face it: Most members of marketing departments are not living the same lives as their target audiences. Today, Procter & Gamble spends more money on this kind of ethnographic research than anyone else. For years, Intuit, the makers of Quicken, the leading software for personal financial management, have actually observed consumers using the product to continue making improvements in ease of use.

Besides these five pointers, there is one more way to come upon a different idea. Rule number three alludes to it and my former boss and mentor Peter Georgescu mentioned it earlier. That's the "a-ha" that comes from an observation of the obvious. Some of the best brand ideas have come from insightful people who were able to see something incredibly obvious, something the rest of us didn't see, until it was pointed out to us. The things that make you slap your forehead and say, "Why didn't I think of that? It's so obvious."

I know someone who does this better than anyone else out there. He's the master of the observation of the obvious. He's not a brand industry guru, but he's an insightful guy who'd be brilliant on any brand team. His name: Jerry Seinfeld.

I became aware of Jerry's masterful talent early on in the *Seinfeld* years. I was hooked on the show. I still watch reruns whenever I get the chance. The plots—if you can call them plots—are ridiculous and the characters are incredibly self-absorbed. What got to me most, though, were Jerry's very "obvious observations of life," as he called them. Jerry has the ability to capture profound truths about very ordinary things, things people found acceptable without considering how unacceptable they might be.

"Did you ever notice that people only eat the muffin tops? Why is it that muffin makers don't just make muffin tops instead of wasting all that batter?"

"Did you ever wonder what really happens in the clothes dryer when you leave the laundry room? Why do those socks want to hide? What's with that?"

"Did you ever notice that a date is like a job interview that lasts all night?"

"Did you ever think about the fact that the road less traveled is less traveled for a reason?"

"Did you ever wonder why dogs have no pockets? It's because they have no money, but somehow they manage to get by."

I could go on and on, but for the sake of brevity, Google "Seinfeld" and read more of Jerry's observations online.

Jerry's somewhere in the back of my mind whenever I sit down with a client to address a brand challenge. That's because sometimes the right way to reveal the simple difference at the core of the brand is to approach the brand and the category with the intent of looking for an obvious and universal truth no one else has seen. What simple reality hasn't been challenged? Find a way to answer it. Look for some situation that is unacceptable that people have come to accept anyway without thinking. Is it a brand idea you can make profitable? Here are a few examples of what I mean:

Ever wonder why a hand-operated can opener makes your hand sore?

Why does aspirin formulated for arthritis come in hard-to-open bottles?

Why do they give you those tiny little headphones on airplanes and expect you to be able to hear over the roar of Rolls-Royce engines?

Why do we assume that bottled spring water is better than other water?

Why do the people who make shoes never think about the fact that it rains?

Why are instruction manuals longer than *War and Peace?* I never finished *War and Peace* either.

These are obvious scenarios that were once accepted. They were taken at face value until some curious people came along and approached them like Seinfeld might have.

In 1990 Sam Farber, the founder of OXO Good Grips, had an "a-ha!" of an observation. His wife, Betsy, who was a wonderful cook, had developed arthritis. She needed kitchen tools that would work for her. The Farbers took a good look at the industry and what they discovered on their expeditions through high- and low-end gadget stores was that most kitchen tools were poorly made and didn't really work well for *anyone*. They were commodity products, mediocre in design and functionality. Why not make sturdy, well-designed kitchen tools that work well for everybody?, the Farbers asked themselves. So they did. OXO Good Grips is now a household name. It's a brand that makes clear the simple difference between its kitchen tools and all others. A meaningfully different idea was born from a long-overlooked and frustrating detail of modern life. OXO hooked up with a company called Smart Design to help them design and manufacture their tools—a smart way to keep its business strategy moving forward.

Although I've never met the Farbers, I do use their sturdy tools in my own kitchen, and I've learned from the story of OXO's origins that even the most mundane categories can be improved. I've seen lots of cases where companies try to make incremental changes in existing products. Incremental isn't good enough or different enough to create a stir. The Farbers and the industrial designers at Smart Design started with a clean sheet of paper. They asked themselves how they would do it if they started from scratch. Slightly different and better is only slightly different and better; it's not meaningfully different and better. The OXO kitchen tools are its most powerful branding signals, incorporating the elements of exemplary functionality and universal design. All you have to do is hold one of OXO's Smart Design products in your hand and you'll experience the simple difference they make in the kitchen.

Bose is the brand that took on those megaton Rolls-Royce engines, plus a few other obvious things that other brands had overlooked. In fact, the history of Bose's success is filled with examples of how it looked at things no other companies had thought to look at.

It started with clock radios. It must have become clear to Bose that a lot of companies were looking for ways to make the clock better and completely ignored the radio. The numbers on the clock were made bigger, digitized, illuminated. The alarm function was made louder, more musical, given a voice. All the while, the radio functionality got worse and worse. Bose observed the obvious—no one was taking on the challenge of better-sounding radios. "Ever wonder

Everything about OXO products, like this Good Grips Peeler, signals comfort in the kitchen.

why clock radios sound so awful?" Bose rhetorically asked. "What would happen if we were counterintuitive and developed an incredible-sounding clock radio, without sacrificing either of the functionalities?" What happened is that Bose made a clock radio with extraordinary auditory and speaker quality. A radio people could listen to while reading in bed, working in their offices, or chopping vegetables in the kitchen without having to sacrifice acoustic pleasure. Bose found a differentiated brand idea by looking at and listening to the obvious and doing something about it. Bose has supported its business strategy with the technology and manufacturing that make it possible and, in doing so, has created a remarkable brand.

Here's another Bose insight. Where do people sit for long periods of time with nothing to do, overwhelmed by the cacophony of engine noise, crying babies, and talkative strangers? Airplanes, of course. No other brand was thinking about a product that could block out airplane noise while also giving you the ability to listen—audibly—to music or books on tape in order to make flying more enjoyable. "Hearing is believing" is the simple mantra behind the Bose Quiet-Comfort 2 Headphones. These lightweight headphones are adjustable to any head size, provide high-quality sound, and cancel out the loudest airplane noise. With a set of Bose headphones, the delight of Beethoven's Ninth can overpower the drone of those noisy engines. Bose identified another simple and meaningfully different idea by, once again, looking at what no other brand was doing and going in the other direction.

Obvious ideas have been brought to life in brands of all sizes. Gary Briggs, a former client of mine and a former marketing executive at Pepsi, talked about one of Pepsi's moments of obvious obser-vation regarding its bottled water brand, Aquafina. "Pepsi was among the first to really do research on bottled waters," he said. "Most bottled water brands are based on derivative ideas. Pepsi took a good look at the category. One of the first things it discovered was that while people may buy bottled spring water, when the bottle is empty they fill it up at a cooler or at the tap. Craig Weatherup, who was the Pepsi CEO at the time, was the first to ask the logical ques-tions. 'Why do we need a spring water source to sell bottled water? Is this a critical cost of entry in the bottled water category?' Pepsi had incredible production facilities and powerful distribution channels. It also had a name people trusted. We decided to see what would hap-pen if we marketed bottled water that didn't come from a spring—but came from Pepsi's plants.

"We did what's called permission research. We asked people whether they would buy a bottled water product from Pepsi know-ing it wasn't derived form a spring source. The answer was yes. People did trust the Pepsi name, and it seemed spring water wasn't an issue. The water would be just as good and also be much cheaper in price than spring water. The other insight Pepsi had rel-ative to the category was to change the shape of the bottle in order to distinguish Aquafina from other brands of water, and to make the bottle easier to drink from. Aquafina's revolutionary wide-mouthed packaging sets it apart from other brands and signals its difference as soon as you reach for a bottle in your local conven-ience store."

Aquafina now enjoys great market share as a result of asking a simple question no one had thought to ask before.

As a final story about finding a brilliantly simple but different idea in the obvious, I want to talk to you about my shoes. Not the shoes I wear to work, but the ones I love wearing on weekends, my Timberlands. The family that founded Timberland had two observa-tions of the obvious. One had to do with product innovation that was catapulted into a progressive business strategy supported by an ingenious brand strategy; and the other had to do with the choice of a brand name. It's a great story, and I'll let one of the founding fam-ily members tell it.

"The business, then known as Abington Shoe, started in Boston about 1955," Sidney Swartz, former president of Timberland, told me. "We were typical of the small, family-owned shoe companies. We made footwear for the working guy. It wasn't pretty or profitable, but we made a living. We moved to New Hampshire in the early sixties because skilled labor was becoming more difficult to find. There were very few brands; none of the major shoe brands we know today existed yet. We did okay, but selling unbranded footwear to discount stores seemed a dead-end street. One day I noticed a guy working for us was wearing a very different boot. He wore it in all weather conditions. It wasn't waterproof but water-resistant. We called our father, Nathan, who had retired to Florida and asked him to come back. He had been a boot maker when the company was founded. He took a look at the guy's boot and reinvented it—made a boot that was better looking and more functional. We had begun to use a manufacturing process called injection molding, which sealed the sole to the leather. This eliminated stitching and holes. This made the boot much more waterproof. We took the boot, invented a name, spent a little money to market it, and Timberland was born. The brand now includes many types of footwear and is sold worldwide."

Sidney went on to tell me that people thought the idea was crazy. Smiling all the way to the bank crazy, I'd say. Sidney's observation of the ordinary led him to brand success. Not focus groups of linemen for the county, construction workers, or the residents of Seattle, but an innovative idea based on a simple observation. While the Timberland product was innovative, the name choice was inspired. "Timberland" says professional gear for real outdoors folk. Because the products are manufactured to stand up to the weather, the name is brilliant in its signal of authenticity. Timberland has expanded its line of shoes and clothing, but it has never veered from its original differentiated brand idea of producing shoes and clothing for the outdoors, and as a result, it has remained in a leadership position. A simple lesson to any brand considering stretching its customer base.

It's a skill to be able to look at something obvious and see it as a universal truth—something that will address an unacceptable situation in the category. Why do we all have four or five TV remotes sitting on the coffee table? Why are CD cases so &%^$# hard to open? Why is it so difficult to reprogram my VCR, and why must I rely on my twelve-year-old nephew to do it? Why are the alarm clocks in hotels so hard to operate? Why does spaghetti sauce always stain my Tupperware? Why is flying such a miserable experience? Keep an eye out for the obvious things in life that have been overlooked and see if there's an opportunity for an untapped business idea—and a brand idea.

Sometimes Seeing the Obvious Requires a Different Position

In my work with clients I've learned that sometimes in order not to miss something obvious, it helps to look at something that's right in front of you from a different perspective. Take a look at your category from a position that you'd never considered. It may be leaving your comfort zone, but that's okay. You can't be visionary if you're standing with your nose pressed to the glass, or if you look at the same thing the same way everyday. If you keep looking at the brand category from the same point of view, you won't see anything different. Often, this can be challenging for people sitting inside the company. Not because they're not capable, but because they're focused on day-to-day deliverables and management. However, a brand's long-term success depends on making the time to get out of the forest and see the trees.

It can be scary to take a different position. Conformity is comforting. Consistency is comforting—but dull. One of my favorite authors, Ralph Waldo Emerson, made that clear in his essay entitled "Self Reliance," when he said, "A foolish consistency is the hobgoblin of little minds." While we don't want to go so far afield in a brand category that we appear foolishly naïve, neither do we want to appear foolish for not going far enough and being considered just another same-as, same-old brand.

When we all dressed alike in the 1970s (much as kids are all dressing alike now), and when we all drive the same cars as our like-minded brethren, not to mention decorate as Martha does, we're not set apart.

We're just in a comfort zone. If you want to set your brand apart, you have to be prepared to move away. Not make your idea irrelevant, certainly, which would be extremely foolish, but find a way to be meaningfully different.

I spoke to Kevin Keller, E. B. Osborne Professor of Marketing at the Tuck School of Business at Dartmouth, about this topic. "When it comes to establishing a unique position for a brand," he told me, "there's one technique I use that's incredibly effective. I also think it's crucial that anyone responsible for a brand do this. I call it 'points of parity, points of difference.' It allows you to fully capture the competitive landscape.

"The first step in this tactic is to look at your competitors' intended points of difference—things they would like to do better than you to gain a competitive advantage. Figure out how you can develop product strategies, communication strategies, and so on, that result in a consumer believing that you do this well enough—even if not exactly as well—so that you neutralize your competitors' points of difference. You achieve what I call a point of parity. Then go on and list things you can say about your brand that are truly unique. Identify things that the other brand absolutely can't say, and find the one thing that you can bring to life better than any of the other things to create your own point of difference."

I asked Kevin for a couple of examples to illustrate what he meant. "Visa is a great example," he said. "Visa came out with a Gold and Platinum version of the card and wanted to take on American Express, which had gained much status and cachet through the years. They looked at the image of the Visa card versus the image of the American Express Card and said 'Let's make prestige a point of parity. Let's take it off the table. Our card is accepted at many of the prestigious locations the American Express Card is accepted, so let's look for a point of difference that American Express absolutely can't claim: overall acceptance. Visa's campaign, 'It's everywhere you want to be,' was the way they articulated this difference to consumers. They showcased prestigious, out-of-the-ordinary venues, restaurants and events that wouldn't accept the American Express Card to make their point. Visa was a widely accepted card with a positive image. The campaign ran successfully for years."

Kevin also talked to me about Miller Lite and Budweiser. When first launched, he explained, Miller made taste a point of parity with Bud and, in doing so, made the beers equally acceptable in the minds of consumers. The point of difference Miller laid claim to was that it was less filling. Bud couldn't say this, until it came out with Bud Lite. At this point, Miller went back to taste, while still emphasizing that it had fewer carbs than Bud Lite.

The two lessons here: When you're looking to find a different position for your brand, first you must successfully neutralize your competitors' intended differences. Make sure there are no reasons for consumers to decide *not* to choose you. Then keep checking on your point of difference to see that it's not in danger of becoming parity. You want consumers always to have a reason to make your brand their brand of choice.

A points-of-parity, points-of-difference exercise is a great way to get outside your brand. It's easy for anyone involved with a brand day in and day out to become insular in his thinking. You've got to look at what the competitors are doing to identify an idea that's genuinely unique. I find that to get out of your narrowly focused point of view, to lay the groundwork for the competitive reality, it helps to start with a basic positioning framework. Here's an example of how it's done.

Exercise: Build a Framework

To take a different position, it helps to start with a basic positioning framework: a BrandSimple framework. This basic framework is built on three questions. The final outcome, however, should be a simple, cohesive one-sentence answer. All of these questions are interrelated, one being dependent on the other. Change the answer to one question and the whole framework position will change. I use this framework with clients.

It's hard to create anything simple when you're working with a committee or groups of different players, which I assume you are. It takes discipline. It takes making choices. It takes saying no. People working with you on the brand position must agree not to push everything back to the lowest, safest common denominator. You have to agree not to let research drive you into endless rounds of analysis, which leads to "analysis paralysis." You also have to make sure the position you take is supported from the top down. The people in charge must endorse the position, believe in it, advocate it, and live it themselves. CEOs and presidents who are their brand's strongest cheerleaders lead the strongest brands. They are guardians of the brand idea.

Take a risk, but be bold with parameters. Your objective is not to be simple and different for the sake of being different, but to find an idea people have never thought about and can care about.

Here are the questions you must answer to build your BrandSimple framework.

1. *Make a choice. Who do you really want to talk to?*
   You can't talk to everyone. Refine your audience. Make a choice, then refine it again. Remember that there are lots of brands, lots of commodity claims, and many ways to segment an audience. A good position, like a good brand idea, is not relevant to everybody, and it shouldn't be. That would be a simplistic and a costly mistake. Don't think just that you'd like to target forty-year-old men; narrow it down to forty-year-old men who wear jeans and sneakers on Saturday night versus forty-year-old men who put on a shirt and tie to do the town. Don't direct your brand idea simply at moms or even working moms; refine it to working moms who put their careers on hold and are now back in the workforce full time trying to juggle issues of personal identity with what to make for dinner. Your brand idea is not for any thirteen-year-old, but street-smart thirteen-year-olds who ride the bus and subway rather than thirteen-year-olds who live in the suburbs and whose moms drive them to the mall. Do you want to talk to real athletes, or weekend athletes? The people who really hike, or the people who want to dress like they're hikers? Think hard about your choice of audience. It's a degree of difference that could make a huge difference in how people view your position in the category.

2. *Who do you want to beat?*

Whose mental file folder do you want to delete? I know this sounds kind of aggressive, but you do want to win, don't you? If you don't assess the competition aggressively, someone else will. Who's your competition? Don't generalize in your response. There can be only one leading sports drink, home computer, search engine, overnight delivery service. Don't stop at obvious analysis. If your business strategy is to sell toys, do you compete with baby toys, action toys, or educational toys? Do you want to appeal to the luxury, spare-no-expense stroller crowd or the all-natural backpack crowd? If your business strategy is to make money selling computer hardware, do you want to compete with the PCs—home PCs or business PCs—or is it complete enterprise solutions? Let's say you're a car brand. Are you a family sedan or an SUV? If you're an SUV, are you a family SUV or an SUV for weekend athletes who wear all-natural baby backpacks? The sharper you focus on who it is you want to delete, the sharper your brand idea will be and the sharper and more effective your branding signals.

3. *How will you beat them?*

This is the Seinfeld-like observation of the obvious question. What has the competition overlooked? What obvious and universal truth might they have stumbled over without recognizing the brilliant idea left behind? People don't like it when the microwave bakes the lasagna and at the same time bakes a tomato sauce stain into the plastic container. Consumers get nasty when the plastic wrap takes on a life of its own. They'd like to have fewer remotes on the coffee table. They'd like flying to be fun. They'd like it if dogs had pockets. Let the dog carry the plastic scooper to the park. Determine why the road is less traveled and fix it. Find out why clock radios have lousy radio speakers. Why shoes don't keep your socks dry. Why most can openers should be canned. Take a position no one has taken and see if it's a relevant point of difference. Does it have profit potential? Have you *really* examined the competition? Have you looked at

75

the category from every which way and found something the other guys haven't? Can you really claim the territory you're after? If you see any flags on the top of that mountain, find another mountain you can call your own.

Again, Can You Make it Happen?

I'll say it once more. Does your company have the resources, the operations, and the people, not to mention the financial capability, to deliver on the position you'd like to take? Can you tangibly make good on the goods and service, on the promise of your brand idea, over the long term? We live in the age of skepticism and cynicism. Make sure you can sell what you promise to sell. People won't give you the time of day if you don't live up to your promise.

American Express has credibility as a provider of security and top-level service, not only because the company replaces lost Cards within twenty-four hours, but because it will assume the responsibility for a questioned charge on your account by removing the charge until the situation is resolved. Barnes and Noble and Amazon can let you know when the books will arrive. They've made the appropriate investments in online technology to ensure it happens. When the online grocery delivery service doesn't deliver in the time frame it has promised and I've got an appointment to get to, it's a problem. The company may not have resources necessary to make good on its position. When an 800 hotline tells me my "wait time is three minutes," and someone picks up in two and a half, I trust the brand. The brand has the resources and functional ability to make it happen. Make sure you do before you commit to a position.

"It's not about finding a position," says Peter Stringham, group general manager of marketing for HSBC Holdings, the world's third largest bank. "That's soft. You have to look at it as *taking* a position. It's active, it's assertive, and it implies being preemptive. It takes work. Starbucks didn't find a position. They went to a new place and took one. Coke didn't find it. They took it. BMW didn't find a position, it took it. Virgin Airlines didn't find it. They, or Sir Richard, took it."

By taking a position, you're putting a stake in the ground. You must do this if you want to transcend your current position, or find an entirely new one. Taking a position is the first step in identifying the simple, different, and relevant idea on which to build your brand—and on which to base your branding. A BrandSimple position is the cornerstone for your BrandSimple idea and for all the branding signals to follow. Once you take a position, you'll be able to close in on the core brand idea. All the words, images, and emotions you want people to associate with your brand will start to take shape.

The Basic Framework

Here is the basic BrandSimple framework. It's what the best in the business use to influence their thinking process: to frame their position. It's not a game of Mad Libs. Don't expect to do this on the back of a napkin over a couple of cocktails. It takes work and lots of intelligent discussion. Make hard choices about your audience, which brands you want to delete from mental files, and what real point of difference can offer to do this. Strong positions and the BrandSimple ideas they spawn lead to terrific branding.

To create your BrandSimple positioning framework, decide:

1. Who you're talking to
2. Who you want to beat
3. How you're going to beat them

Change a component or two and the whole position will change, and along with it all the branding signals you send. Here's what I mean:

To *young, single urban women,* Victoria's Secret is the brand of *alluring lingerie* that will make them feel *secretly sexy.*
   or
To *married women over fifty,* Victoria's Secret is the brand of *alluring lingerie* that will *re-ignite their marriages.*

Big difference, wouldn't you say?

Here are the basic positioning frameworks created by a few well-known brands.

Motel 6

> To *frugal people*, Motel 6 is the *alternative to staying with family and friends* that provides a welcoming, *comfortable night's rest at a reasonable price.*

Who you're talking to: Motel 6 could have chosen travelers as its target, but by choosing frugal people, it chose a mind-set that is extremely positive to those who share it. Frugal people aren't skinflints. They want good value for their money.

Who you want to beat: The most interesting decision made by Motel 6 is what it *didn't* choose as its competition. Motel 6 realized there was a gap in the market that no motel or hotel was tapping into: people who stayed with family or friends to save money. So instead of saying it was competing with motels and hotels, it positioned itself as the alternative to the lumpy, bumpy couch or sleeping in the kids' bunk beds.

How you're going to beat them: Motel 6 isn't about bells and whistles. It knows what it is: a clean and comfortable room with friendly service and good prices. It isn't about special amenities but about doing basic things right with a homey charm. (Among its original branding signals were the warm and homey voice of Tom Bodett and a promise to keep the light on—just like mom would.)

Johnson & Johnson

> To *today's new mothers*, Johnson & Johnson is the leading brand of *baby skin care products* that understands that *having a baby changes everything.*

Who you're talking to: Johnson & Johnson (J&J) has been the leader in baby care for the past century. To expand its franchise, it needs to constantly appeal to new, contemporary parents and ensure that its brand never seems like it was for my Mom, not me.

Who you want to beat: As the leader in baby care, J&J needs to combat other brands that want to break into its stronghold, some of which have baby equity, as well as generic brands.

How you're going to beat them: While J&J has significant heritage in safety and specific product benefits (No More Tears® baby shampoo), in today's market, to fight off interlopers, it needs to connect emotionally with its target. How better than with a powerful emotional understanding of the sea change every mother goes through when her child is born? It does change everything; as no greater emotional connection exists than that between mother and child.

Target

> To *value-conscious consumers of all income levels,* Target is the brand of *discount retailer* that delivers *great design at reasonable prices.*

Who you're talking to: Target recognized that there are value-conscious consumers at all income levels. Its marketers saw Mercedes and BMWs in the wholesale club parking lots next to Honda Civics and realized they could appeal to a wide range of customers by offering great value.

Who you want to beat: Target set out to change how consumers think about discount shopping. With a department store heritage, it saw its competition as not only Wal-Mart and Kmart, but warehouse clubs and department stores too.

How you're going to beat them: Target's on-trend merchandise at affordable prices launched a new era in discount retailing. Its first prototype "T–1" store was easy to shop, attractive, and always clean, offering high-quality, stylishly designed items plus all the essentials for your life, displayed in a welcoming and organized environment.

"Design for All" is the philosophy that drives all Target merchandise. The company recognized that you can add high design to your life for every room at reasonable, even surprisingly low prices. Target has teamed up with world-class designers in home, fashion, accessories, beauty, furniture, and outdoor living to offer exclusive products (very powerful branding signals) that support its stylish promise of value. It has tapped such creative talent as Michael Graves, Amy Coe, Sonia Kashuk, Liz Lange, and Isaac Mizrahi.

Exercise: Define Your Brand Enemy

One of the things Ken Roman, former president of Ogilvy, told me was that "you need to know when to say no. It's one of the most basic but overlooked rules of building a brand. It's easy to say yes. Anyone can say yes and too many people do and then just move on without thinking about what they agreed to. The key to success in the industry is to know when to say no."

Building a brand is, in very good part, about saying no. The fact is, knowing what is wrong or off the mark relative to your brand or branding signals is as important as knowing what is right on the mark. In a universe where there is very little distinction between one brand and another, you can't just be a little different. You must be *really* different. I'm not talking 10 percent, or even 50 percent. You've got to transcend your category. Categorically set yourself apart. Make sure your brand breaks barriers.

Sometimes the best way to set a brand apart, to find the one meaningfully different thing you can own, is to start from the "no" side of the equation. Instead of spending endless hours debating what you *want* your brand idea to be, spend the time and effort concentrating on what you *don't* want it to be. Establish a sharply defined contrast between what the competitors are doing and what you can do. Someone once told me that the best way to determine the kind of boss you want to be is to look at the kind of boss you don't want to be. It's sort of the same concept here.

Consumers need all the help they can get figuring out if something is actually different. With all the changes in the marketplace, you can understand why this is so. Sometimes the only way to make what your brand stands for obvious is to make what it *doesn't* stand for obvious. To clarify this for yourself, take out a sheet of paper. Make two columns on the page, one labeled "is" and the other "isn't." Think about your brand idea and fill in the columns. Often the "isn't" column will help you define and focus better than the "is" column. I like to take this exercise further by taking on an enemy.

Choose an enemy brand representative of your category and make an "Is/Isn't" chart for what consumers believe about this brand. Study the contrasts. What is it you *don't* want your brand to represent?

I'm not talking halfhearted or next-best measures here. Derivative will not land you on *Brand Week*'s top ten list. With a nation suffering from brand attention deficit disorder, a little bit different is a sure-fire recipe for not-so-benign neglect.

Examine the competition from all angles. Evaluate its modus operandi and every other modus about it, including its advertising, its online experience, and its customer service. Identify the key emotional associations the brand elicits. What do customers have in mind when they think of this brand? What specific audience does the brand appeal to? Who are the brand's most profitable customers, and why?

Go on to explore what the brand enemy uses as its most powerful branding signal. Is it in product design or functionality? Is it a special level of service, or is it in the people it hires? Has the brand stayed ahead of technology in some way? Has its research and development been given the go-ahead to invent a unique formula for spot removal? Does the brand differentiate itself with its telemarketing operations or its distribution logistics? What is this brand doing that you haven't considered but that might be more relevant to the audience you'd like to target? Is it the "no-questions-asked" guarantee? Maybe it's merely price point or general value equation. Maybe it's the buzz the brand generates. How'd the buzz get started?

What overall expressions come through its branding signals? What channels or forms do these signals take? Has the enemy brand established a blog network as advocates? Does it count on word of mouth? Does it elicit endorsements? Is it listed as a good choice by the American Association of Retired Persons or *Consumer Reports*? Are its signals in any way proprietary? In other words, is it possible for anyone to use the same branding tactics the enemy employs? For example, could Wal-Mart have a private sale for preferred customers, or is this a signal only high-end retailers can use?

There's more. (No shortcuts here.) You've got to examine the customer's experience at various points of contact with the enemy brand. Where does the enemy brand make its greatest branding investments? On which branding signals does it spend the most money? Is it in training the telephone reps? Is it the retail environment, catalog, direct mail, or its collateral material? Maybe it's sampling, free downloads, or free trials. How much does the brand invest in specific branding activities, and why? This is not a casual assignment. Looking at the enemy brand is a battle plan.

Mind the Gaps

In every London subway station there's a sign I find funny: "Mind the gap." There it's obviously referring to the space between the platform and the train doors, but I always think of the sign when I take on a brand enemy exercise with my clients. What space exists between "them" and you? Where's the gap between the enemy and you? You don't want to fall into it, you want to widen it.

When you evaluate and consider the options consumers have within your brand's category, look for gaps in the experiences that consumers have to deal with. Examining the customer's journey with your brand (which I'll explain in chapter 6), considering all the customer touch points—or interactions—may yield opportunities for differentiation. What are the critical moments of truth with your brand? If you are a twenty-five-year-old guy wanting to impress his date by making a savvy choice, approaching the bar is a moment of truth. Is your brand the bold and cool choice, the safe choice, or the brand no one asks for?

The point is, where do you see potential for counterpoint compared to your competition? By clearly evaluating what competitors do and how they do it, you'll begin to see what *you* could be doing and how you could be doing it. You'll begin to see what options you have to take for an alternative yet relevant position. Once you consider these options, you'll have a better understanding of how to capture it in a simple idea.

Found the Gaps

What brands have taken on the enemy with distinction? There are quite a few of them. Most brands I talk about have done this in some way or another, but let me give you a couple of examples.

HBO Took on TV

To *astute TV viewers*, HBO is the brand of *television network* that provides *programming you can't see anywhere else.*

As Larry David, star and creator of the popular HBO show *Curb Your Enthusiasm* might say, "It's pretty, pretty, pretty, pretty unique." And that was exactly the point Eric Kessler, president of sales and marketing at HBO, wanted to get across in taking on both regular and cable television networks as the enemies. He knew exactly what he did and *didn't* want HBO to represent in the market. I met Eric when we worked together at Lever and was interested in getting his insight on the HBO brand.

HBO was unique starting out of the gate. Regular network TV was free, and basic cable channels came packaged together. HBO was the only individual brand of TV network you paid for. It's currently in 90 percent of all cable packages. The challenge Eric and HBO faced, as home-based entertainment choices began to proliferate, was convincing consumers that HBO was still different and better and worth paying for every month. In the age of satellite dishes and video downloads, the business strategy faced a pretty, pretty, pretty, pretty big challenge.

"If it was the type of program you could see on a regular TV network, we wouldn't do it. Basic cable? Let's do it differently," Eric told me. "We needed to take a position that was different and we needed to deliver on it. We needed to prove HBO was worth the price of admission every month."

HBO did so and continues to live up to its different idea month after month. HBO found its brand idea by going through a positioning exercise, deciding what kind of network it didn't want to be, and taking the very strong position mentioned. The enemy was the ordinary TV fare found on other networks. HBO articulated the position in a simple message: "It's not TV. It's HBO." A simple statement like this that captures the essence of the brand idea is something we at Landor call a brand driver, which I'll explain in complete detail in chapter 5. (Note that, in most cases, a brand driver is not the brand's advertising tagline. In HBO's case, however, it happened to work beautifully.)

HBO's brand driver encapsulated its position and in doing so gave the organization something that became the driving force behind all of its branding signals. HBO succeeds not merely as a result of having established a meaningfully different idea that is simple to grasp, but because its business strategy is in alignment with its idea. What HBO sells is innovative programming unlike any other programming found on television. It spends its creative energy and its money creating this type of programming to guarantee viewers perceive it as something worth buying.

Like all the best brand drivers, HBO's became a self-fulfilling prophecy. "Hey, if we make a claim like that, we've got to develop programming that supports it. We need to *transcend* the category," Eric explained. "Getting to the simple idea was the hardest part. Once we got the simple idea, the programming actually took on a life of its own."

Getting to simple, finding something obvious and making it revelatory, is the hard part. Once you get there, the rest should, by rights, take on a life of its own.

In the case of HBO, the programming is actually one of its most powerful branding signals, along with the cast members of these outstanding programs. As a result, HBO knows it should commit the bulk of its branding dollars on programming. Knowing what consumers expect from you and where to make investments that allow you to meet expectations is essential to effective branding.

Carrie Bradshaw and *Sex and the City,* Tony Soprano and his band of merry men and not-so-merry women, *Six Feet Under,* the fellows on *Entourage,* and Larry David of *Curb Your Enthusiasm* came about as a result of the driving force behind the line "It's not TV. It's HBO." The creative minds at the network use it as a touchstone for developing programming. You won't find anything like this programming on the other networks. Eric told me people at the network have an intuitive feel for what will work and what won't. They know what being HBO means and what it doesn't mean.

HBO's advertising and marketing teams picked up on the idea and ran with it. Michael Patti, an executive creative director, now Vice Chairman at Y&R, New York, who worked on the original advertising, won an Emmy for the initial campaign—the first ad in history ever to earn this distinction. The ad, filmed on a preserve in Africa, "starred" some chimps who mouthed movie lines made famous by actors such as Marlon Brando, Sly Stallone, and Tom Hanks.

Michael, who worked with Eric on the brand positioning exercise, told me, "There's HBO and there's everything else. You intuitively couldn't do a TV promotional spot like anything else any more than you'd do ordinary programming. We weren't TV, we were HBO. We needed to live the brand and live up to the bargain."

The photography in HBO's print advertising is shot by Annie Leibovitz, whose work has appeared in several contemporary art museums worldwide. Her photographs for HBO programs, most notably *The Sopranos,* take advertising to levels above even Hollywood's high standards for its film advertising. These photographs are bold, provocative, and intriguing. HBO's advertising is a branding signal that no ordinary television network could use. Like the programming, the advertising is groundbreaking. As such, it resides in many a consumer's mental file folder. HBO is a perfect example of how *not* to do what everyone else is doing. It's not TV. It's HBO.

Pixar Took on Animated Movies

To *parents with young children,* Pixar is the brand of *animated movie entertainment* that *appeals to audiences of all ages.*

The folks at Pixar had two fabulous insights, both of which made my life as a dad exponentially better. The first was that kids are a whole lot more sophisticated today than they were ten years ago. They don't go for cute mice and bunnies anymore. They've been influenced by video games, GameBoys, and computers. The movie entertainment choices for the ten-and-under crowd were not reflecting that.

Curb Your
Enthusiasm

HBO

HBO
IT'S NOT TV. IT'S HBO.

HBO's "Curb Your
Enthusiasm" print campaign
perfectly illustrates the unique
programming that is the core
of their brand.

The second insight was that even though seven-year-old kids are too cool for dancing mice and bunnies, they don't go to the movies by themselves, either.

Although these points may seem obvious, as the best brand ideas are, they hadn't become obvious to anyone until Pixar, more formally Pixar Animation Studios, spent some quality time viewing what its enemy brands in the industry were showing at the local cineplex. Their response to what they saw was incredible. Create movies that parents would want to take their kids to and even movies that adults would gladly go see on their own. Do what no other film brand was doing and create marvelous computer-animated movies that both the most precocious kid and sophisticated parent could love. Pixar saw a gap in the marketplace and figured out how to fill it, hour after entertaining hour.

Once it had established a different brand position that was viable from a business perspective, Pixar captured the essence of this position in a simple idea: stories and characters the entire audience can believe in.

The ingenious people at Pixar knew intuitively what to do with such a focused and simple idea: use it as inspiration for everything, from story lines, to lovable characters, to the famous folks employed as voices for the characters, to investments in their amazing technology. Pixar knew that doing so would send exactly the branding signals required to connect with children and parents of all ages worldwide.

Pixar's films are magical because they work on multiple levels. As I said, they appeal to both my kids and to me. The dialog is simple enough for the kids to follow but clever enough to keep me transfixed. Also, although Pixar has extraordinary technology, it doesn't allow this extraordinary technology to overwhelm the story line. The stories are inventive, but simple, credible, and familiar. What parent hasn't been awakened at 3 A.M. by a child who thinks there's a monster in the closet? What kid hasn't fantasized about toys or cars coming to life? And who says a superhero can't be an insurance salesman who needs a few weeks on the Atkins diet?

Pixar movies, much like HBO's programming, are the brand's most powerful signals, worthy of incremental branding investment. We believe in Pixar. Its feature-length films, its DVDs, and other related products created in partnership with Walt Disney Pictures are the signals that give us permission to believe. Pixar was bought by the Walt Disney Company in 2006, which was a smart move for both companies, as they each bring something important to the table. Disney is a perfect fit for Pixar because it understands how to weave family entertainment into the fabric of life. With Disney's help prior to the merger, Pixar was able to jump-start its brand and branding initiatives with licensing and merchandising support. Pixar is perfect for Disney because it knows how to take Disney magic to the next level. Every brand needs to keep reinventing itself, find ways to keep its differentiation fresh. Pixar will be able to put a new buzz in Disney's portfolio of creative products. The best brands put a lot of thought into their partnership or merger arrangements and don't sign up unless it is a good fit for each party, from both a long-term business perspective and a brand image perspective.

Pixar has created and produced one hit after another: *Toy Story, Toy Story 2, A Bug's Life, Monsters, Inc., Finding Nemo, The Incredibles,* and *Cars. Toy Story,* released in 1995, received two thumbs up from parents and kids alike and became the highest-grossing film that year, generating more than $362 million in worldwide box office receipts. *Finding Nemo,* released in 2003, generated $865 million worldwide and received the Academy Award® for Best Animated Feature Film. How's that for sending the right signals?

When I told you both the brand and the branding had to be aligned with the business strategy, I wasn't kidding. Just ask Pixar's very grown-up shareholders if they're happy. By the way, I'll be watching *The Incredibles* on DVD for the fifteenth time with the kids this weekend. I hope I can find my Supersuit.

Crest Vivid White Took on Toothpaste

The oral care category is crowded, to say the least. Consumers are overwhelmed by a kaleidoscope of colors, claims, benefits, and products in the oral care aisle. The category is hard to shop, and consumers find it hard to locate "their" product on the shelves. There are hundreds of oral care products, from toothpaste to floss, whiteners to gum treatments. When Crest decided to enter the market with its new

Vivid White and Vivid White Night toothpaste products, it decided to look at what the other brands in the category were doing and go in the opposite direction. A lot of toothpastes claimed to have whitening power, but there was a broad unmet need for a whitening product that actually performed.

I spoke to Matt Barresi, a Landor client and P&G's associate director of North American Oral Care, about the business strategy and the brand idea behind Vivid White. "We had a wonderful technology breakthrough," he told me. "Being part of P&G, our technology group was among the best. It had developed a product that had the ability to genuinely whiten teeth more effectively and safely. This is a functional need consumers have: whiter teeth. Our goal was to identify a brand idea that tapped into a more emotional consumer need. In research we discovered that consumers felt more confident when they knew they looked their best, and that a whiter, cleaner smile was part of this. We had our technology breakthrough. Our brand breakthrough was to make Vivid White part of a beauty regimen. Make the attainment of a whiter smile part of the consumer's beauty routine, not a part of their dental routine. In other words, take a cosmetic position with the brand. No other brand had done this."

Matt and his team knew that to make this brand position credible, Vivid White's branding signals had to express the fact that the brand was not like any other toothpaste available and, in fact, was not a dental product but a beauty product. They worked with Landor to identify the name and the packaging that would best express this message and send the associations it wanted people to have about the product. The name "Vivid White" is both functionally descriptive and aspirational in its language. The packaging doesn't look like toothpaste packaging, but more like cosmetic packaging, employing rich, elegant colors and minimal, sophisticated copy. The advertising, used as branding signals, is designed to look like ads for cosmetic products and, unlike ads for most other toothpaste brands, appears in all the most popular fashion magazines. Promotional brochures, echoing the quiet elegance of the ads, can be found in spas and health clubs.

"We had a clear sense of where we wanted to play," Matt said. "The number-one P&G mantra is that the consumer is boss. Understanding the consumer's needs is everything. We took our technological advancement in the category and found a position for it that was unique and distinctive and relevant. Doing this allowed us to do our branding in a simple and focused way. We needed to make a choice about what to communicate. We decided to communicate what no one else was communicating. We decided to make Vivid White a beauty product and not just a whitening product because we understood that consumers feel better when they look better. Our simple brand idea, 'the first beauty toothpaste,' made it a simple idea to execute."

Five Important Lessons Learned in the Search for an Idea

I've given you a couple of exercises to give you a sense of how to go about establishing a simple and differentiated brand idea. What I'd like to do before we go to the next step, which is capturing the essence of your brand idea in a brand driver, is to emphasize five important lessons I learned along the way to identify BrandSimple ideas for my clients.

Striking design and an innovative marketing campaign helped Crest Vivid White to stand out on the shelf.

1. *There are no magic bullets.* Just because the engineers invented it, doesn't mean you'll be able to sell it. Brand positions and the ideas they generate need to address things people really need. Just because your inner Seinfeld says, "Ever wonder why . . . ," you haven't necessarily hit on an idea people will find acceptable. Sometimes an idea has been overlooked all these years for a legitimate reason. In 1988,

for example, R.J. Reynolds (an RJR Nabisco subsidiary) spent over $300 million to market its Premier Smokeless Cigarettes. However, Premier didn't last long after its launch in test markets for two essential reasons. First, Premier was priced almost 25 percent higher than other cigarettes, although price was not the greatest concern. It seemed that smokeless cigarettes didn't appeal to smokers, but rather to non-smokers.

2. *Don't get caught up in group-think mentality.* David Ogilvy summed up this lesson in typical apt fashion. "Search all your towns and all your cities, you'll find no statues of committees." Don't take what seems to be a bold and brilliant idea and let rounds of research push you back to comfortable category norms. To out-cool an iPod, to un-cola a cola, to out-latte a Starbucks, or to out-Target chic cheap takes leadership.

3. *Make sure your idea is durable.* With the pace of technological breakthroughs, scientific discoveries, and globalization of ideas and production capabilities, you have to do some smart, proactive thinking to stay ahead of the brand idea curve. We've all seen technical products become obsolete quickly. Every SUV can seat seven passengers comfortably. A lot of products allow you to download music. Base your brand idea on something that transcends product features and benefits—that transcends battery life or the half-life of a pharmaceutical, for instance. Otherwise, any competitor with similar research and development capabilities will be able to beat you at your game. If your brand lives in a fast-changing category, the position you take cannot be based on a rational or transitory point of difference. Any brand can be a trend. This is not your objective. Instead of giving you an example here, I'm going to wait until I tell you the story of GE in chapter 5. Given all the changes the past century has brought, GE has continued to innovate and bring meaningful services and technology to the market—and unify its thousands of employees—by way of simple, differentiated, over-arching brand ideas. Stay tuned.

The last two lessons require more by way of example and case history to bring them to life. I've seen a lot of brands fail for the next two reasons, so I want to give you more food for thought in these areas.

4. *Don't be afraid to make a clear choice.* You can't be all things to all people. Focus your audience to ensure that your brand idea is relevant to the right group. As I said earlier, sometimes having a smaller audience is more profitable because it allows for greater operating efficiencies and greater margins. For example, not everyone needs a $500 vacuum cleaner. Richard Dyson invented "suctionless vacuuming" and made it meaningful to a very high-end audience, and in doing so he made Dyson a very profitable brand. His great design was also a powerful branding signal. IAMS Eukanuba pet food is another great example of making a choice in your market. For some people, nothing is too expensive for a beloved dog or cat. The only food these people will feed their pets is Super Premium pet food. Bugaboo baby strollers, called by some the Hummer of strollers, is supercharged with performance tires, premium fabrics, and the ability to transform as your baby grows, and they command a price premium three times that of more common alternatives. Another classic niche brand is Waterford Wedgwood. The heritage and the fine craftsmanship of Waterford crystal and Wedgwood china make it a brand of distinction with a very distinct audience and the mark of quality for wedding gifts.

A lot of brands have started out with narrowly focused target markets and then have gone on to expand the base of customers. Here are a couple of cases of what happened.

NIKON: One Way to De-Niche a Niche Brand

If you've got a niche brand and you're thinking about expanding your customer base, it's critical not to erode your brand's position of authority with the people you chose to talk to in the first place. Nikon kept its original users in sharp focus as it looked to widen its appeal. My work with Nikon a few years back gave me a good sense of how to de-niche a niche brand.

Nikon has long been known as a manufacturer of camera equipment for professional photographers. In the 1990s, when I worked for Ammirati & Puris, the agency was in a pitch against other agencies for the Nikon advertising account. Nikon's objective was to see if it could translate its professional credentials to compete with Canon and Minolta in the point-and-shoot consumer market without undermining its respected standing as *the* camera for professional photographers. Nikon wanted to appeal to a wider range of people. At the same time, it wanted to combat Canon's inroads into the professional market with its EOS line of equipment.

Any time you pitch a piece of business, it's critical to demonstrate to your prospective client that you understand their business, and that you understand the core audience. Without doing this, it's impossible to be credible in terms of any strategic business, brand, or creative recommendations you make. In the case of Nikon, this meant demonstrating our understanding of professional photographers and their relationship with their Nikon equipment. We wanted to prove we understood the DNA of the brand—what "Nikon-ness" meant to its most critical audience. Perhaps nothing makes you more credible than going straight to the key user and getting their insights.

We knew various levels of amateur photographers made up part of the general Nikon audience, but it was the real pros, the prime influencers of the brand, whose insights we wanted to capture. These were the incredibly creative people who worked for *National Geographic, Sports Illustrated,* and *Vogue.* However, at the epicenter of this group was another audience: the photojournalists who went to war. We wanted to get their point of view on the brand.

Unfortunately, there has never been a shortage of wars. Our pitch to Nikon came during the buildup of the first Iraq war. We felt that in order to get a handle on what Nikon-ness really meant, we should talk to the people who, in the words of Eddie Adams, a well-respected war photographer, "get the world's worst assignments."

We made contact with a producer at ABC News who had access to the photographers and journalists who covered the war for *Time* and *Newsweek*. We asked if he could talk to these people for us and get their feelings about Nikon. We developed a questionnaire that he used as reference for his interviews, which we requested he film. The questions we posed captured exactly what we were looking for. When the producer sent back the taped interviews, it became apparent that the three-minute segments of war coverage we see on the evening news don't come close to portraying what these photojournalists go through to get a story. To say that the people who cover war are an intrepid bunch is both an oversimplification and an understatement.

With background scenes of swirling desert sands, rocket launchers, tanks and military vehicles, the photographers talked at length about what the Nikon brand meant to them. Relating a story about coming back from a mission, one photographer said, "We were hanging onto the truck's roll bar with one hand and our cameras with the other, and realized that the only piece of equipment with us that wasn't a Nikon was an M–16 rifle." Another told us, "It's not like that Volvo ad where the car gets rolled over by a truck. Our equipment and lenses get rolled over on a daily basis and survive." And another: "I can honestly say that after riding in the back of military Hum-vees, dealing with blowing sand and 100-degree temperatures, and crawling through the trenches with the troops, it's the only camera I'd take into war."

Using these interviews as both strategic foundation and visual backdrop, we demonstrated our understanding of the Nikon brand and its audience and won the assignment. As we began to work on the business, our key challenge was to develop a simple brand idea that would appeal to both the core audience of users—the professional photographers—as well as a broader audience. In BrandSimple terms, we were looking for a brand driver that would allow Nikon to serve both audiences well.

Excited by the idea of expanding its customer base, most brands have a tendency to chase after the new audience without thinking about the equity it has established with its original audience. This isn't smart. The first rule when seeking to broaden the appeal of a niche brand is that you must identify a way to hold down both bases, or risk losing everybody. With Canon nipping at its heels on the professional side of the business, and Canon and Minolta raising the stakes in the point-and-shoot market, Nikon needed a brand driver that would enable it to take on all competitors—to do battle on all fronts. The brand driver we arrived at with Nikon was "Approachable Authority." It was an idea that would allow Nikon to maintain its image and its reputation as the authority in the professional market, as well as allow it to court consumers who were simply interested in taking great pictures—simply. "Approachable" implied user-friendly, whoever that user might be.

I spoke to Sue Manber, a brand planner with whom I worked at Ammirati & Puris. "Nikon's credentials were impeccable," she told me, "but we watched Canon and Minolta begin to grab the lion's share of the burgeoning 35mm point-and-shoot market and we knew Nikon faced a challenge. Canon had introduced the EOS—a new camera that was enabling it to break into the professional market and chip away at Nikon's traditional stronghold, particularly among sports photographers. As a brand driver, 'Approachable Authority' served as a catalyst that allowed Nikon to enter the growing consumer market of photography buffs without sacrificing its high-end professional business."

According to Sue, Nikon chose to use a particular type of visual imagery to bring the idea of "Approachable Authority" to life in its branding signals. Canon and Minolta positioned their brands as cameras that made family photography easy and they used images of frolicking families as part of their branding efforts. Nikon, on the other hand, used images in its branding that were of a more technical nature—things that demonstrated how easy it was to take pictures without the red-eyed stares and blurring that frustrated so many photography buffs. This more technical imagery, to which people reacted favorably, allowed consumers to associate Nikon with high quality photography anyone would appreciate, even those who simply wanted to show off their frolicking families. Nikon's branding signals, based on the idea of "Approachable Authority," conveyed that because of its heritage only Nikon had the expertise and knowledge to make a camera for anyone who's serious about taking good pictures—even the point-and-click folks.

"On the professional side," Sue said, "despite Canon's inroads among professional sports photographers, Nikon's imagery as the authority in lenses continued undiminished. The solution to audience expansion for Nikon was taking on the role of 'Approachable Authority.' Building on its heritage along with its original tagline, 'We take the world's greatest pictures,' Nikon showed how even the average consumer could take fabulous pictures automatically."

"Approachable Authority" encapsulated Nikon's brand idea in a way that could be understood by both people inside the company—the ones engineering the technology—and the people outside the company—the ones taking the pictures. In its subsequent advertising, Nikon has shown images of how its professional audience has used its cameras in the most challenging situations, among them, the first Iraq war. Nikon has also made smart use of evolving technologies that make cameras even easier to use.

Nikon is a perfect example of how a strong niche brand broadened its base without undermining its original brand integrity. It identified a simple brand idea that captured and reinforced the brand's relevant difference for two very distinct audience segments.

Black & Decker: Another Way to Build Your Base

Nikon had one approach to its niche challenge. Black & Decker is a good example of another way to approach an audience expansion challenge.

The Black & Decker brand had built its reputation in the power tool market by touting tough performance. It became the favorite brand of professional contractors as well as serious users of power tools in the do-it-yourself market, a situation analogous to Nikon. Black & Decker wanted to expand its product line and purchased the home appliance division of GE, makers of toaster ovens and Dust Busters. All of a sudden, the Black & Decker name started appearing on coffee makers and irons, as well as power drills and sanders. Although it had seemed a logical strategy—Black & Decker for the entire house—it was not the best move.

The core DNA of the Black & Decker brand—tough performance in power tools—had been eroded. Its credibility was damaged with the contractor market. No serious contractor would show up on the job with a power tool that carried the same name as the toaster his kids used. Black & Decker had forgotten its core users as it went from the garage to the kitchen. Fortunately, Black & Decker recognized the problem and dealt with it quickly and effectively by way of promoting another brand it owned, DeWALT.

DeWALT was a brand for which professional tool users had a high regard, and in 1992 Black & Decker launched a line of electric tools under the DeWALT name. It knew it had to market these tools in a completely different manner from how it marketed its home appliances. That's why you won't find a DeWALT product on the shelves at Wal-Mart, but you will find it at Home Depot. To support the brand idea even more, Black & Decker started investing DeWALT promotional dollars in NASCAR events. The key to Black & Decker's success was tapping another brand in its organization to help it be most relevant to the target audience of professional power tool users. In fact, DeWALT has become one of Black & Decker's most profitable companies.

5. *Make sure your business strategy and brand idea are fully aligned.* I started the chapter with this thought, but it's such a critical issue I want to emphasize it again. I've seen too many great brand ideas struggle or fail because they weren't aligned with the basic business strategy. These brands just couldn't deliver on the promise of the brand idea. They didn't have the technology, or the production facilities, or the training for employees. If you take a position based on low airfares, make them low, but make sure you can stay in business when the price of fuel goes up. If your position is based on the fact that you don't charge interest for the first six months, you have to check the same thing—can you make money? If your point of relevant difference is based on a 100 percent money-back guarantee, can you afford to take the position? It may make a relevant difference to consumers, but it could be a killer to the bottom line.

Here are the stories of two brands, both started with the best of intentions. The brand ideas behind each of these well-known brands were simple and different, which was a good thing. Let's see how each of these brand ideas is being challenged by the business strategy.

TiVo: Hardware Brand or Software Brand?

I have TiVo. I admit it. I also admit I have a couple of questions. The first question has to do with the number of remote control devices I have on my coffee table along with the "cheat sheet" sitting next to them explaining which remote does what. Why do I need so many remotes? As a branding professional, the more important question I have is this: Is TiVo's business strategy still relevant and in alignment with its initial brand idea?

As quick context, TiVo began as a wonderful brand in the making. It was a totally new product—a digital video recorder (DVR) that made recording your favorite TV shows significantly easier than using your old video cassette recorder (VCR), not to mention making it possible to skip over advertising. When nothing seemed new anymore, TiVo established a refreshingly new brand idea. In doing so it captured great space on our mental desktops. A brand cult and culture quickly grew—very hard to achieve—and TiVo took on the status of Kleenex, Google, and FedEx. If I need to find something on the Internet, I Google it. If I need to get a package somewhere overnight, I FedEx it. I won't be home tomorrow night to watch the season premier of *24*, so I'll TiVo it. And by the way, hand me a Kleenex.

One of the initial challenges faced by the company was how to explain what TiVo was. People had no context. It was totally new technology. I talked to Nick Copping, a founder of the strategic positioning firm ZOOM, who worked with ZOOM co-founder Ellie Victor on TiVo's initial positioning. "The folks at TiVo ran around in the beginning telling consumers it was a 'personal television system.' The problem was everyone had a different perception of what 'personal television system' meant. It could have been any number of things. No one imagined it in exactly the same way, and the people at TiVo went to extremes not to use the term VCR in any of its explanations. The company tried to use quirky advertising to get people's attention, thinking that by doing this, the idea would take hold. But the advertising, although entertaining, still didn't tell consumers exactly what TiVo was in a way that made sense. People remembered the ads, but not what they were for. Consumers needed some type of familiar context to understand what this new technology was all about. At least tell me what TiVo was similar to? When TiVo finally began to explain that it was like a VCR without tapes but, rather, with a hard disk, people began to get it. ZOOM called it a DVR, rather than a personal television system. It was a simple way to get the TiVo idea and brand into people's heads.

"Okay, we finally had a simple way to explain it. That was the first step," Nick continued. "The second challenge was to create an emotional hook. Why do I need TiVo in my life? We began to do focus groups in order to get an understanding of how the market perceived TiVo. We immediately realized we had a gender issue to deal with. We all know men and women differ in how they perceive things, which has been written about extensively in books such as *Men are from Mars, Women are from Venus*. The way men and women perceived TiVo was really different. It's a generalization, but men loved the hardware. They just loved talking about the technology aspect. We found that what women liked about TiVo was that it was one of the only household electronic devices that allowed them to schedule life on *their* time. It was TV on their schedule. When Oprah referred to TiVo as the "ultimate girlfriend appliance" on one of her shows, the marketers at TiVo knew they were onto something. When a *Sixty Minutes* report referred to it in a similar manner, relative to its appeal to both genders, the company knew it had its emotional hook. 'TV you can control.'"

TiVo had a simple, different idea people could get: Like a VCR, but without tapes. TiVo created the DVR category and, with it, a relevant emotional hook: "TV on my schedule." And the good news is that the DVR culture is thriving. It's predicted, in fact, that more than 40 percent of U.S. households will have some sort of DVR device by 2008. The current challenge for TiVo is that the cult and culture are starting to move to other DVR providers for that dose of TV they can control—cable, telephone, and electronics companies. Although TiVo did an amazing job creating emotional space in the consumer's mind, it may have made itself the unwitting sacrificial version of the DVR world by giving up its innovative name to the generic category. People may say they are TiVo-ing *Desperate Housewives,* but they could be using another kind of hardware to do it.

TiVo is in danger of losing its difference and relevance in the category. It's becoming apparent that if TiVo continues to base its business strategy on hardware, it may not be able to compete with the cable, telephone, and electronics companies that have entered the field. The scale on which these companies operate gives them a great advantage.

To continue to capitalize on its name, it may be necessary for TiVo to consider evolving to a software-based business strategy. It designs incredible software, including a wonderfully easy and intuitive interface that makes it simple to scroll through and program the viewing options available. It's this simple and engaging interface that has enabled TiVo to create such a loyal brand following and on which it should consider differentiating itself from its competition. In other words, it may be time for the company to ask, "Should we be positioning ourselves as a hardware brand or a software brand?" It spent a lot of good time, money, and energy focusing on a brilliant brand idea, but has been losing its edge on the hardware side of the business. It's less than a parity product on this dimension.

It's tough to play catch-up, especially in the tech space, but many brands have done it. TiVo got the most difficult part of building a brand right. It attained the brand fan club other brands only dream about. My suggestion is that the company take another look at its business strategy. Redefine it and realign it with the fun and innovative associations that have been linked to its brand name. Then, send the signals—software and services—that put users in control of TV in a way DVR hardware brands can't. Although I'm not sure about how to solve the remote control situation, you have my answer on the other, more important, question.

IRIDIUM: Great Idea, Great Business Strategy— Second Time Around

> To *Masters of the Universe* Iridium is the brand of *global telephone network* that allows you to *call anywhere from anywhere*.

Motorola, a great company, founded Iridium several years ago after the wife of one of its engineers provided it with an interesting "a-ha." She needed to get in touch with her husband, who was working on an oil rig in the middle of the ocean. How could she do it?

Motorola came up with a magical solution. The team on the *Starship Enterprise* would have been impressed. It launched sixty-six close-range satellites into low-earth orbit and turned them into receivers and transmitters for a special breed of portable telephone. Masters of the Universe, the business jet-set, were impressed—at first.

Motorola hoped that Iridium would take on the position of the unquestioned market leader and number-one provider of global wireless communication solutions. When global business leaders think about staying in touch, the company wanted them to think about "Iridium." At the time, it was able to promise that a single phone and a single phone number would work anywhere on the planet.

Its position was terrific at first glance. Several of its branding signals were terrific, too. The team at Landor developed a logo fashioned after the Big Dipper along with the line, "Communication Anytime, Anywhere." When Landor showed the proposed identity to the target customers, whether they lived in Chicago or Rome, it had the desired magical effect. Anyone who looked at it was reminded of gazing at an endless, starry nighttime sky during childhood camping trips. Given that the brand was based on a man-made solar system created by Iridium, the branding signals were brilliant and established all the right associations.

Iridium continued creating branding signals, from a website to customer service kits, to packaging, and then hit a snag—a pretty major snag: the phone itself. The most vital branding signal of all wasn't too terrific.

To begin with, the product design didn't sync with the target audience. Neither did the functionality or the price point. The phone was big and clunky. It didn't fit comfortably into the Armani suits or Hermès briefcases favored by Masters of the Universe. The satellite thing didn't work too well either, particularly for those who were more often inside an office building or a Michelin-rated restaurant than on a mid-ocean oil rig. Most times you needed to be on the street to pick up a clear signal, and that was not a good branding signal. And the price point was too high, even for the highest fliers. The phones sold for about $1,000, and the calling charges were about $5 per minute.

Time also wasn't working for Iridium. The cell phone landscape on earth was rapidly evolving. During the early 1990s, traditional tower-based cell phones were beginning to be able to send and receive from more and more places in the world. In addition, due to legislation, local phone providers were starting to link up so that cell users could keep a single telephone number even if they changed carriers. Cell phones could be used inside buildings, and they fit nicely into pockets and briefcases. Perhaps most important, the prices of cell phone calls continued to drop, making the technology attractive to everyone, jet-set VIPs and everyone else.

Within a few months of its launch—literal and figurative—Iridium clearly was not going to come close to making even its minimum sales targets. And with billions of dollars invested in rockets and satellites, the investment bankers threw in the towel. Iridium went bankrupt. In 2000, new management was brought in to see what could be done.

The new management team decided to look at different and smaller market segments. (The original audience had to be enormous for the company to recoup its initial investment.) Management went back to the original insight: the guys on the oil rigs. Cell phones didn't work on oil rigs at sea and cell phones didn't always work in the Gobi. Perhaps most critical, cell phones didn't always work in times of emergency, natural or man-made.

Iridium's management decided to change two components of its positioning statement in order to succeed:

> To *people who must get in touch no matter what,* Iridium *is the brand of global telephone* network that allows you to *get in touch when it's mission critical.*

Iridium took the position of fail-safe communication system. From a business strategy perspective, cost of entry or price per call aren't barriers to this audience. These people *had* to get in touch.

Iridium is now a highly valued and respected supplier of satellite-based communication systems to the people who must get through no matter what and will pay to do so. These people are willing to carry bigger handsets, and are willing to pay more than three cents a call. During Hurricanes Katrina and Wilma, for example, Iridium technology was working when cell phones went silent. Iridium technology can be found on container ships at sea, and serves the needs of first responders in every part of the world, from defense departments, to emergency management departments, to healthcare and environmental organizations. Iridium signals are now genuinely life-saving.

I learned a number of important things from my Landor project with Iridium. First of all, building a brand in the technology category is a constant challenge. Tech brands face a rapid pace of change. A product can go from amazing to ho-hum in a matter of weeks. Building a brand takes time. If you base your brand idea on something that will be old news by the time it gets to market, you're in trouble.

To succeed in any category, especially the technology category, you've got to find an idea or position for your brand built on something less limiting than a feature or benefit, which can easily become obsolete by the time you get to market. The challenge is to find a position based on an emotion or a frame of mind. In Iridium's case, this meant moving away from a position of "any place, any time," which the cell phone industry co-opted, to a position based on secure communication. A claim based on the idea of security could grow and evolve as Iridium's technology changed. It also gave the organization a focal point for all brand initiatives. Iridium supports the simple idea of security not only by overall network capabilities, but by providing backup batteries to customers and offering phones that can be recharged by way of light sources and are guaranteed waterproof.

The second thing that became obvious in my work with Iridium is that no amount of advertising or branding, no matter how brilliant, will make up for a business strategy that doesn't deliver. Iridium promised the ultimate business communication tool for globe-trotting executives but could not make good on its promise. The bottom line: Even the greatest branding can't overcome a brand idea that doesn't align with the business strategy and deliver as expected.

Where We Go Next

I've talked about stepping back. In the next chapter, I'm going to talk about closing in. Once you've examined your business strategy, created a brand framework to position your brand, and established a simple and different brand idea, it's time to get simpler still. It's time to get to the essence of your idea. In order to create successful branding signals, you have to reduce your idea to a brand driver. You got a hint of this in the HBO story. Chapter 5 will give you the details.

5

Step Two: Capture the Essence of Your Idea

Did you ever play the game of Telephone when you were a kid? You'd sit in a circle with a bunch of friends, whisper a phrase or sentence into your neighbor's ear, and it would be passed along person to person. The last person to hear the whispered phrase would shout out the message. The more tangled the phrase, the more fun it was. Misinterpretations were expected, and anything of a crude nature was a bonus, especially to twelve-year-old boys.

The next step in achieving BrandSimple status is sort of like a game of Telephone, but with one huge difference. You do *not* want your phrase or sentence to get mangled or tangled or misinterpreted in any way (especially in a manner amusing to twelve-year-old boys). Your message has to be heard, understood, and passed on person to person exactly as it started.

In chapter 4, I discussed the need to use the BrandSimple framework in order to get to a simple and meaningful idea on which to build your brand. The first big mistake people make when they face a brand challenge is to rush into the branding signals before they've established the idea on which to base those signals. The second big mistake people make is not taking the time to reduce this idea to its simplest state. Your idea may be different and relevant, and you may think it's stated succinctly, but your branding signals will be less than effective unless your idea can survive a game of Telephone.

After you've identified a simple idea to call your own, it's critical to successful branding to take your general idea and reduce it to a single phrase or sentence that captures the core meaning of the brand idea. Much like reducing a sauce, you must take your idea and boil it down to its essence. It must be something that evokes imagery *beyond* the phrase itself. We at Landor call this a brand driver, for the simple reason that it's meant to have the ability to drive every branding signal, brand behavior, and brand association. Some folks in the brand business call this a brand handle, brand axis, or brand DNA. I like the action implied by the term "brand driver." It forces you to make the phrase or statement something that motivates and inspires those charged with bringing it to life in a way that will connect with the customers you want to impact. A brand driver should be something that people can grasp intuitively, without any guidelines or explanations.

Establishing a brand driver is critical to winning the brand equivalent of a game of Telephone. That's because you'll be playing it with the hundreds, perhaps thousands, of people inside your company, advertising and public relations agencies, as well as those who may be manufacturing parts, products, or operational systems for you. You want everyone to not just hear the same message, but understand it in the same way.

A strong, well-articulated brand driver makes it possible to communicate your brand idea to the people who will be responsible for creating the branding signals and ensures that they understand its intent without any misinterpretation. It allows everyone in the organization to internalize the "brand recipe." This vital step in the brand-building process ensures that your branding signals will be consistent from customer touch point to customer touch point, wherever your customer interacts with your brand. It will ensure that all signals are in sync with each other, and in sync with the brand idea. A good brand driver ensures that the brand idea is conveyed with cohesion, consistency, and coherence.

If your advertising campaign signals one message about what your brand stands for and your product functionality signals don't stand up to the promise, you've got crossed signals. If the design and voice of your catalog signals one thing about your brand and customer service doesn't follow through, you've got your signals crossed. If your packaging states that the product inside is easy to assemble and it isn't, your engineers don't have the same brand recipe the package designer does. Someone didn't understand the message. This sends a message to your customers that you'd prefer they didn't get.

Here's a quick example of what I mean by crossed signals. Fighting to regain share lost to low-cost airlines, United Airlines adopted a new brand position captured in the idea of "Rising." It sounded optimistic, the driving message seemed actionable—let's rise above the competition, or let's rise above consumer expectations, as in "we're coming back." The airline had two problems, however. First, it became clear that the idea wasn't articulated in a way that employees could fully understand what it meant. Second, and more critical, the branding signals conveyed to customers weren't in any way aligned with the brand idea or with each other. Customer service was poor, planes were constantly late in departing, luggage was lost on a daily basis, meals were eliminated, and it appeared that the only things that were rising were the ticket prices. The brand idea and the ensuing branding signals were the antithesis of "Rising." The business strategy was sinking as a result of these crossed signals and because airline management hadn't really thought through the basic implications of its brand idea to begin with. The airline went into Chapter 11. The lesson: Nothing kills a brand faster than not delivering on your promise.

It's imperative to establish a brand driver that can be unconditionally understood by everyone in your organization so that they can successfully deliver the promise inherent in your brand idea. A brand driver provides the clear direction—the recipe—that all the branding signals should follow. It ensures that your customers get the message you intended them to get wherever and however they interact with your brand.

Clarity Is Critical

If you can't preserve clarity and coherence of the brand idea with groups inside your organization, you'll have enormous difficulty with effective branding—sending consistent and focused signals—outside your company. Managing clarity of idea is the most challenging and the most significant part of the brand and branding process. Play that game of Telephone with a thousand or more employees in multiple locations worldwide and you can imagine the distortion of meaning that can arise.

In many of today's global, matrixed organizations with numerous marketing teams, agencies, and distributor partners, the challenge of creating a clear and focused brand driver is considerable. Just think about the sheer number of people involved with expressing the Coca-Cola brand idea. There are global marketing managers based at the company's Atlanta headquarters, and there are Coca-Cola marketers in most major markets around the world. Both groups have multiple agency partners to help express the Coca-Cola brand through branding signals including advertising, packaging, promotions, public relations, sponsorships and events, and the Internet. In addition, in some countries, marketers focus on just Coca-Cola in bottles and cans, while others focus on Coca-Cola sold at soda fountains. Furthermore, to manufacture, sell, and distribute Coca-Cola in bottles and cans, enormous networks of franchisees have a direct impact on how the Coca-Cola brand appears at retail locations. And by the way, Coca-Cola also has a large and very profitable team that licenses the brand name for merchandise, such as T-shirts and baseball caps. Without exaggeration, literally tens of thousands of people are charged with bringing the Coca-Cola brand idea to life. Without a clear brand idea, distilled to a brand driver, a game of Telephone could easily break down fast.

Successful branding occurs when your brand idea can stand up to a game of Telephone without any slips between one messenger and the next. A general position or idea is neither portable enough nor focused enough to ensure your message can come across unscathed and intact. A compelling brand driver—a phrase that captures the philosophy behind your idea—will ensure that everyone gets all that the brand idea implies without the need for remedial assistance. A good brand driver intuitively enlightens employees and anyone else responsible for branding signals. It tells them how to do what's right for the brand. It establishes and promotes a strong brand culture. A good brand driver is self-instructive and helps everyone understand how to "be the brand," and why.

A Brand Driver Is the Perfect Internal File Name

The success of a brand is determined in large part by its relevance to a specific group of people and its differentiation from competitors. If a brand doesn't tap in to consumer needs, if it doesn't speak to them, it won't sell, nor will it be able to command effective margins. A brand driver gives focus to the meaningful difference you offer and gives the people in the brand organization a shared vision. It pinpoints ownable qualities and provides direction for all creative and strategic endeavors. A general idea or position can get fuzzy in interpretation. A brand driver, if crafted well, cannot. Clear and effective communication is at the core of the brand business. A brand driver is the shorthand required for effective, unmistakable communication. It will conjure up all the right mental associations. Actually, it's the perfect internal mental file name.

A Political Specialty

Successful politicians and their speechwriters are quite adept at taking a general idea, based on a campaign platform, and making it into a brand driver. (Yes, politics is about brands.) They can encapsulate a range of promises in a succinct and pithy manner. Much like skilled brand managers, these people know exactly what's needed to mobilize and motivate legions of voters. They can take a candidate's entire philosophy or ideology and capture it beautifully in a phrase or slogan. They make it a bumper sticker of an idea.

"A chicken in every pot and a car in every garage" was the clever brand driver taken by Herbert Hoover in his first campaign in 1928. Although he may have meant it literally, it conjured up imagery ("We're in for good times!") beyond the specific phrase. People got it and held on to it. Four years later, in the throes of the Great Depression, Hoover had to create a much different image: "We are turning the corner," he tried to tell a beleaguered nation. No brand driver, no matter how well intentioned or well crafted, could have saved him in his run against FDR, whose brand driver was based on another, more relevant position and ideology: "I propose a New Deal." It was a statement more people could relate to. The nation got it and all it stood for.

Ronald Reagan asked the nation, "Are you better off now than you were four years ago?" It was a clear, concise representation of his philosophy and the imperatives he embraced. He didn't need to go into long explanations. His supporters knew intuitively what he meant. The first George Bush defined his message with the brand driver, "No new taxes." His platform encompassed the complex reality of the conservative stance he represented. Again, there was no need for details, facts, or figures. And there was very little room for misunderstanding. For those who might have missed the exact words, however, he advised us to "Read my lips." And, as with traditional brands, when Bush failed to deliver his brand promise and taxes did increase, he suffered politically. Some say this disconnect with his brand driver was key to his reelection loss to Bill Clinton.

People Listen with Their Guts

I had a conversation with Thomas Friedman, columnist for the *New York Times* and author of many books, including the bestseller *The World is Flat*. The central theme of his book is that as a result of many things, including exponential advances in communications and technology, the world has become flat. This flattening of the world allows us to do business and almost everything else with billions of people across the planet faster and more easily than ever before.

Among the many things Tom writes about is the intersection of business and politics, the people, events, and global implications. He talked to me about his experience traveling across this flat new world and what he discovered in conversations with corporate, cultural, and political leaders. "People listen through their stomachs, not their ears," Tom said. "If you connect with people on a gut level, they'll say, 'Don't bother me with the details, I trust you with my gut, go ahead.' If you don't connect with them on a gut level, you can't offer them enough details or statistics to bring them around. You have to connect on a gut level first."

"GE gets it," Tom told me. "Jeff Immelt, their CEO, gets it. He's got a huge multifaceted, multinational organization with thousands of employees and hundreds of products. But he has boiled down what GE stands for into a simple, gut-level idea that everyone can connect with, inside the company and outside: 'We're going to be about imagination.' It defines the culture and it's believable. Why? Because coming from GE, imagination is credible. It's authentic and doesn't feel contrived. If you promise something that seems inauthentic, people can smell it from a hundred paces."

Tom told me that the same thing applies with politics and politicians. "The best politicians out there know they have to reduce their platform to a simple message—something that connects on a gut level in an authentic way. You have to believe the message and the messenger. There is nothing wrong with complicated ideas, but if you want to convey a complicated thought to a mass audience, you have to first condense it into something digestible and believable. Once you grab someone's attention, you can pour in the details.

"You have to be able to understand something in its complexity to be able to express it with simplicity. The best political leaders, the best business leaders are able to simplify the essence of things without dumbing them down or making them silly."

Complicated ideas don't work in politics any more than they work with brands. People need a simple message. Think of it as a literal and figurative bumper sticker of an idea: "Peace and prosperity in our time." "Don't swap horses in mid-stream." Neither Tom nor I are talking about just the simplicity part. It's getting your brand idea down to a simple, actionable phrase that will be perceived as genuine. It must connect on a gut level to have real impact.

Great Brands, Strong Brand Drivers

Strong brands have strong brand drivers. It's demonstrated by the way their branding signals are brought to life. The signals resonate with the brand idea and the associations they want consumers to have click with us. These brands have become shortcuts. The people who work for these brand organizations get what the brand stands for and, as a result, we do, too. Let me give you a few examples. Then I'd like to share an exercise you can use to help you generate your own brand driver.

Town Market: eBay

Join me at the Town Market. Over 100 million of my closest friends and neighbors will be there. What can you buy at this Town Market? you ask. Almost anything imaginable. Baseball cards and housewares, antiques and dolls, used books, used cars, new cars, clothing, electronics, tickets to Broadway shows, and airline tickets are all there for the bidding and the buying. Who will you be bidding against or buying from? More than 100 million of your closest friends and neighbors. All like-minded folks who just want an equal opportunity to buy and to have a little community fun doing it.

Town Market is eBay's brand driver and its business strategy rolled brilliantly into one simple phrase. It's the simple idea behind eBay that captures its essence and makes its branding signals intuitive.

In 1995 Pierre Omidyar, cofounder and chairman of eBay, had an insight about the Internet. Call it one of those Seinfeld-like observations most of us overlook. Pierre realized that people talked a great deal about what businesses were going to be able to get out of the Internet, but no one was talking about how to use the Internet to give market power to the individual consumer. He was interested to see how the Internet could create a fair opportunity for all consumers. Allow them to get fair prices with no markups on whatever they wanted to buy, with no middleman, and with the fewest people touching something along the transaction route.

I talked with David Knight, eBay's vice president of international marketing, about Pierre's insight. "When Pierre launched the site, it was almost as a hobby," he said. "He was intrigued with the idea of giving like-minded people the opportunity to create a commerce connection. But unlike controlled Internet business models, Pierre left it to the community to evolve the business model—to see if users could develop the rules to make things faster and more efficient as they went along. eBay gave them the tools and resources, but it was the eBay users who built the brand. Our customers are all brand managers."

Allowing users to make the rules is what has allowed eBay to evolve into a global Town Market. One of Pierre's guiding principles is that people are basically good. The system of self-policing on the site—a set of simple and highly effective rules—bears this out. The values on which eBay grew came from its users. David emphasized that it's their site. eBay has put in place technological and privacy guidelines, but the day-to-day guidelines are provided by the people who come to the Town Market every day.

And people do come. Of the more than 70 million people who use eBay in the United States, 724,000 of them use its commerce connection as the sole source of family income—and they're incredibly successful. The people who work at eBay are encouraged to use the site as much as possible to experience what happens there on a day-to-day basis. David said, "Unless you're on the site, you can't possibly understand what a vibrant network it is for people. We have an event we call eBay Live once a year. Last year in San Jose ten thousand people showed up. We maxed out the convention center. We had roundtable discussions with both users and employees, so that there was dialog about what was going on, what improvements could be made, what innovations to explore. We gave workshops on how to optimize an individual's business on eBay, how to deal with imports and exports, with taxes, anything that could help our community of users. Our brand is not a supercontrolled environment, which is what makes it what it is. eBay is not just an experience, it's a movement."

eBay is a simple idea. It's a global Town Market that creates incredible opportunities for anyone who visits. The branding signals that have grown out of the Town Market brand driver are absolutely in sync with its intent. The name, among its most powerful signals, is easy and approachable. It's a friendly word, and it sounds simple. eBay's other branding signals come through in the wide variety of educational tools, features, and services the company makes available. It provides resources that enable users to buy and sell on the site quickly, safely, and conveniently, as the brand driver implies will be the case. The site itself, the most powerful signal, is enjoyable and simple to navigate. As the brand signal responsible for generating the greatest return on investment, the website's design, functionality, and technology are among the company's highest priorities in terms of branding investment. Note that eBay didn't get so enamored with or distracted by its technology that basic human needs or the promise of the brand were overwhelmed. In other words, the technology became a means to achieving its business strategy and delivering its brand idea. (Pixar, as I said earlier, understands this, too. The simple and innovative stories told in Pixar movies are never undermined by its incredible technology.) The folks who work at eBay know the brand is about the people they serve in the Town Market, and they never let anything get in the way.

Town Market, like every great brand driver, expresses all the intended associations behind the brand's philosophy, and then some. It clearly says, "We're a friendly and accessible place to come and buy or sell your wares."

Pierre Omidyar, cofounder Jeff Skoll, and CEO Meg Whitman (or "Mayor," as she's affectionately called) have turned eBay into a global trading platform where individuals have balanced opportunity to buy or sell practically anything. Today the eBay community includes more than 100 million registered members from around the world. People spend more time on eBay than on any other online site, making it the most popular destination on the Internet. The signals it sends have played a significant role in reinforcing the fact that it is a trustworthy and welcoming Town Market.

"Imagination at Work": GE

"'We bring good things to life.' You don't walk away from a tag line on a whim," Beth Comstock, president of NBC and former corporate vice president and chief marketing officer of GE, told me of her company's catchphrase. "And we didn't. But twenty-five years after that incredible line was created, GE was still being associated with refrigerators and light bulbs in the mind of the consumer. While we still do that, and do it well, GE now represents a lot more. We've got six different business units ranging from health sciences to consumer finance to entertainment. We needed a vision and a vision statement that encapsulated everything that we are now. Something that could be both inspirational and act as a message of aspiration to everyone in our company."

Michael Patti, then the creative director at BBDO who worked with Beth and her team, along with GE's CEO Jeffrey Immelt, explained. "Jeff said to us at our first meeting, 'In my mind, GE makes things that make people go wow! We need a vision that captures that wow factor.'" "To do this," Michael said, "We went back to GE's genesis, its heritage: the imagination of Thomas Edison. From day one, GE has been able to imagine things that other companies couldn't and make them real. They could make things that made people go wow. Imagination was the big thing. It was simple and it was authentic. It became obvious that imagination was at the core of everything GE has done, and still does."

Taking this general framework as a starting point, Beth and her team along with the team from BBDO reduced the idea to the brand driver, "What we can imagine we can make happen." But, being the innovative people they are, they did more than that. They took the phrase and found an imaginative and intuitive way to tell its story in a format that everyone in every GE business unit in every country worldwide could connect to. They took the new GE Equation, as they called it, and drew it on chalkboards to creatively telegraph its meaning.

In executing the new brand driver in this format, GE not only got it on one page, but also made it instantly comprehensible. When you're trying to teach thousands of people a new idea, a straightforward, engaging execution is far more memorable, and has greater impact, than a tedious PowerPoint presentation. The chalkboard execution allowed everyone in the GE organization to grasp exactly what was meant without any extraneous explanation. It was an ingenious brand recipe, easy to understand and on which to follow through with actions and branding signals that could make it a reality.

"Imagination was a concept everyone could take hold of and make applicable to his or her area of expertise," Beth said. "Jeff challenged each business group to identify breakthrough ideas for growth. He called them Imagination Breakthroughs—ideas capable of generating at least $100 million of new revenue in three years. Ideas that could help our customers in ways they never imagined.

"We've seen the result of Imagination Breakthroughs in exciting, more effective designs for medical imaging equipment, in solutions for smarter energy sources like wind and solar power, in consumer finance opportunities. Imagination has become a cultural touchstone and a business engine. It's become part of the criteria HR uses in hiring practices and is the foundation for our employee awards program.

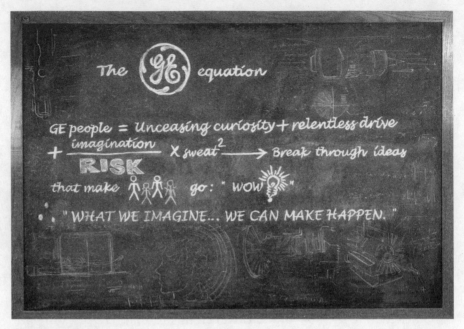

The (GE) equation

GE people = Unceasing curiosity + relentless drive
+ imagination / RISK X sweat² ——→ Break through ideas
that make 👤👤👤 go: " WOW 💡"
∴ "WHAT WE IMAGINE... WE CAN MAKE HAPPEN."

Imagination became a Brand Driver that aided GE in both internal and external branding.

People intuitively understand how it affects them and how they can make things happen."

GE's powerful internal signal, the chalkboard equation, became the catalyst for an incredible range of external branding signals, from inventiveness in product design and functionality, to package design, to family entertainment. "What we can imagine we can make happen," and its simple, evocative execution, have become the literal and figurative brand driver for one of the most respected brands in the world.

I talked in chapter 4 about things to watch for in the establishment of a brand idea. One was to make sure you had an idea that was durable and not built on a product or feature that could become obsolete quickly in a fast-evolving marketplace. There are few businesses as complex or as diverse as GE. It's the third-largest company in the United States with multiple business units, products, and services. Yet, as complex a company as it is, GE was able to hit on an idea and a brand driver that could last as long as necessary. It connects on an emotional level and is aspirational. GE looked to its roots and in doing so found a brand driver that was both authentic and relevant to everyone inside the organization, no matter what their line of business or their role in the company.

"Complete Confidence": Cleveland Clinic

The Cleveland Clinic is one of the most highly respected medical institutions in the world. Founded in 1921, it is home to a world-renowned group of physicians, surgeons, specialists, researchers, nurses, and support staff. Working together, they explore, discover, innovate, and invent better ways to care for the people who depend on them. They demonstrate measurably superior medical outcomes and work to improve them every year. *U.S. News & World Report* has included Cleveland Clinic among the best in hospital rankings for eleven years in a row. In 2005, the Cleveland Clinic ranked fourth overall out of over five thousand hospitals in the United States. Eleven out of sixteen medical specialty areas rank among the top ten in the nation.

In 2004, Cleveland Clinic decided to take a fresh look at its brand idea and its branding signals. It wanted to raise its profile in order to establish name recognition and presence equal to its peers in high-quality medical care. It also wanted to raise its top-of-mind awareness beyond its facilities in Cleveland. Its medical facilities had grown in both physical size and stature, and patients come from as far away as the Middle East. The staff at Cleveland Clinic has been treating the king and the royal family of Saudi Arabia for more than thirty years and, in fact, is building a facility in the Middle East, but Cleveland Clinic has been perceived as a regional resource. It was seen as such due to its name, which, unlike the names of many of its competitors—Johns Hopkins, the Mayo Clinic, and Sloan-Kettering, for example—is geographic in nature. A name change, however, was not a consideration.

Cleveland Clinic gathered staff from every area of the organization, along with a team from Landor, to develop a clear idea for its brand. The way it had been presenting itself was somewhat muddled and its branding signals—the way it presented itself both internally and externally—were inconsistent.

Beyond building image and recognition beyond the immediate market area, Cleveland Clinic was clearly interested in attracting more patients from across the country. This was a business imperative. The best hospitals in the country reach beyond their city borders for growth, the growth that will fuel their research, innovations, and other life-extending skills.

Generally speaking, people won't travel far when they're ill unless they are very ill or suffering from a complex medical condition. In those cases people often search out the best the nation has to offer. Cleveland Clinic needed to reach out to these people and to referring physicians to let them know the facts. The question became: What could the brand promise and deliver?

When people are confronted with a potentially life-threatening illness, fear is a very real, present, and powerful emotion that must be addressed. One of the first things any of us who have dealt with just such a situation tries to do is minimize the patient's fears. We want to console and offer hope to those who fear they may end up seeing the wrong doctor. They may be fearful of being misdiagnosed or undergoing the wrong treatment. They may fear being treated like a number. Ultimately, like any of us, they may fear their own mortality.

While minimizing fear was a powerful and credible position to take, Cleveland Clinic chose instead to take a position that reflected the polar opposite. It wanted people to come there with a sense of complete confidence. It wanted prospective patients, their families, and referring physicians to know that they were making the very best decision in their choice of medical care. In taking this position, Cleveland Clinic was speaking directly to fears and uncertainty, but at the same time instilling the sense of confidence that comes from knowing you're making the right choice.

I spoke with Jim Blazer, director of marketing at Cleveland Clinic, about his team's brand positioning work. "Sometimes the best ideas are the simplest ideas," he told me. (I agreed.) "What we wanted to get across in our message to prospective patients and their families was that if you chose Cleveland Clinic for your medical care, you could have complete confidence that you'd made the best decision.

And there it was, 'Complete Confidence.' It was a eureka moment for us. It captured the position we wanted to take in such a concise and compelling way that it became the phrase we used to get the message across internally. It took about three seconds to get across, if that long. While it was something that always existed in the care we provided, we hadn't codified it in this way.

"'Complete Confidence' as a driver of all of our initiatives was so obvious. It was differentiating and galvanizing at the same time. It kept the focus on our patients, while also having the power to inspire a culture to continue to drive us all toward the best outcomes for our patients," Jim said.

The simple, credible position Cleveland Clinic took became its brand driver, something that could raise its presence externally while sharpening its focus internally. As I mentioned earlier, it's not often that a general idea becomes the brand driver, but when it does, it is, as Jim said, a eureka moment. (Remember, don't disregard the obvious. Recognize a good idea when you see one.)

Based on its internal driver of all brand behavior, Cleveland Clinic employees now ask, "What else can we do to instill complete confidence in our patients and their families? What can we do for them that would convey confidence to them?" These are questions asked and answered by everyone from researchers and technicians, to nurses and nutritional staff, to doctors. From a business strategy perspective, the position and the brand driver are in perfect harmony. When the staff of a medical organization is inspired to instill complete confidence in its patients, it not only yields better medical outcomes, but makes good business sense. The branding signals that wield the most significant influence are those made possible by the extraordinary research, care, and service provided day in and day out. These are branding signals Cleveland Clinic conveys with every patient treated.

To get the new brand driver across to more than 33,000 employees of Cleveland Clinic, Jim took on the role of branding ambassador. With the support of teams from every department, he went through a series of presentations and activities that helped instill the idea. "Actually, it was easy," Jim said. "'Complete Confidence' speaks for itself."

Effective branding is the reflection of an effective brand idea. With the new idea in place at Cleveland Clinic, it was time to align the branding signals with the idea. They weren't dealing with a "throw out the baby with the bathwater" do-over. There was local equity (and certainly internal passion) connected to many elements of Cleveland Clinic's original visual brand identity, for example. But the fact of the matter was that Cleveland Clinic didn't look as if it were world class, one of the best in business of health and medical care. It didn't look current or innovative. Most of all, it didn't look confident. The Landor team, along with the team from Cleveland Clinic, created a new website, new collateral materials, and a host of training initiatives, but the phrase itself motivated the most appropriate branding initiatives of all: We will do anything and everything necessary to instill complete confidence in our patients. It's our reason for being.

"Good Journalism about People": *People*

Nothing interests people as much as other people's lives. "Good journalism about people" is the brand driver that drives every story in *People*. And it's what drives more than 36 million people a week to read it.

People was founded more than thirty years ago as a chronicle of popular culture when the editors at *Time* magazine realized how much people enjoyed reading its "People Pages"—the weekly section that lets us know what's going on with people more famous than we are. It covers traditional milestones, such as birthdays, births, and deaths, as well as news of what newsworthy people have been up to lately.

People responds to the inherent interest we have in the "people behind the headlines," as managing editor Martha Nelson refers to her subjects. *People* differentiates itself from its many competitors by giving us more than just gossip, but well-researched and well-written profiles that give us insight into people's lives. *People* keeps us abreast of what's happening in the world of celebrities and entertainment as well as what's happening in the world in general. It doesn't shy away from hard news. In fact, it brings hard news closer, makes it real, by telling us the behind-the-scenes stories of the people who've been part of what we see on CNN's breaking headlines.

Martha told me that *People* has always held its editorial staff to standards of rigorous journalism. It is serious about the reporting and stringent in its fact-checking, and won't write stories based on rumor. Martha said that what sets *People* apart from other chroniclers of famous names is the quality of the reporting. "We may be a touchstone for popular culture and current events, but we operate with a high degree of journalistic professionalism and integrity. Trust with the reader is our number-one priority."

I asked Martha how the editorial staff goes about choosing the people for each week's edition. "First and foremost, we identify people who are genuinely interesting," she told me. "There has to be a real sense of newsworthiness to the story. If we sense there's a saturation point in the market, we don't do the story.

"When *People* started," Martha explained, "we didn't have too much competition. There was no *Entertainment Tonight,* no *US* magazine, no *Access Hollywood,* and no Internet. While the market has changed, we maintain the integrity of what made us different—good journalism about people in the news. This means a wide range of news. We report things on a human level. The good things and the sad.

"After the space shuttle crashed, for example, we told the stories of the astronauts. Our readers were interested in the lives of the people on the shuttle. They didn't look to us for scientific coverage, how the tiles came off, or any of the technical details of the tragedy. There are other news sources for that kind of reporting. Our reporting is and always has been about how events touch people. We tell human stories.

"After the wrath of Katrina, we never once referred in our stories to how the levies broke, or the physics of storm surge, or wind velocity. We told compassionate stories about the people who experienced the terrible storm—the incredible hardships, the bravery, and the tales of individual heroism. That's what our readers expect from us—well-written and researched stories about people." She went on to say, "It's not called *Famous People* magazine, it's called *People* magazine."

With such a focused brand driver, indoctrinating new editorial staff at *People* is not difficult. Martha told me that the staff has a gut instinct about what's on-brand and what's off, what makes for an appropriate story, and what is not appropriate to the magazine. *People* gets to the heart of the story and is able to address what's on people's minds from a personal perspective. Martha told me that she's had trial lawyers, university professors, and literary intellectuals of every genre tell her they read *People* as a way of staying in touch with what's really going on out there. It helps put the world in context from a social and cultural point of view.

I asked Martha what happens as *People* gets bigger. "We keep focused on our original DNA," she told me. "Our DNA travels with us from project to project, from assignment to assignment. We've never strayed from our core values. We apply the standard of good journalism to stories about people, without descending into gossip. We can change what we do on a day-to-day basis, but we'll never change who we are."

People's competition does keep increasing, and not only by way of derivative magazines. Our news and views about noteworthy people come from a fast-multiplying array of sources, including all those blogs I mentioned. What will keep *People* relevant and differentiated is staying true to its brand driver, "good journalism about people." *People* will continue to look for innovative ways to signal the fact that what sets it apart is its professional standards of journalism. I expect that in the years ahead we'll see new venues and channels for *People*'s stories and innovative journalistic techniques to give us the compellingly different and personal perspective we've come to look forward to each week. The beauty of *People*'s brand driver is that it's not just relevant to traditional print formats but to new media vehicles as well. It's actually a brand driver that transcends format, which is critical in this media category. A good brand driver should have the strength and elasticity to move across its specific product categories.

"Ideas for Life": Panasonic

I spoke to Tom Murano, director of brand strategy at Panasonic of the Americas, who told me an interesting story about the company's founder and the company's first product. "At one time there was only one source of power in a room. In order to plug in an iron, for example, you had to unscrew the light bulb from a lamp and use the socket connection to plug in the iron. The company's founder looked at this and asked, 'Why?' As a solution, he created a Y-configured piece into which you could connect a light bulb and an iron plug at the same time. This simple idea made life more convenient for people. And making life more convenient and better for people is what Panasonic is all about. The simple idea behind the Panasonic brand, the brand driver, is: 'We take ideas *from* life to create ideas *for* life.' In external communications it has been expressed as 'Ideas for Life.'"

Although I didn't share my Seinfeld theory with Tom, the fact that this is what drives the company's innovative solutions was immediately obvious to me. Kind of "Ever wonder why you have to iron in the dark?" Tom told me that Panasonic had once operated almost like a group of separate companies. Each produced wonderful things, but there wasn't a single focused idea on which the company operated as a whole. Bringing the nine divisions together to talk about this issue, Panasonic discovered that while the brand was certainly being driven by engineering innovation, this idea hadn't been codified in any way that would allow the brand organization to take full advantage of it. As part of the internal exercises undertaken to establish a cohesive brand idea, the teams drew two pyramids, one representing Panasonic and one representing an enemy brand—the brand they saw as their primary competition. At the top of the enemy's pyramid, they wrote the word "Engineering." Although the team considered engineering essential to success, they went back to the origins of their brand and wrote, "Help contribute to society" on the top of the Panasonic pyramid. They recognized that driving toward that goal would yield far greater success and gratification than simply focusing on engineering for engineering's sake. It was this "a-ha" moment that led the team to the brand driver: Taking ideas from life will drive ideas for life. It was already in Panasonic's DNA. They just had to formalize the idea and present it to Panasonic employees as a way in which they could drive the company into the future in a unified manner.

"It's a simple concept but such a profound business driver," Tom said. "It's consistent with our heritage, and it allows all of us to use the inherent strength of our creativity and technology to solve common problems. It's the powerful thread that connects us internally. It's authentic. It's what we've always been about, and you can see the proof in solutions that come from every one of our divisions: security, broadcast, and consumer electronics. We're not about bells and whistles but what's genuinely important to your life."

Plasma television technology is one of the first things that come to mind when you think of Panasonic. Its market share in this category is second to none. I asked Tom how it captured this market. He talked about the customer experience. "It can be a circuitous journey," he said. "Believe it or not, it takes about nine months for a customer to make a decision about a plasma TV. We knew we could shorten this journey if we understood why it was taking so long. We realized there were three key areas in the consumer consideration process. First, consumers considered which size to buy. Then it was the plasma versus LCD question. Then it was installation issues."

"We looked for ways to simplify the journey, make the process more convenient and more rewarding. Our brilliant technology people figured out a way to let a consumer take a photograph of their living room, upload it onto the Internet, and 'drag' different-size TVs to the spot in the room they were considering. Try it before you buy. It's been working incredibly well. More than this, because we know installation is a hurdle to purchase, Panasonic offers information and rebates on the installation process." *Consumer Reports* rates Panasonic best in its top five categories.

Panasonic is a leader in global consumer electronics. The pride it takes in engineering, manufacturing, and marketing is evident in everything it produces, from TV sets, to DVD players, to high-definition cameras. Its brand driver, "Ideas for Life," reflects its corporate structure, its forward-reaching innovation, and its heritage of being in touch with customer needs. The benefits of its products to the consumer are powerful.

"Answering The Call of the Wild": American Zoo and Aquarium Association

It's time to give our animal friends their fair share of ink. This final story will do just that. The American Zoo and Aquarium Association (AZA) is an association of 210 accredited member institutions in the

United States and Canada. These members receive accreditation by meeting the association's rigorous standards of animal care, conservation, and education. Until 2005, the AZA's role was solely member services. However, the board, staff, and members wanted the AZA to play a more public and protective role in guiding and championing the future of their industry. Negative campaigns by their detractors, particularly People for the Ethical Treatment of Animals (PETA), and In Defense of Animals (IDA), were increasing and the need to rally behind a clear, focused idea that defined the valuable role zoos and aquariums play in society was urgent.

When the AZA came to Landor, we realized that the challenges were as much about education as inspiration. The brand committee at AZA was made up of directors of zoos and aquariums with a history of zookeeping, not marketing. Clarifying the role the association itself played versus its member institutions was a major hurdle. Zoos and aquariums provide family-focused, entertaining living classrooms; the association, however, needed to reflect something more visionary and authoritative, without losing the inspirational nature of the industry as a whole. Getting member buy-in was critical but had never been achieved in the past. The AZA needed a compelling brand idea to unify the three thousand attendees at their annual conference.

After rigorous assessment, Landor and AZA landed on an aspirational position for its differentiated idea: "Building America's Largest Wildlife Conservation Movement." This was not the brand driver, but the idea the team wanted to communicate.

"Building" implies that AZA is just getting started. It's a goal and something to which the organization aspires. "America's Largest" is a fact. No other conservation group has access to the 143 million people who visit zoos and aquariums each year. (This attendance number is higher than for all sports events combined.) "Wildlife Conservation Movement" means the guests of AZA zoos and aquariums will learn something about how their actions affect animals and nature and will be inspired to act on their behalf.

This idea was all well and good, but it was neither simple enough nor compelling enough for a brand driver. Three thousand zookeepers, veterinarians, scientists, and other members of the association had to get its inherent meaning, embrace it, and rally around it quickly enough to prompt direct action and the appropriate branding signals.

After more discussion, the teams from Landor and the AZA association arrived at a brand driver that captured the spirit and the intent they were looking for: "Answering the Call of the Wild." This brand driver embodied exactly what AZA wanted to get across to association members. It addressed the need to maintain the highest accreditation standards with regard to the care of animals within institutions. It also reflected a commitment to conservation education and action nationwide and on a global scale.

The AZA presented the new brand idea and the brand driver to its members, who warmly embraced both. Since its inception, the brand driver has led to a host of educational programs within and outside accredited zoos and aquariums, a unified industry with the ability to lobby Congress for better endangered species protection programs, plus partnerships with like-minded conservation organizations. All of these initiatives are strong branding signals to AZA's internal and external audiences. In addition, AZA is developing a number of other branding initiatives, including a new logo and set of graphic guidelines to signal the valuable role the association plays in animal care and active wildlife conservation. With the millions of visitors to AZA zoos and aquariums every year, this means millions of people who can be made aware of AZA's promise to 'Answer the Call of the Wild,' and make it their own.

Exercise: How Visuals Can Help Establish a Brand Driver

It can be challenging to articulate a brand driver—to get to the three or four words that capture exactly what you're trying to convey. This is especially true when working with groups of very smart people, which is almost always the case when working on brand assignments for universities, law firms, and nonprofit organizations.

I spoke to Roy Bostock, with whom I worked when he was CEO and chairman of D'Arcy, McManus, Benton and Bowles. He's now consulting with nontraditional brand organizations. "People have a tendency to overcomplicate things," he told me. "Group dynamics can be difficult. I've found this to be even truer in academic environments, in legal environments, and with nonprofit institutions. The people in these fields have intellectual freedom. They don't want to make choices. It's hard to get people in these sorts of environments to give up their ideas in favor of someone else's. It's not a typical marketing environment like a P&G, for instance, where there is extraordinary discipline when it comes to brand thinking. It's the reason P&G is so successful.

"What happens when you can't agree on the one thing you'd like to represent is that you end up with an amalgam of an idea. There's a desire to include everyone's idea—he wants it red, she wants it blue. Okay, let's make it purple. Two weeks later someone is asking 'How the hell did we get to purple?' When I work with people who do have great intellectual freedom, I point out to them that what is excluded is more important than what is included. You've got to choose the words you want to use carefully. You need to be precise. Get focus."

Getting people to focus and helping them choose exactly the right words to capture a brand driver can be extremely challenging. It's one of the reasons many people in the business use pictures. Pictures have the ability to elicit words and feelings that people can't come up with on their own when they are prompted for adjectives. A picture gets people to say things more personally meaningful, which is exactly what's required to capture the essence of a brand's differentiation.

Larry Lubin, with whom I worked on a Landor assignment for PepsiCo, is a researcher who uses pictures in a lot of his sessions. He shared a story about some research for a relaunch of Lay's Potato Chips (a Frito-Lay brand within the PepsiCo family). Frito-Lay owns top-selling potato chip brands around the world. The company believed that people worldwide, despite cultural differences, enjoy the chips for similar reasons. The company embarked on a study to verify this premise and identify shared marketing opportunities.

"We decided to use pictures to help us identify a unifying brand idea," Larry said. "The pictures we use in a traditional visual-prompt

focus group come from a lot of sources. We cut them out of magazines. People bring them in from photo albums. In a photo-sort
group, we generally show people an assortment of pictures and ask
them to pick out the one they think best represents their idea of the
brand. I can't remember exactly where we got one particular picture
we used for the Lay's group, but it was the best picture I ever used in
my work. It was a photograph of four mischievous little boys in a tree
house. They had a bucket attached to a rope. In the bucket was a
dog with a bag of potato chips in its mouth. The rascals were pulling
up the bucket with the dog and the chips. I included this photo in
focus groups with people of all ages, from teens to grandparents,
and took it to groups in places as diverse as China, Spain, and Brazil.
Every single person almost instinctively reached for that picture. Not
only that, they told great, long, evocative stories about the picture
and what it meant to them.

"One teenage girl in Spain talked about how stressful her life was,
how her parents didn't understand her, how her teachers were hard.
'There was a time I was happy,' she said, 'when the only job I had was
to be happy—just like those boys in the tree house.' A father who
chose the picture talked about how nice it was to see teamwork in kids,
how they must have worked to come up with a plan and about how his
own kids just fought all the time. A mother went on and on about what
little rascals they were and that they wouldn't be able to eat their dinner, and how long it must have taken them to train the dog to steal the
bag of chips from the kitchen, but that boys will be boys."

Larry told me that this image crystallized the brand idea for the
team working on the project, which was expressed in the Frito-Lay
brand driver, "Simple pleasures that connect us all." The study confirmed that Lay's Potato Chips shared a common appeal worldwide
and it was used to reinforce this idea without undermining the
strength of each brand's equity in its own market. Landor's job was to
create a global branding design system that would consistently signal the Frito-Lay brand essence. The advertising that was used worldwide as a branding signal told stories very similar to the story of the
four mischievous little boys in the tree house, each ad adapted to
correspond with the specific cultures of the country.

A traditional picture-sort group is one way to use images to prompt the words you're in search of to articulate a brand driver. My colleagues at Landor London developed a more structured way to help people choose words as precise as they must be to establish a meaningful brand driver. We use this exercise when we need people to think in more abstract terms than they're used to.

The exercise begins with a listing of the brand's general attributes by the team participants, who include client representatives and folks from Landor. We then determine "necessary" brand attributes, "nice to have attributes," and "truly different" brand attributes. It's the truly different we're looking for. We come to an agreement on the one truly different attribute we would like to make the focus of the brand driver, and for which we would like to find just the right words. The starting point is usually a general attribute, such as "innovative," or "intelligent performance," or "functionally accessible." Although these are fine attributes, they make less-than-motivating brand drivers.

The next step is to have each participant choose a picture he or she believes captures the idea we're after. Not any picture, as in a typical photo sort exercise, but a photo aligned with one of nine specific categories, each category more abstract than the one preceding it. For example, the first category might be animals, the second, a car or a drink, the third might be a style of architecture, a piece of furniture, a typeface, a textile, or a color. Using this structured approach helps people drill down to the root of the message they want to convey. When people look at visuals of furniture or architecture or typefaces, they are forced to think of words they don't use every day. Each team participant explains why he or she chose a picture, which prompts group assessment. This gets them to work together to discover what they're looking for.

Using pictures rather than words in an exercise like this one results in creative, more imaginative thinking. It gets you back to more childlike observations. You learn not just from what people say about a visual image they chose, but why they chose one image over another. People feel freer discussing pictures than they do discussing words, especially in front of their bosses or, in the case of an academic community, their peers. As Roy implied, words can be hard to agree on when you're working with people of an intellectual mindset. I've found that when there's a CEO or another senior executive in the room, using pictures makes it easier for subordinates to express their thoughts. Pictures disarm people.

Discussion alone can't always help you identify the words you need to make a point. And often, when working to build a brand across multiple countries, language differences prove even more problematic. Visuals, however, often can help people communicate the idea behind the brand driver across geographies. Visual prompts can help sharpen your focus. When you want to reduce a brand idea to a brand driver that's as precise and compelling as it should be, pictures help.

The Benefits of a Strong Brand Driver

A brand driver is essential to building strong brands. It serves as the catalyst for all branding signals, from visual identity to naming, advertising to marketing, product design and functionality to services, environments, and experiences. Here's why it's essential:

- A brand driver will establish your focus and long-term vision.
- It will quickly distinguish what is unique and ownable about your brand.
- It will pinpoint your brand's meaningful difference.
- It will point the way for new brand initiatives, including new products.
- It will provide clear direction for those creating your branding signals.
- It will ensure that your employees understand how they should behave as representatives of your brand.
- It will direct all strategic and creative expressions of your brand.

Most Critical: The Financial Benefit

Strong brands are built by establishing a simple, different meaning for the brand and delivering it consistently through the appropriate branding signals. When your brand driver is succinct and compelling, your branding signals will be more effective and more efficient. A great brand driver will not only result in communicating a brand's differentiation and relevance, but most likely increased revenue. A consistently delivered brand driver that prompts strong, memorable branding signals will also minimize branding expenses. You won't waste time or money creating any stray, false, or unnecessary signals. The ultimate benefit of a good brand driver is the financial benefit.

The best brand drivers generate branding signals that hit the target with laserlike accuracy. When it comes to branding, clarity is efficient, lack of clarity is expensive. It's your choice.

With your brand driver in place, you're ready to think about your branding signals. There is one step that comes first, however: getting the people responsible for creating the signals fully engaged with the brand idea. In chapter 6, I tell you how to do this.

6

Step Three: Get Your Employees Engaged in the Idea

You've got a BrandSimple idea, and you've got a brand driver—the short phrase that captures the essence of your idea. This means you're almost ready to start considering your branding signals: the expressions of your brand that inspire the images and feelings you want inside the people's mental files. Branding signals produce what I call the *brandness* of the brand: The Apple-ness, the NFL-ness, the BP-ness.

Before you consider the branding signals, however, think about this first: Who creates the branding signals? It's imperative that the people responsible for creating the branding signals—your employees—are totally engaged in the brand idea. Your goal is to help them internalize the BrandSimple idea and make it their own. You've got to make the promise inherent in your idea understandable to everyone in your company. Everyone has to have the same brand recipe and know it by heart. Doing so will ensure that all branding signals are consistent with the brand idea and, more important, are conveyed consistently to consumers. To "be the brand," your employees must understand what the brand means.

Step Three in BrandSimple is to do internal branding: Communicate your idea inside the organization. For a brand to be successful, it's essential to take the time to do this. Whether yours is an organization of ten people or ten thousand, if the people who represent the brand don't understand what drives them, they won't be able to create branding signals that resonate effectively. A good internal branding program will ensure that employees feel confident making decisions relative to the brand. You need to demonstrate what it means to make "on-brand" choices in day-to-day activities. It's actually much more efficient to undertake a brand engagement program and encourage employees to do what's right for the brand than to try and control things from the top. If the people inside your organization aren't able to personally connect with the brand idea, the customer won't connect with the brand idea. It's that simple. Remember my example about how many people work on and touch the Coca-Cola brand? The power behind getting every employee engaged is amazing.

When you were a kid, you learned to tie your shoe. It didn't happen because your mother told you to tie your shoe. She showed you how, you tied it a few times yourself, tripped up a few times, and then eventually got it. Engaging the people in an organization in the brand idea and the promise they've got to deliver is the same process: It's not going to happen if you *tell* them to tie their shoes, you've got to make sure they *know* how to tie their shoes and why. You don't want anyone to trip up.

The most successful brand organizations know it takes more than an e-mail message from the CEO or the human resources department to get everyone on board. You've got to do things to get them jazzed up. In order to get people excited about what you and they do, get them engaged in an interesting way.

The management and marketers at BMW, "the ultimate driving machine," can preach its catchphrase all it wants, but if the engineers working on the antilock brake system don't understand how their design relates to an ultimate driving machine, I'd have to wonder about those brakes. Fortunately, BMW is an ultimate brand. We know BMW-*ness* when we experience it because its branding signals reinforce it. The people in charge at BMW make sure everyone inside the organization knows the recipe for "ultimate driving machine" and can instinctively make it happen without having to consult a brand cookbook.

Mazda is another automotive company that doesn't rely on a cookbook to keep its brand recipe intact, but rather on the judgment of its people, and more so today than ever before. While it had always been a good company, Mazda began to lose its edginess in the late 1990s. It was beginning to blend into the auto landscape by trying to chase competitors like Honda and Nissan and, as a result, lost what had initially made it stand out. In 1998, Mark Fields was brought in as president to help get the company back on track and the employees reengaged. (Mark became president of Ford Motor Company's business in 2005 to help it achieve the same goals.)

"Mazda had walked away from its roots," Mark told me. "It was trying to be everything to everyone—allowing the competition to define it instead of defining itself. It was clear we needed to get back to a strategy of differentiation. We didn't want to invent an entirely new position because the company had good DNA. But, we needed to go back and identify what we did well and link it to the needs of our customers.

"After four or five months of working with people from across the organization, we established a position based on the idea of being spirited, insightful, and stylish. It was founded on Mazda's product and R&D philosophy. Spirited, for example, was representative of functionality like dynamic handling. Insightful was representative of the brand's ergonomically-inspired features. And stylish was based on the unique shape and look of the cars. We wanted people to be able to recognize a Mazda from 50 feet away. While these three words were all well and good and true, we knew we needed something more emotional—something deeper—an idea that could excite and engage our employees around the world from Japan to Europe to the United States. Because we were a global company, but a smaller global company, we couldn't afford to mean different things in different countries. We had to find a way to unite everyone inside the organization. Everyone had to understand what the brand meant if we were going to succeed."

To do this, Mark explained, management challenged its advertising agencies worldwide to frame the brand idea in a way that would convey its essence in a universally emotional way, on a global scale. W. B. Doner, the company's agency in the United States, "zoomed-zoomed" in with the solution.

"Zoom Zoom." "It was the Holy Grail of branding," Mark said. "It was a simple evocative line which encapsulated the brand idea perfectly. It captured our differentiated position and became shorthand for our brand DNA. While we were thinking spirited, insightful, and stylish with our branding heads, our branding hearts were

135

saying 'Zoom, Zoom.' It was emotional in nature. It became organizational lexicon."

In order to help everyone get it, management at Mazda invested time and money to help its employees intuitively understand what "zoom zoom" meant when it came to delivering the brand promise. They asked employees in every department how they would deliver "zoom zoom" when it came to product development or manufacturing, what it meant relative to parts distribution, to purchasing, to sales. The company even incorporated the idea into employee performance metrics. "You can't get the brand idea across in a speech," Mark told me. "You need to reinforce over and over what the brand means and how it benefits customers. Everyone in the company has to speak the same brand language."

Making it possible for everyone in the organization to speak the same language is incumbent upon making your brand idea simple. Your employees are busy. Make it simple for them to get what their brand stands for, repeat and reinforce, and then allow them to use their judgment to make on-brand decisions. I spoke to Carin Van Vuuren, an industry expert in internal branding. She has assisted many companies with employee branding programs and has great expertise in the area of brand engagement. "Brand perceptions are shaped through words and actions," she said. "It's the responsibility of the employees to shape relevant experiences for the consumer. This point is conditional. Employees can only shape these experiences for consumers if they understand why what they do is relevant. You need to make the picture clear to them. The goal is that the brand becomes a filter for their decision making. Companies invest tons of money in their brands. They have a financial imperative to protect this investment. Engaging the employees in the brand creates an organization focused on the consumer. Doing anything less than this would be irresponsible to a brand's stakeholders. It's imperative that management is involved and actively supportive of brand actions."

Why Brand Engagement Is Critical to Success

How a company behaves on the inside is an indication of how it will behave on the outside. Earlier I mentioned "being the brand." Getting your organization engaged is the key to being the *successful* brand for five reasons.

First, engaging the organization adds another tool to the branding toolkit. Strong brands like IKEA, Starbucks, Apple, BP, and FedEx are considered leaders because of the relevant and unique experiences they offer their customers. These experiences are consistent, and familiar in approach and feel, no matter where a customer interacts with the brand, whether it's a website, a retail site, a fuel pump, or a catalog. Engaging your internal audience in your BrandSimple idea will ensure they are aligned around a common goal. As Carin said, an employee branding program will arm employees with the tools and information they need to deliver the customer experience in a uniform manner.

Second, organizational involvement allows you to control the customer experience. Remember brand attention deficit disorder? It's difficult to grab a customer's attention and keep it long enough to make an impression. Branding signals are everywhere. The best way to build a strong brand is to manage the customers' experiences wherever they interact with the brand. If you help your employees get engaged in the brand idea, you'll be able to manage and convey an integrated brand message, no matter how many actual signals are involved. Manage the fragmentation, ensure consistency of expression, and you'll have a better chance of creating a mental file that consumers will find worth "saving as."

Third, engaging the organization allows you to manage employees cost-effectively. Although the activities involved in getting an organization on board with a brand idea may seem like an expensive proposition, consider the idiom "Penny wise and pound foolish." The effort may cost you money up front, but you'll make up for it in many ways as you build your brand. The true value of getting your organization on board will become obvious when you compare that cost to the cost of making up for employees who don't understand the brand promise they're supposed to be delivering. Employees who don't get the brand message actually put their companies at risk. A brand engagement program that involves departmental brand leaders and includes hands-on training activities, role-playing exercises, succinct graphic guidelines, and even off-site activities, will give people the information and skills they need to make their own appropriate brand-inspired decisions. It will allow them to "be the brand." Your cost savings, as a result, will quickly add up.

Fourth, organizational engagement builds a strong culture. Great brands are built from within. Your employees are your brand's most important audience. To send compelling branding signals, to create a sustainable and credible brand promise, the BrandSimple idea and all it implies must be ingrained within the organization's culture. If that is the case, all employees will deliver the brand message not just intuitively, but enthusiastically. Taking the time for brand engagement will guarantee that everyone inside has an innate sense of what needs to be signaled outside, and what role they play in making it happen. Consider Coca-Cola for a minute. This brand believes strongly in internal branding. Its employees, regardless of their roles or responsibilities in the organization, play an important part in sending external branding signals. Employees think of themselves as brand messengers—when they meet neighbors, chat on an airplane, apply for a mortgage, or are asked where they work. What they say about the brand are branding signals. Take an organization with twenty thousand employees and you have great word-of-mouth branding potential.

Finally, engaging the organization increases productivity and creativity. People want to be innovative and creative. They want to feel that they're making a genuine difference. It takes the routine out of the day and gives them the power to drive the brand in the right direction. Ensuring that employees are truly in sync with what the brand stands for will give them the freedom to be innovative—within the appropriate guidelines. Employees who understand and are inspired by the brand idea will automatically look for ways to bring it to life. They'll come to you with new product ideas, introduce ideas for better service, and immediately cut short any off-brand activities, either their own or the people they manage. This means more time savings, more money saved, and an incredible degree of brand advocacy. Who better to be a brand advocate than an employee?

Packaged Goods versus Corporate or Retail Brands

Any brand organization can benefit from engaging its employees in the brand idea. But with a packaged goods brand, you might need to focus on a different set of objectives than if you had a corporate, service, or retail brand. Getting the employees of service brands on board, for example, can literally transform the way the company works from the inside out. People *are* the brand in this instance. They create the brand experience. In this case, you may be dealing with a change or, at least, an evolution in corporate culture or behavior, especially true when there's been a merger or an acquisition of another company. In this case, management might see the need to build bridges to get everyone on the same side. Here engagement exercises are doubly important in circumstances such as this.

Engagement programs for packaged goods brands can be targeted to only those people who influence the brand's delivery. This might include the research and development team, promotion or advertising agencies, package or industrial designers, and the sales department. You'd need to give these folks the resources and information they need to understand the product rather than a whole new way of working. For example, a brand engagement program would be entirely different for Pampers than it would be for FedEx. In the case of FedEx, which I'll actually go into later, employees are the brand's most powerful signals.

Start with an Engaging Journey

The objective of bringing a brand to life is to turn concept into reality. You're not sitting in a conference room getting all excited about your theory. It's time for the real thing. One of the most useful ways to illustrate the brand idea to a whole group of people is literally to illustrate it. Draw a map for your employees. In this case, it's a map of your customers' journey with the brand showing all the places your customers interact with your brand. It's the route the customer follows.

I've loved maps since I was a kid. GPS and other technology may be great, but there is nothing like a map as fodder for imagined journeys. I love visually tracing possible routes with my finger, stopping on places with intriguing names and envisioning the experience of being there. But, once you take the actual journey, reality takes over. Some places are just as you'd imagined they'd be, but others are disappointing. It's not anything like the experience you'd expected to have.

Whatever the outcome, those stops along the way morph, taking on a life and a personality of their own. They amass in a mental file folder as "the trip to . . ." You remember the trip as the synergy of encounters.

Building a brand these days is much like any journey. Customers travel from interaction to interaction and pick up the brand idea signal by signal along the way. The journey morphs into the brand. The goal of the organization is to make sure the journey holds together as a positive holistic experience. You must ensure all the signals are aligned with the brand idea, and with each other. You don't want the customer's journey to be disappointing in any way. We all know it's not just the marketing department that is responsible for the brand. It's everyone in the organization. That's why I use a map of the customer journey as the first step in any brand engagement program. The journey taken by the customer, shown from the customer's perspective, is one of the most instructive internal branding exercises you can undertake.

It's a nifty way to get everyone engaged. It allows employees to see where the customer interacts with the brand and the role they play in the interaction. With a map, everyone in the organization knows exactly which route the customer is following.

The second thing a map of the customer journey can do is give you an idea of where your branding signals will be most effective in signaling the message you want to get across. I call the branding signals at these points of interaction *power signals* for the simple reason that they have the greatest potential to send and reinforce the right brand associations relative to your brand idea. Obviously, you've got to know what message you're trying to send in order to create effective power signals.

It stands to reason that the points of interaction for which you create power signals are those points at which you'll likely be making your greatest branding investment. I talked about HBO. One of its power signals is its innovative programming. It's the signal that most clearly expresses the simple idea behind the HBO brand. A lot of branding investment goes into its programming. Likewise, because

Pixar's simple brand idea is based on technological breakthroughs in cinematic storytelling, its branding investments would be made in areas that support this idea.

Not every customer interaction is equal in its ability to cement brand associations. You can't do what is referred to as 360-degree branding—touch customers at every point they interact with the brand. It's neither efficient nor effective. Although no analytical model will give you a definitive analysis of return on investment in this arena, a map will give you perspective on where to signal most powerfully and where to invest.

Last but not least, a customer map will show everyone how all brand interactions interact with each other—or don't. It will let employees see how to create a consistent brand experience. No matter how many signals you send you have to make the brand experience a cohesive one. You might have a great product with every kind of whiz-bang feature available, but if the engineers aren't using the same map as the copywriters who write the instruction manual, you've got a disconnect.

Not All Journeys Are Created Equal

The fact that not all customer journeys are created equal is an obvious statement, but a very important one. Just as there are lots of different types of brands, it follows that there are different types of journeys, running the gamut from simple, point A to B to C, to very complex ones requiring a lot of

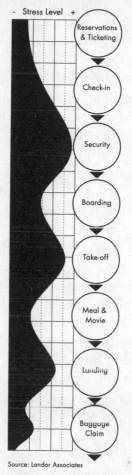

Simplified Customer Journey Map For an Airline Brand

- Stress Level +

Reservations & Ticketing

Check-in

Security

Boarding

Take-off

Meal & Movie

Landing

Baggage Claim

Source: Landor Associates

A customer journey map illustrates where a brand and its consumers interact, and where the brand can most have an impact. This simplified example plots the consumer experience from making a reservation to picking up baggage, showing which points are the most stressful for customers.

signal coordination. A journey with a packaged good brand, for example, would most likely be much more linear than a journey taken by the customer of a service brand, such as a financial institution.

An entertainment brand, such as *Sesame Street* or the NFL, has yet another kind of journey, possibly including interactions outside the brand itself (licensees, perhaps). Move across the spectrum even more, and you encounter experiential brands: fashion brands, cosmetics, even airlines. Even though there are, of course, tangible branding elements to these types of brands, it's more a matter of coordinating interactions to create an outcome of a more emotional nature. Here the journey is more like orchestrating an event. It's theater.

The branding signals you create are a function of your idea, of your brand driver and ultimately of your organization's capabilities and your budget. Whether you win big is certainly a function of your creativity and your execution. A map of the customer journey will give you the strategic focus you need to concentrate on the right branding signals. It will help you pick your battles and win.

No matter what category your brand falls into, a map of the customer journey is an important strategic tool. It will show your employees how and where the customer interacts with the brand. It will allow you to identify which points of interaction—the power signals—will be most effective in getting your message across. And it will allow everyone in the organization to deliver the reality of the brand.

Now that I've talked about maps and journeys, I'd like to show you one. I think you'll find there's more to a customer journey than you imagined.

An Engaging Bunch

A map of the customer journey is simply the first step in a good employee engagement initiative. There are lots of exercises you can use to follow up and support this effort. What you do and how you do it depends on the culture of your organization and what type of brand you have. Here are some examples of great brands that undertook very successful internal branding programs.

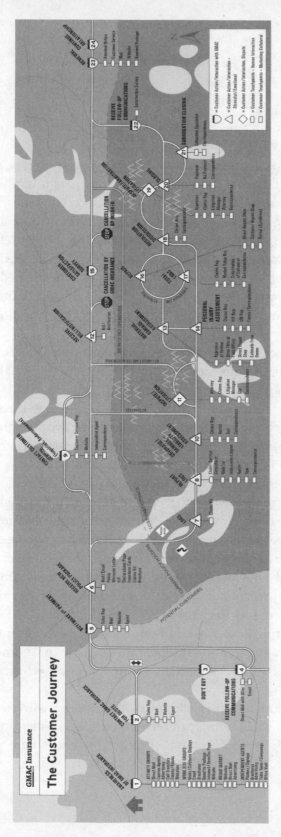

GMAC Customer Journey

"Working with Landor, we developed a Customer Journey for GMAC. Research told us that while our major competitors were nipping around the edges of what was important to consumers, no one had landed on the core idea. This tool was a way for us to spec out all of the points where customers touch our brand and identify a core brand idea that mattered to consumers. It also allowed us to think about the operational requirements necessary to deliver on a brand idea—deliver our brand promise. It became clear to us that what really mattered to clients is what happens during the insurance claims process. Everything else is cost of entry, parity. If you can make all points of touch associated with the claims process different and better, you've succeeded. As a result of looking at the GMAC Customer Journey we were able to differentiate our brand. It transformed the way we handle clients. Recent research told us over 70 percent of clients and claimants would recommend us to friends."

—Gary Kusumi, CEO, GMAC (General Motors Acceptance Corporation)

Are You Ready for Some Football?: The NFL

Think of a brand that doesn't need help in clarifying its meaning to anyone. Does the NFL come to mind? The NFL *is* football. It's an idea even a seven-year-old can understand. It's Sunday afternoons and Monday nights. It's an all-American passion. Everyone gets football, don't they? The fact is that up until a year or so ago, everyone didn't get football. The NFL brand was being signaled inconsistently and, at times, in a less-than-desirable-manner. That's because the NFL itself controls only a small percentage of how its brand is experienced. Although a good number of us think football is fun to watch, the people responsible for protecting the integrity of the NFL brand didn't think it was so much fun, until they engaged in a serious game of brand engagement.

Michael Capariso, vice president and executive creative director of the National Football League, talked to me about the real challenge of a weekend of football. "Being able to communicate NFL as a brand in a consistent manner is a challenge," he said. "You've got sprawling networks of groups sending the message. First, you've got the people at the league, itself, along with all the business partners and sponsors including Pepsi, Visa, and Coors accompanied by a wide range of sporting equipment manufacturers. Then you've got the broadcast partners, each of which covers the game in a different manner. Add to this the thirty-two teams, which are all sub-brands of the NFL. Next, you've got to include all the advertising agencies employed by these groups, the promotion and sports marketing people, the legal firms, and any internal communication groups. Our challenge was to get control of the brand idea and codify it for all of these groups. We wanted to find a way to help all of these separate entities—all with the power to influence consumer opinion about the brand—to understand the implications of their branding signals. To do this we had to help them get the brand—what it means to be the NFL."

Michael and his team did this by embarking on a customer journey with the brand. They appropriately called it a "fan's journey." It was essential for the NFL to see exactly how and where it was connecting with its fans, what the milestones were as the season progressed. It had to determine the mind-set of the fan during the season and to see at which points the fan came into contact with the brand. It wasn't just the games, but the behavior of the players and the officiating staff, the halftime show entertainment, promotions at local fast-food emporiums, branded credit cards, public relations events, and a host of other activities. The NFL also needed to carefully discern where it could control the interactions directly, where it could influence them, and where it had no control whatsoever.

What the NFL discovered on this fan's journey was that there were hundreds of places the NFL brand was signaled. It also came to the important conclusion that while the NFL couldn't control all of the activity directly, it was essential to guide or influence all NFL branding signals. Every action and communication, every branding signal undertaken by the NFL employees, business partners, sponsors, and team players, had the potential to impact on the NFL brand significantly. Michael and his team recognized the responsibility they had in upholding the highest standards. The NFL's large and diverse audience expected no less.

"As you can imagine," Michael said, "getting the brand message simple was mission one. We had to make sure people got the message and knew how to send it. There was potential for infinite complications and miscommunication. To mitigate this we undertook an employee branding initiative. We wanted to make sure everyone internally knew what it meant to stay true to NFL values in their actions and behavior. And with regard to partners and other outside groups, we had to show them how *their* value would be affected by intersecting with ours."

The NFL held a series of training sessions with every group with whom it interacted. Prior to these sessions it had sent out a survey to gauge general understanding of the NFL brand. The activities at these sessions were customized to address the specific audience—a sponsor or advertising partner, for example, needed a different type of information from an NFL team player or official. The engagement strategy used had to be appropriate to each group so each group could respond with the appropriate actions. The NFL had carved out a powerful brand position—one that was relevant to its audiences and distinct within the world of professional sports and entertainment. It didn't want the brand position undermined.

The brand engagement sessions included a number of participatory activities. Working from a brand playbook, participants were taken on the fan's journey, then through the rules, the roles, and the responsibilities of upholding the NFL brand, its values, and its promise as it related to them. Then Michael made sure employees could determine which actions, behaviors, ads, promotions, spokespeople were on-brand and off-brand. "Because the network of branding participants was so diverse," he said, "we had to make sure their net take-away was on target—what was intuitively right or wrong for the brand."

The participants were presented with a number of questions, along with visual aids:

- Was John Madden's choice of a particular photo for his "Best of NFL" video on brand or off? Why?
- Was the new Visa ad campaign scheduled to air during the games right for the brand or not?
- Would the choice of a certain performer for the halftime show support the brand or not? Why?
- Was the product being endorsed by a particular coach appropriate to the brand?
- Were the promotional tie-ins being considered by a specific NFL team right for the brand or not?

This exercise really drove the message home.

The people responsible for any brand have the power to strengthen it or destroy it at any point of interaction. The NFL asked the right questions of those with whom it worked: Are you conducting business in a way that supports the brand promise, values, and personality or not? Are you producing a product or communication that supports the NFL brand image or not?

The NFL, like all good brands, understands that a brand is an asset to be protected and defended. When it came down to protecting the NFL brand, the NFL engagement activities considered both great offense and great defensive strategies. See you at the game.

A page from the NFL brand book, helping NFL brand partners to understand what they stand for.

Think Globally. Act Locally: HSBC

The material HSBC Bank put together as part of its employee branding initiative includes the question "What is our unique point of view on the world?"

The answer HSBC provides is: "In a world where homogeneity and standardization dominate, we are building our business in the belief that different people from different cultures and different walks of life create value. We believe that it is the combination of different peo-

147

ple, and the fusion of different ideas, that provides the essential fuel of progress and success."

This sums up both the position HSBC, the world's third-largest bank, has taken and the position it takes toward its 260,000 employees. To succeed as "the world's local bank," you must treat everyone as an individual. In one of the first business school classes prospective MBAs take, they learn that the way to take on a global business is to act local. It's one of the simplest marketing theories, but it's very hard to put into practice.

I spoke at length with Peter Stringham, group general manager of marketing for HSBC Holdings, PLC. I asked him how HSBC had grown to be the world's third-largest bank, and how it had managed to assimilate so many employees in a relatively short period of time in such a "local" way. To answer the question, he suggested we start with a little history.

"HSBC goes back to the 1860s," Peter explained. "It was started by a Scotsman as a bank for tradesmen—the adventurous folks who traveled from one part of the world to another trading goods. Although it quickly established trade offices worldwide, as a retail bank it first expanded into various Asian markets and by the mid-1900s had moved into European, South American and North American markets. In the latter part of the twentieth century, most of the growth came through acquisitions. By the 1998–99 time frame it had acquired 80 different banks across many geographies, along with 80 different brand names. It was decided that success was incumbent upon bringing all of these entities together under one brand with a set of consistent guiding principles.

"How do you dissect eighty cultures? It is impossible to describe in a Venn diagram. We had only basic graphic guidelines to pass on, and that certainly wasn't enough to build a brand on. We did, however, have a cultural heritage we could share and instill throughout our geographies. We took a look at our roots. Because we had started as a trade bank, we had an intuitive 'cultural awareness.' Among our cadre of international managers who spend their entire careers with the bank, there is a saying: 'We've always been guests everywhere we go.' As we moved from country to country, we learned to respect and adapt to the culture of our hosts. The ethos of our company is 'respect for local culture.' We see everyone as an individual.

"It seemed so obvious to us," continued Peter, "that the way you get people to 'be this brand' is to respect them as individuals. We remind ourselves that we are guests in their communities and try to understand what they deal with relative to the local culture. More than this, just as we ask them not to treat our 110 million customers as numbers, we in turn don't treat our employees as numbers.

"It should be top-down," said Peter, "from the CEO, to the international and local managers, to the tellers and customer service staff, to IT and the HR department. It is very gratifying that you now hear our people in meetings ask the question, 'As the world's local bank, how should we approach this problem?' The answers that come back have helped propel our progress. We really believe that our diversity of experience is an asset that can fuel innovation and growth. The key is to get the whole organization to understand that and draw on each other's ideas every day."

What's absolutely brilliant about the HSBC position is that it's Marketing 101 brought to market. Although companies worldwide always have talked about being global but acting local, none in the banking category, one of the most global categories, had done it successfully. HSBC saw the idea in the obvious, made it its own, and made it real—not just in terms of its core brand idea, but in how it goes about getting thousands of employees comfortable with the idea. HSBC realized it was already in the brand DNA.

In our conversation, Peter told me HSBC's internal branding initiatives were created to help employees clearly understand the kind of behavior customers would expect from "the world's local bank." It didn't matter which division they were in—retail, corporate, lending, or savings. There were applicable behaviors for every business unit and every employee in the bank. Provided with guidelines, HSBC employees are encouraged to identify activities, products, and services that support the brand promise.

HSBC took its heritage and made it the foundation for its internal branding initiatives. Any brand can follow this critical lesson in brand engagement. Start from cultural attributes that already exist in your company and work forward from there. You're never going

CANADA
Football

UK
Football

AUSTRALIA
Football

Never underestimate the importance of local knowledge.

To truly understand a country and its culture, you have to be part of it.

That's why, at HSBC, we have local banks in more countries than anyone else. And all of our offices around the world are staffed by local people.

It's their insight that allows us to recognise financial opportunities invisible to outsiders.

But those opportunities don't just benefit our local customers.

Innovations and ideas are shared throughout the HSBC network, so that everyone who banks with us can benefit.

Think of it as local knowledge that just happens to span the globe.

HSBC ◆X◆
The world's local bank

Issued by HSBC Holdings plc

HSBC's brand promise is that despite their global reach, they can bring personal solutions no matter where you call home.

to achieve 100 percent cultural transformation, but starting from a familiar place will allow you to change your company's behavior in measurable increments.

By looking at what it already had—its brand DNA—HSBC was able to turn this DNA into a key motivating factor in its internal branding. As HSBC grows and expands internationally, it continues to knit together disparate cultures seamlessly and deliver on the experience one would expect from "the world's local bank." HSBC makes good on the idea, internally and externally, every day.

They All Think Flying is Fun: JetBlue

Here's a simple story about employee branding that isn't necessarily the result of any formal training (although it exists) but is more the result of the intrinsic culture of the company, and the people who choose to work there. By way of introduction, let me provide a personal anecdote.

My eight-year-old son, Josh, is really into airplanes. He can tell you the difference between a 737–400 and a 737–500 and will do so any chance he's given. He knows an Airbus when he sees one and, as net-savvy as kids are these days, he's bookmarked the Boeing site. The first thing he wants to know when I get home from a business trip isn't whether there's a gift in my briefcase for him (unlike his sister), but what kind of plane I was on. Was it a 747, an A320, or a 777?

When I mentioned one day that we were planning a family trip to Florida, I knew he would be excited. He was. "Dad, can we fly JetBlue?" was the first thing he said. I was stumped by his request. He's never flown on JetBlue, so why would he care which airline we chose? I braced myself for a barrage of details about engines, cruising altitude, and range, and asked, "Why JetBlue?"

His answer? "Because JetBlue is fun!"

There it was, over breakfast with my kids. Proof that despite everything that may have changed since I began my career many years ago, what once made for brand success still makes for brand success: The power of a simple idea to grab someone on a gut level. In this case, the idea was that flying could actually be fun.

For those too young to remember, flying did used to be fun. In fact, it was downright glamorous. Remember the movie *Catch Me If*

You Can? It's a true story about a real fake. It takes place in the early 1960s. Leonardo DiCaprio plays Frank Abagnale, a fast-talking teen who cons his way into a number of professional situations—doctor, lawyer, and a pilot for Pan Am. The kid is after excitement, and at the time the airline industry was exciting. The people who worked for the airlines loved what they did. They had a passion for flying, and their passion was infectious. Passengers were well cared for. Service was a high priority. The employees delivered a magical experience because they were jazzed about their jobs. We got dressed up to fly—it was that special.

Then it became not so special. The airline business began to get big and complicated and messy for a lot of reasons. In the midst of the messiness, management lost sight of the fact that keeping customers happy was important. Dollars were squeezed out of the system. Pennies were squeezed, and we passengers started to get squeezed. The people who worked for airlines began to lose their passion for flying and the industry in general. They were unhappy with management and in some cases became downright surly with passengers. Flying wasn't fun anymore, until David Neeleman asked why it couldn't be.

David Neeleman, CEO of JetBlue, loves airplanes and he loves flying. He's excited by everything about the business. His gut-simple idea was maverick back in 2000. He wanted to make flying fun again, and he succeeded. David created an airline that's fun to fly, and his passion for the idea is contagious. The reason JetBlue is fun to fly is because David knew that in order to make flying fun, it was a matter of "putting the humanity back into flying." This is JetBlue's brand driver and as a result, its internal brand engagement comes naturally. JetBlue is all about the people.

I spoke to Doug Atkin, director of strategy at the well-known ad agency Merkely and Partners, about JetBlue. He worked with David Neeleman as part of the original brand strategy team. "It was an opportune time for the emergence of another airline," Doug said. "The airlines that had dominated the market were struggling. They had reached the bottom of what is called the "S Curve" of change. The whole universe operates on the S Curve of change—countries, empires, stars, industries, brands. Something grows, it develops, it dominates, it dies, and then a new idea takes over. We looked at the JetBlue business plan in terms of the airline industry and where it would sit on the S Curve of change. The intersection at the bottom of the top curve on an 'S' and the top of the bottom curve is what we call the 'chaos box'—the intersection of the old and the new. We recognized that the airline industry was in the chaos box. The old, accepted way of doing things was dying. It's where the old category idea is dying that you have the opportunity to apply dogma heresy, or heretical thinking. That is, looking at the category in a totally new, heretical way. It's here that there is an opportunity for a new idea to emerge and take hold based on breaking with accepted business practices. JetBlue's business idea took hold because it was heretical. It broke with the accepted practices, the dogma, that had been associated with the major airlines that preceded it. It started a new S curve.

"Everything JetBlue did was heretical," continued Doug. "The design of the planes was different, the uniforms the flight crew wore were different, the website, which was revolutionary for its time by virtue of its aesthetic quality and its easy functionality, was different from what people had experienced. Perhaps the most heretical thing JetBlue did, however, was to create a culture where people looked out for each other and valued each other. 'Putting the humanity back into flying' influenced how JetBlue hired people, why it fired people, and how it trained people."

Doug went on to explain that by taking this contrarian point of view—which I referred to earlier in the book as taking on a 'brand enemy'—it was able to wholly differentiate itself in the category. It had identified a totally unique and relevant idea. The JetBlue brand driver, "putting the humanity back into flying," allows it to deliver a different brand experience that is built on a loyal community of people. One of the reasons JetBlue doesn't have a time-consuming food service on its flights (in addition to the fact that it's hard to make airline food humanly palatable) is because this would take time away from the flight crews' interactions with customers. They're not distracted by functional activities. The more time customers spend time interacting with brand employees, the tighter the bond between them. People don't tell you they like JetBlue because of the low fares or the in-flight entertainment, but because of the people who work for the airline.

Another of the things that Doug told me is that during JetBlue's initial research it asked consumers which organizations or business categories they hated most. The answers ranged from the IRS, to car mechanics, airlines to HMOs. The reason was due to the amount of stress generated by these categories. Stress is a function of how much control one has over a situation. When you choose to fly, it's extremely important to get where you're going, yet passengers have no control over the situation. The fact that JetBlue took the contrarian view to "put the humanity back into flying," was a recognition of this fact. It wanted its customers to feel good and experience as little stress as possible.

Because JetBlue uses only two types of airplane in its fleet, if something breaks down, chances are there are spare parts—or spare planes—standing by, making its arrivals and departures more dependable. When your departure is not delayed, the stress level definitely decreases. And, anyone who has used JetBlue's website knows that it's just what Doug said it is. It was created with humans in mind. The website is friendly and simple to navigate. In addition, when traveling with my family, I know that when I arrive at the JetBlue terminal, the check-in process will be as easy and stress-free as any airline can make it. I know I'll find plenty of kid-friendly food choices in its departure lounge areas, and a place for my WiFi connection. The ticketing kiosks are intuitive to negotiate. And, for the less than tech-savvy, there's always someone standing by to help out.

The humanity associated with JetBlue actually starts with its name. It's not serious or geography-centric, but an emotionally whimsical name suggestive of soaring across a clear, blue sky. Its tagline is also fun and indicates the presence of real human beings: "We like you, too" establishes the fact that the whole experience will be friendly. Hey, you always have more fun when you're with people who like you.

The people who work for JetBlue *do* like you and they understand what it means to "put the humanity back into flying." They are genuinely passionate about flying and about their jobs. As a result, the JetBlue experience is delivered consistently from the customer service phone lines, to ticketing, to baggage claim. When Josh said he wanted to fly JetBlue, he had obviously picked up on branding signals that told him flying can be fun, and that JetBlue is the airline with the kind of people who make it fun.

JetBlue, like a great many successful brands, was started by a renegade who questioned the status quo and continues to be chief steward of the brand vision. The brand has become successful not simply as a result of the initial idea, but because Neeleman created an unmistakable JetBlue culture. Its culture and its business strategy are one and the same. It's a culture that brings about a smile and friendly words from the flight attendants, elicits a helpful response to questions asked of the gate personnel, and ensures the baggage claim process will be as stress-free as possible. People are happy to be working for the company and, because they are, we enjoy flying on the airline.

JetBlue identified a great business opportunity by identifying a simple, different and relevant idea, and made this idea the foundation of its culture. JetBlue's simple, differentiated idea is its magic ingredient and the secret to its employee engagement. In fact, employee brand engagement is an almost redundant term for JetBlue to use. Employees are the brand—an organic part of the brand. The people who work for JetBlue like what they do. Other airlines might have toyed with the idea of creating a different kind of airline experience; JetBlue followed through with it, people and all. It created the signals necessary to transmit its idea in a genuine, emotionally connected way. Its business strategy enables it to do a very good job at being on time and not losing bags—fundamentals that, if they fell short, would negate much of the humanity. Everyone associated with JetBlue gets what the brand stands for: likely, most joined the company because they do. The lesson to be learned here is that if you make your brand idea clear and simple to understand on the outside, the people you want inside will know what they're getting into and raise their hands to show it. JetBlue is a different kind of airline. It makes flying fun because it's put the humanity back into flying.

A Few Tips on Employee Branding

It would be ideal if you could wave a magic wand and get everyone in your organization instantly in sync with your brand, unthinkingly making on-brand judgment calls. I have yet to hear of such wands. Given this, here are a few tips to keep in mind as you design and implement an employee brand engagement program:

- Be clear about what you want to communicate. Make sure *you* understand what your brand stands for and what it means to your employees before you try to educate anyone.

- Make sure your simple brand idea is really simple. You need to capture the essence of what your brand stands for in shorthand—the brand driver. People need to be able to get it, internalize, and act on it instinctively. They need to know the brand recipe by heart. Make it a simple recipe.

- People also need to understand where they fit into the whole and why it matters. Ensure everyone in the organization understands the customer journey and their role in it. You need to give them context for their actions.

- I speak passable grade-school German. My friends who spent their junior year abroad living with families in other countries not only speak the language of these countries fluently, but with all the right inflections and cultural nuances. Think of brand engagement not simply as teaching employees a new language, but a new culture, a new set of behaviors. The best way to do this is through immersion—hearing, watching, learning, and doing. You can't possibly get what you want from people by holding a company-wide teleconference call. Think about creating a virtual "brand lab" with exercises and workshops designed to actively involve employees in the behaviors you want them to adopt. Remember what I said about the engineers designing brakes for the "ultimate driving machine": The ultimate brakes on the BMW are the result of engineers who have internalized the BMW brand idea and act intuitively. They have an innate sense of brand. They don't need a cookbook for the recipe. They know the ingredients.

- Manage your expectations. Changing behavior is challenging, especially across an organization. Don't give people fifty things to change at once. Start with four or five specific behaviors you feel will make a measurable difference. Then point to and celebrate success as it happens.

- Share ownership of brand engagement with employees. Encourage creativity. Yes, develop a brand engagement program with clear guidelines, but don't be so prescriptive as to leave employees without room to make their own on-brand decisions. You want people to feel engaged, not to feel they are being dictated to. Brand engagement should be engaging. Make it fun.

- Your objective is to reach an internal a-ha! We get it! We know what our brand stands for and how we, as employees, contribute to what it stands for with our customers. We know how to "be the brand!"

7

Step Four: Consider Your Brand's Name

It's time to talk about branding signals—the things that express your brand idea. As I've told you, all branding signals are not equal in their ability to influence perception in the market. Some are just more powerful than others. These are the ones I call power signals. And these are the signals you should focus on first as you move from brand to branding. One power signal is the mother of all others: your brand name. As the ultimate power signal, your brand's name is the ultimate conjurer of images and associations.

Sometimes you're lucky enough to start with a clean slate and get the chance to create a name for your brand. I say lucky because you're not saddled with existing baggage. Some would say unlucky, because finding a suitable name is one of the hardest jobs a brand organization faces. Either the name has to say inherently everything about you, or you have to actively invest the name with everything you want it to stand for.

More than anything I've talked about, choosing a name forces you to get ultra-simple—you're about to put everything you want people to associate with your brand into a single word. You reduced your BrandSimple idea to a brand driver. Now, you've got to reduce your brand driver to a name. Remember, once you do, once your name is burned onto the label of a mental file folder, it's hard to get consumers to rename the file. So focus. You rarely get a second chance to make a first impression. (I talk about the challenge of renaming at the end of this chapter because it's worthy of its own explanation.) I'd like to tell you about the challenges and delights of starting with a clean name plate.

What Makes a Name Good and a Good Name

Selecting a name for a brand begins as a game of numbers. You can come up with 800 names, and your legal department will shoot down 794 of them. Although there are many things to consider in naming a brand, perhaps the most difficult thing you'll encounter is whether the name is taken. Does someone own it? With so many brands, sub-brands, and categories, the legal hurdles in this arena can be significant. Unless a name is totally made up (which creates its own set of challenges), it's almost impossible to find a viable name that doesn't already exist.

Another challenge in naming is that no word or name exists without both positive and negative connotations. A brand can redefine a word. It's your job to feed the name with positive associations. People make snap decisions, so it's imperative to get the associations with the name right—right out of the gate. A brand name will be accepted in its ultimate context, if you control the context.

Let me give you an example: Mountain Dew. Think about all of the possible associations this word might bring to mind. On the one hand, there's the serene, relaxing scenario of a quiet morning amble along a peaceful mountain trail. The folks at Mountain Dew, however, wanted to associate the brand with another sort of mountain activity—the aggressive, incredibly cool, extreme-sports type of activity. Mountain Dew is for people who push themselves and consider the outdoors an adventure waiting to happen. The Mountain Dew brand team did an incredible job managing the image they wanted us to save in our mental files relative to its brand associations. As a result of its branding work, Mountain Dew, both as words and as a brand, has been defined as anything but a serene experience. Given vigilant branding oversight, our context for the word is just what Mountain Dew wants it to be. The chart below will show you what I mean.

The sweet spot of naming is finding a word that magically signals the idea behind your brand driver as simply as possible. While it doesn't always happen, it's very sweet if you can do it. Whether you

Branding Helps Manage the Message

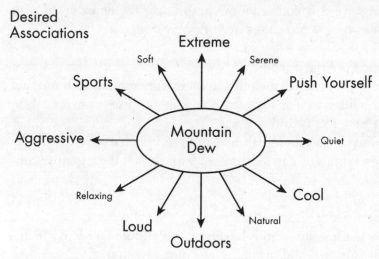

Desired
Associations

Source: Landor Associates

A brand name such as Mountain Dew has numerous potential associations, only some of which the brand will want to reinforce.

do or not, here's what you need to consider in your brand naming process.

To begin with, naming is not just a creative exercise. The best names are built on strong, clear, simple objectives. Your name has to be as simple to get as your BrandSimple idea. All good names must meet criteria in three key areas: strategic, linguistic, and legal. Let's take them one at a time.

Strategic Criteria:
• Does it capture your BrandSimple idea in a meaningful way?
• Is it appropriate and appealing to your audience?
• Is it as brief as possible?
• Does the name connect to what your business is about?

- Does it have the potential to be memorable?
- Without the aid of a crystal ball, could it potentially limit you in any way? If you grow the brand, can the name grow with you into new categories or with new customers?

Linguistic Criteria:
- Is it appropriate in meaning in all major languages? If not, are you willing to live with not being able to use it universally?
- Is it easy to say and/or spell?
- Have you considered all relevant cultural sensitivities?
- Is it so similar to an existing trademark that it may cause confusion?

Legal Criteria:
- Can you use it without infringing on another trademark?
- Can you own and protect it as your trademark?
- Is the domain name available, or can it be modified to own?
- Can you use it and protect it in all relevant geographies?

Name Types

Names are composed of two key elements: construct and content. Construct of the word refers to whether it is real or coined. A real name is a dictionary word. A coined word is a made-up word. Two real words can be joined together in a creative combination to describe what the product does. WhiteStrips, ThinkPad, and DeskJet are good examples. Coined or invented words are composed of unusual strings of letters or word parts that may not be immediately recognizable: Amtrak, Advanta, Qwest, for example.

The second element to be taken into consideration when choosing a brand name is its content. It can be generic—a common descriptive name that cannot be trademarked (cereal, tissue, or cleanser). It can be descriptive—a name that's easy to understand and that explains a benefit or attribute. Brands that have taken this route include SoftScrub, Easy-Off, and ChapStick.

A name's content can be suggestive—it implies a key idea or concept but doesn't tell you directly what the product does. Good exam-

Name Types

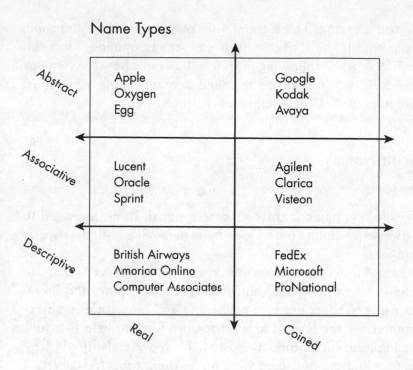

Source: Landor Associates

This chart divides up the
different types of construct
and content.

ples are Vanguard, Fidelity, Lucent, and Agilent. Finally, name content can also be fanciful or arbitrary. An arbitrary name has no meaning but develops meaning over time through branding signals and customer experience. Here you'd include Google, as I said earlier, as well as BlackBerry, Aveda, and Apria.

The most essential thing to remember about a brand name is that it is your most visible and your most significant power signal. Whether you've made up the name or it's meant to communicate your claim to fame overtly, it will be completely useless if you don't imbue it with the associations you want consumers to have. You must deliver on the idea behind it. Think carefully and strategically about your name before you commit to it and start investing in it. Once you do, make sure it has positive meaning. Think about your own name. How do people think about you? It's hard to change minds once an opinion is formed.

Take a look at the following graph. It illustrates how the two key elements—construct and content—make a brand name what it is. Then take note of these inspired success stories.

Good with Names

Baby Einstein

The Baby Einstein name is truly its power signal. It has managed to capture its essence and its brand idea in its name. It's both descriptive and whimsical.

The Baby Einstein brand was the result of one sweet "a-ha." In 1997 Julie Clark, a new mom and former teacher of art and literature, was eager to share her love of the arts and humanities with her own daughter. As she looked around for products to help her, Julie discovered that no such products existed. There were plenty of learning tools for children, but there were no learning tools for babies. A gap in the market!

To fill this gap, Julie took out her video camera and started to film ordinary household and natural objects, flowers and trees, fruit, toys and even the family pet. She reorchestrated classical music to make it simple and baby-friendly and ran it with the video images. With her baby daughter in her lap, she screened the video, pointed out the simple objects and hummed along. To her delight, the little girl was equally delighted. This mom had become a true "mother of invention."

As mom-to-mom word of mouth traveled quickly and demand for the product grew, the successful Baby Einstein brand was born. I asked Rashmi Turner, Baby Einstein's vice president of marketing, communications, and educational productions, how the name came to be. "Julie knew Albert Einstein was a lover of arts and the humanities and, as a scientist, was insatiably curious and had a passion for discovery. From the beginning, Baby Einstein products were created to tap a baby's natural sense of curiosity and to provide parents with tools to help expose their little ones to the world around them in playful and enriching ways. When Julie thought about the perfect name for this brand and product, 'Einstein' seemed like an obvious fit."

Rashmi went on to explain the company's overall philosophy, noting that The Baby Einstein Company understands that babies are fascinated by the sights and sounds around them and that every moment of a baby's day is an opportunity for discovery. This simple principle, coupled with the belief that parents play a critical role in the discovery process, is the foundation for the brand idea and its entire product collection.

Very little advertising was required to get the message of Baby Einstein across. Moms did it for them. Word of mom is a very credible branding signal. Moms trust other moms. This continues to be among Baby Einstein's most powerful branding signals.

Since its acquisition by The Walt Disney Company in 2001, The Baby Einstein Company has enjoyed enhanced visibility and has expanded its distribution channels and developed product extensions, including playthings, toys, baby gear, and apparel. Baby Einstein is a leading infant brand that now extends far beyond the video aisle.

Baby Einstein is a baby brand that, like any baby, had to be nurtured very carefully. The Baby Einstein team, along with its parent, The Walt Disney Company, treats this special brand with TLC. Baby Einstein enjoys 93 percent awareness among its target audience, thanks to word-of-mouth endorsement and the perfect name.

CureSearch

CureSearch is another name that involves children, but children in a totally different world—those children suffering from childhood cancers. It is a name that signals the best of all things: hope.

The National Childhood Cancer Foundation (NCCF) is a fundraising organization that was created to raise funds and build awareness for the number-one network of oncologists in the country, the Children's Oncology Group (COG). Their shared objective is to create awareness of the number-one disease killer of children and ultimately to find a cure.

Relative to this naming story, few people knew of the COG network or understood its relationship with NCCF. The groups were operating with two separate names and vastly different identities that had no visual or verbal linkage, which also didn't help. Any branding efforts were getting lost in the alphabet soup of other organizational names and a market flooded with requests for money. The fact that the NCCF name was shortened to initials further decreased the chances of making an impact.

The organization came to Landor to get some guidance with its branding. "NCCF is the leader in the field," they told us, "but no one sees us." Even the smallest hospitals were raising more funds. Landor's goal was to enhance visibility and recognition of both organizations and to help external audiences understand the relationship between them. Equally critical was a need to focus on their unique point of differentiation—a fundraising organization supporting a dedicated medical research organization. The ultimate business objective was to increase awareness in order to build financial and sponsorship support.

It quickly became apparent to the Landor team that the branding challenge the organizations faced was in good part due to the name—or names. Although the NCCF and the COG hadn't come to Landor seeking a name change, it was going to be difficult to address the branding issue without addressing the name issue. The Landor team tried to get the initials to work. But no matter how they arranged and rearranged, they couldn't get any combination of the acronyms to work in a way that would break through the clutter of an already alphabet-laden category. (Unless you're an IBM or GE, acronyms are tough, in general.) The team then decided to approach the naming challenge from a different angle: to create a new name all together. Let the two names reside comfortably under an umbrella name that would unite the two organizations and give them the branding power necessary to have the impact they needed to meet their objective.

After rounds of work, the team unanimously agreed on the name CureSearch, an identity that works well with both organizations. The name is descriptive. It highlights research as its main point of differentiation as well as the common goal: finding cures for childhood cancer through research. The logo created for CureSearch is simple and focused. A clever visual cue enables the name to express two levels of meaning. The two words that make up the name evoke "search

Before the cancer, hair was all that mattered. CureSearch.org is a comprehensive website that can help you deal with all aspects of childhood cancer. It connects you to the network of doctors and scientists whose collaborative research has turned childhood cancer from a nearly incurable disease to one with an overall cure rate of 78%. So now you can learn how to make her skin grow a little thicker until her hair grows back.

MORE »

www.curesearch.org

How do you convince a 14-year-old girl that hair doesn't matter?

Ad Council.org

CureSearch™
National Childhood Cancer Foundation
Children's Oncology Group

You're not as alone as you feel.

This ad, part of the campaign launching the new branding for CureSearch, raised its visibility as a leading national children's cancer organization.

for the cure," while the design catches the eye by emphasizing the letters -RE- to simultaneously reveal the word "research."

I spoke to Paul Burke, president and CEO of CureSearch National Childhood Cancer Foundation, about the brand name and the impact it has had. "The simplicity of the name is remarkable," he said, "but it says exactly who we are and what we do. We are searching for a cure through research. Earlier attempts we made to name the Foundation didn't yield the significant distinction we needed in a very competitive environment. To our knowledge, the NCCF and COG model is unique. NCCF is the exclusive fundraising agent of COG. The Children's Oncology Group is the world-class network whose work has helped transition childhood cancer from the nearly incurable disease it was about forty years ago to one with an overall 78 percent cure rate. Together these organizations are united in their purpose to achieve a cure for childhood cancer. The umbrella name captures this without undermining the integrity of the individual names."

Paul explained that the Internet is among the places the CureSearch name has worked best. "CureSearch.org is a comprehensive online resource for childhood cancer information, referrals and family support," he said. "This site was a dream of ours when we first came to Landor with our branding challenge. Currently CureSearch.org receives about 90,000 unique visitors each month and the number of visitors is growing. If you want a lighthouse of hope on the Internet, if you want to be able to serve patients and their families, especially at point of diagnosis and be able to provide referrals, the CureSearch URL is that lighthouse. In the past, if you were to Google a request for information about childhood cancer, the search engine would have directed you to multiple sites, but there wasn't one comprehensive site that was providing even near to what the CureSearch site now provides."

The CureSearch story is about the power of a name that works for everyone it touches, inside the organizations, within the professional community, across the fundraising landscape and, most important, the families and children dealing with childhood cancer. The new name and the CureSearch icon, the visual representation under which both NCCF and COG reside, promote one culture and vision shared by these groups. Everyone involved with the naming process agreed that the CureSearch name intuitively captures the essence of both organizations' reasons for being. It became a brand name and a catalyst for action.

Timberland

I want to go back to my story about Timberland, the brand that perfected the waterproof boot. Timberland is an example of a wonderfully suggestive brand name. Although it doesn't tell you directly what the product or company does, it's a real word that evokes certain imagery. These associations summon up emotions and feelings and a sense of "prestalgia"—a funny word made up by a friend to describe feelings you have based on experiences you *wish* you'd had. In the case of Timberland, this prestalgia summons up visions of a walk in the autumn woods, the sun glinting through orange and red leaves, a bracing chill in the air, a babbling brook, and—you get the picture.

As Sidney Swartz, a founder of Timberland, told me, there weren't too many recognized shoe brands, let alone boot brands, back in the sixties when his family business introduced its new line of boots. The Swartz family had the appropriate "a-ha": "Let's brand the boot," Sidney said. The next obvious "a-ha" was that to brand the boot, you had to name the company that produced the boot.

Recognizing the limiting strategy of a product-specific name, Sidney and a friend who ran a small ad agency came up with the name "Timberland." It was flexible enough to grow with the business—a great strategic move—and appropriate to the audience it hoped to attract. Most of all, the name captured a spirit of the rugged outdoors, something different and relevant, and a promise Timberland realized it could own. Into this unexplored territory Timberland staked its claim.

The friend at the ad agency also had the brilliant idea to design a logo that reflected the name—the now instantly recognizable Timberland tree. Timberland found a boxmaker, had the new name and logo imprinted on the boxes, and you know the rest. Since introducing the brand name in 1973, Timberland has become The Timberland Company. In 1978 and 1979 it added casual shoes and boots to its line of footwear. In the 1980s the company expanded overseas and became an international lifestyle brand. In subsequent years it has introduced women's apparel and kids' gear.

Timberland hasn't veered from its roots. It continues to manufacture authentic, rugged outdoor shoes, clothing, and other products. "We got out front with a really simple idea and focused on it," Sidney said. They did, and the Timberland brand name powerfully signals all it stands for, and has stood for, over the years. It suggests and delivers everything Sidney hoped it would.

Crest Whitestrips

As I've said, sometimes the obvious things are so obvious they get disregarded. Not in the case of Crest Whitestrips. All those white smiles out there are proof that sometimes the most obvious names can be dazzling.

Whitening dental products have experienced explosive growth since the late 1990s and early 2000s. Seeing an opportunity in this category, the Crest team at Procter & Gamble developed a new tooth-whitening technology in the form of a simple strip that consumers apply to their teeth. (This R&D investment was the perfect strategic fit for a leading brand in tooth care.) The over-the-counter product offered superior benefits, such as noticeable whitening and easy application. The Crest team asked Landor to help develop an internationally available sub-brand name for this revolutionary new product; a name that would be free of inappropriate meanings and associations.

Although consumers were looking for whitening benefits, they were growing skeptical about an over-the-counter's ability to deliver on the promise. Also, many consumers believed that whitening treatments were complicated and time-consuming. The team had to take both of these factors into consideration. The name also had to be a good emotional fit with Crest. Research had proven again and again that Crest had credibility and that a Crest endorsement would support the brand's promise.

Landor developed the sub-brand name Whitestrips, with a strong Crest endorsement. The simple, descriptive name immediately communicated the "strip" form of the new product, suggesting that Crest

Whitestrips were removed from the realm of cumbersome trays and messy brush applications. The whitening benefit was inherent in the name, a natural fit for Crest. Studies have shown that just two years after its launch, Crest Whitestrips captured more than a 50 percent share of the market category.

As I said in the beginning of the chapter, a good brand name can come from any number of formulas—purely descriptive to highly fanciful. In the case of Crest Whitestrips, the winning formula was an easy, descriptive name that communicated exactly what the product was all about. The name captures the essence of the product benefit in a simple and radiant way.

What Do You Do If Change Is in the Wind?

What happens if you have a name but decide that a change in business strategy is required and your name doesn't reflect your new intent? What happens if the market changes and you're stuck with a name that limits you? What happens if your business strategy changes and you ignore your name and what it means to consumers altogether? Can you survive a name change? Can you survive without changing your name?

None of these questions is simple to answer. Let me start by going back to one of the most essential rules of naming: Your name must be aligned in some way with your simple brand idea and the business strategy it signals. Either your brand name has to overtly signal what you stand for, or you have to spend the time and money to imbue your name with the associations you want people to have about your brand. Changing a name and changing a business strategy in midstream is very difficult, but it's been done. It's harder to change a business strategy and keep a name.

In either case, the way it's done successfully is inside out.

In order to be able to change a name in conjunction with a business strategy change or to align a name you want to keep with another idea, a brand must look inside the consumer's mental file folder. To change the associations with the mental file name, you have to change what's in the file itself. What feelings or promises does the consumer associate with your brand? What was your business strategy when you

171

established your original name? Where are you going and what would you like your name to stand for?

One thing that can help in this process is to go back and look at the map of your customer journey. At what points of interaction were you most powerfully signaling your original idea? Which points of interaction signal your brand name with the greatest degree of impact? Consider your new business strategy and the idea with which you want to align it. What new or different points of interaction require branding signals to get the brand name and idea across? I'm going to tell you the tale of two companies—one a successful renaming story and the other a story of a brand that tried to keep its good name and struggled. I'll start with success.

Beyond "Beyond Petroleum": BP

BP, originally British Petroleum, is the story of a transformation. CEO John Browne, an industry leader, is also a visionary, as leaders usually are. His long-term vision for the company is to have it be perceived as a different kind of energy company: an energy company that transcends the category through expansion into alternative sources of energy, including hydrogen, wind, and solar. His objective is not just to have BP be perceived as a green energy company but to deliver green, environmentally friendly solutions worldwide. To make this vision come to life, he knew it had to be driven internally and signaled externally. In creating this vision, John Browne knew you couldn't just say green, you have to be green and look green.

I spoke to a couple of people who were personally involved in both the brand idea and the brand name transformation. One of them, Courtney Reeser, managing director of Landor San Francisco, who worked on BP for Landor, had many conversations with Sir John Browne (now Lord John Browne) and his managers to get a clear understanding of the direction the company wanted to take. "John Browne had a very clear vision of what he wanted his company to stand for and how he wanted to transcend the petroleum category," Courtney told me. "In addition to this, he wanted to signal that the company was indeed global. While it was British in origin, it had expanded worldwide, and the name was limiting. He also wanted to unite a number of companies worldwide, several of which operated under different names, and go to market as a single brand. In my work with Sir John and his team, they spoke about the need to make the change visible, both internally to employees worldwide and to the consumer market."

The fact that BP was dealing with multiple business units across a spectrum of geographies, as well as 100,000 employees worldwide, made the execution of Sir John's vision seem an interesting challenge, to say the least. David Fowler, worldwide creative director at Ogilvy, the agency that worked with Landor on the project, put the challenge into perspective. "BP is a classic case of not creating a new brand or business strategy but revealing the attributes that already exist," David told me. "The solution was utterly simple once we looked at the facts. Often the essence of the brand you'd like to become lies within a dimension of the brand you have today. The truth is the truth.

"In our research, we found that British Petroleum actually went beyond what people expected from an oil company. It went beyond in its environmental concerns, in its exploration of renewable energy sources, in the way it interacted with various cultures around the world. It was, and is, an extraordinary company. We assembled the facts. It's astonishing this doesn't get done more often. We looked at the facts and discovered that it was a company that was already transcending the category. The simple idea we were looking for was right there on paper. British Petroleum already went beyond petroleum as part of its business strategy. Sir John Browne's vision was already happening. It was real. The company was already going beyond to exceed expectations of what an energy company should be."

This realization of the obvious was serendipitous for the teams working on the renaming efforts. The name "BP" was brilliant for a number of reasons. It could authentically reflect both the strong heritage inherent in the original name and the company's transcendent vision for the future, going "beyond petroleum." It was also a name easily communicated on a worldwide basis. It could unify all of the company's global enterprises. The name literally and figuratively translated well.

BP knew that delivering alternative energy proof points was most critical to changing the associations and perception people had of the brand, and was already on its way to meeting this challenge. In 1998, for example, BP set a target of reducing its carbon emissions to 1990 levels by the year 2010. The company achieved its goal in 2001, nine years earlier than expected. This couldn't have happened without the engagement of thousands of employees committed to making the vision real. At the same, it was critical to send a powerful external signal to announce that change was in the wind (and the sun).

The British Petroleum shield disappeared and in its place appeared the Helios symbol. Looking somewhat like a green and yellow flower, the symbol was named for the Greek god who, each day, steered his chariot across the sky, bringing light and power to earth. Resembling a dynamic burst of energy, this symbol became a daily reminder to all BP employees of their principal objective.

"The combination of the Helios symbol and the words 'beyond petroleum' served as both brand driver and tagline, and communicated instantly what this company was about," David told me. "It said it fast—to its employees, to environmentalists, to government agencies, to consumers, and to Wall Street. The fresh new symbol and the simple language said everything BP needed to say to get the message across."

Because John Browne wanted to make the change in BP's business strategy as visible as possible, as soon as possible, BP quickly changed the signage at its retail locations worldwide. With more retail outlets than McDonald's, this action had a huge impact on quickly getting people to focus on the new brand name and its implications. The advertising created to signal the evolved BP has also had significant impact. It is not meant to look like advertising, but more like a series of messages, which it is. It is messages based on facts. The advertising asks and answers serious questions about energy and the oil industry. The people at BP understand that the energy business is paradoxical. On one hand, it propels the world, and on the other, it has the potential to damage it. By presenting this paradox truthfully in its advertising, BP puts the onus on the thinking that's behind what the company does and explains what consumers can expect from it. BP doesn't spin the message; much like its name and the business strategy behind it, it presents the facts.

BP has taken the time to send internal branding signals as well. It instituted its Helios Awards, recognizing employee teams that go beyond petroleum to identify commercially viable projects that support alternative energy solutions. On a smaller scale, but no less important, is the fact that all of the pencils in the company are made from recycled plastic coffee cups (which is proudly stated on the side of every pencil). Another internal signal is that all of the floral arrangements in company offices are aloe vera, the only plants that produce more oxygen than carbon dioxide.

BP is a company that understood the need to align its business strategy with its name and the idea on which the name was based. It had to change the associations with the brand in the public's mental file folders. David reiterated what a number of good brand people know: Sometimes it's a matter of assembling the facts and seeing the obvious in what already exists. BP is a company that was already going "beyond petroleum" when it decided to change its name to signal the associations implicit in the new name. Part of its success was in recognizing that it had a brilliant idea hiding in plain sight. The other part of its success was in having a leader who knew where he wanted to take the company and became its strongest brand—and branding—advocate.

It isn't the name change per se that makes for BP's continued success, as I said, but changing the associations inside mental file folders and connecting them to the name. BP looked inside the company and identified the things it needed to bring to the surface to deliver on the brand's new vision. It changed the perception of the brand from the inside out. Today the BP name is a powerful branding signal of this change.

A Computer Glitch: Compaq

What happens if a brand decides to change its business strategy—dramatically—without thinking about the impact on its name? I'll tell you what happens.

Compaq was a company with a lot of great things going for it when it was founded in 1982 by senior managers from Texas Instruments who left to start their own company. They launched the company with very little cash, but with a big yet simple idea. They wanted to create a lightweight, portable, high-performance personal computer based on industry standards that was able to run all the software then being developed by and for IBM. To say that they succeeded is an understatement. Compaq raised $67 million in its initial public offering in 1983, just a year after it was launched, and went on to break industry records in its PC sales. In 1986 Compaq joined the ranks of the *Fortune* 500. Its reach and impact was global, from the United States, to Brazil, to Singapore.

Compaq's initial success was due to a couple of important factors. First, its business strategy was perfectly aligned with its brand strategy. Compaq's business strategy was to take the accepted notion of clunky, heavy computers and make it unacceptable by developing and manufacturing PCs that were lighter, faster, and portable. Its brand driver, "simply works better," captured the essence of this strategy, and it was driven into the company from the top down. CEO Rod Canion was perhaps the brand's most ardent cheerleader and his passion was contagious. Everyone in the Compaq organization understood implicitly what "simply works better" meant to them. This phrase drove all of its branding signals, from how things were engineered and manufactured, to marketing and customer care. Everything and everyone "simply worked better" than the competition.

The name "Compaq," a union of COMPAtability and Quality, was chosen as a clear signal of the product's performance. It was a name aptly suggestive of the brand's attributes. The fact that consumers also associated it with the "compact" nature of Compaq's products also helped the brand grow, and grow fast. Computer resellers embraced the brand, given its excellent margins and strong acceptance by consumers and small- to medium-size businesses. A standards-based computer, offering excellent performance and reliability at competitive prices, was a winning business strategy in the 1990s. By 1996 Compaq was ranked the fifth-largest computer company in the world. Pretty good for a few guys with a simple business plan.

Then around 1997 or so, competitive factors drove significant shifts in this business strategy. Compaq's revenues and profit margins were gradually being eroded by Dell, with its direct, made-to-order business model. It offered better PC products in laptops, desktops, and servers, all custom made and sold at better prices. As technology became more standardized and cheaper, more and more companies emerged that could offer many of the same things Compaq was offering but at a lower price.

Compaq wanted to transform its business, and the way it wanted to do this was by extending its business footprint into the large enterprise space to compete with companies like IBM, Hewlett-Packard, and Sun, which offered complex, high-margin enterprise solutions. It wanted to compete with full-service hardware and software companies on every dimension. This was an extremely wide competitive landscape to take on, especially after having existed in such a finite space.

Rather than identifying an internal growth strategy, Compaq jumped into the enterprise game by buying companies that made things it didn't make and then offered the services required to deliver complete solutions. For example, in 1997 it paid $3 billion for Tandem, a California-based company known for very expensive enterprise computing systems for data-intensive industries like banking and telecommunications. Then in 1998 it paid $10.6 billion for Digital Equipment Corporation (DEC), the Boston-based inventor of the VAX minicomputer and known for its midrange server software solutions. These two companies, each different in geography, culture, and business strategy, were now merged with a Texas-based hardware company.

Compaq now had a rich portfolio of hardware or software solutions and was willing to offer whatever made sense for its clients. It didn't see a problem with having such broadly based competition that included companies including IBM, Sun, Cisco, and HP, as well as any business offering PCs. Not seeing this as a problem was a problem of huge proportions. With such broadly defined competition, how do you establish a simple, differentiated meaning for your brand when your name is already associated with something else? While Compaq might have considered its robust product and service offerings as different from anything else available, it became apparent that this was the very thing that was confusing people—both inside the organization and outside.

Compaq certainly had all the ingredients required to do whatever it wanted to do, but it had overlooked the essential ingredient to building—or rebuilding—a strong brand: a simple, crystal-clear brand idea that could support its transformed enterprise under the Compaq name. Compaq was asking its customers to increase the capacity of their mental file folders. It was trying to stretch the meaning associated with its name to include associations that would differentiate it in the world of $1,000 PCs, as well as in the world of $20 million enterprise solutions. It hadn't defined a primary target, and in failing to do so, couldn't define its primary competition. Without doing this, it couldn't establish a clear identity.

I spoke to Giovanna Imperia, who was Compaq's worldwide brand director in the early 1990s, about Compaq's challenge during its brand evolution. "I started back in the days when the notion of 'simply works better' drove everything," Giovanna told me. "We had a crisp idea of what the brand meant. It was based on the idea of doing something relevant and compelling for the customer. What happened after Compaq went into acquisition mode was what happens to a lot of companies that grow exponentially and become complex. It's hard to develop a cohesive, single-minded idea on which to build the brand.

"We were still viewed primarily as a hardware company, fundamentally a PC company," Giovanna said. "We were trying to find an idea that worked on both the PC side and on the enterprise side and we couldn't do it. 'Simply works better' was an easy idea to drive into the company because it was tied to the business strategy at the time. The company never found an idea that could work for multiple lines of business. As a result, the Compaq name became amorphous in meaning."

Having a brand that was amorphous in meaning made it virtually impossible for Compaq to do effective branding. In fact, when Landor worked with Compaq after its acquisitions, I personally underestimated the scope of the brand transformation challenge. Any brand transformation is difficult. Once consumers have saved a mental file folder, changing associations inside the folder even just a little bit is a long-term, expensive, and risky undertaking. It's even harder if you are trying to make a quantum shift—taking the meaning of your brand from the lower end, in this case the PC segment, to the upper echelons, the enterprise solution segment.

To make matters even more difficult, Compaq's strength was in the technology and sales side rather than the brand and marketing side of the equation. As proof of this lack of strength, Compaq went through a period where it tried to use advertising to transform the brand meaning. Over the course of a few years, the global advertising account moved from Ammirati & Puris/Lintas, to Doyle Dane Bernbach, to Foote Cone Belding. Each of these agencies had a strong track record building world-class brands, but none could transform the Compaq brand by way of advertising. As I've said, you can have what appear to be great branding signals, but if they're not based on a simple brand idea aligned with a business strategy, they're irrelevant. This is even truer in the high-tech industry, which moves and changes faster than consumer goods categories.

In hindsight (which, as we know, is always 20/20), you might say that Compaq shouldn't have attempted a brand transformation of this scale. It might have been smarter to have created two companies—one to do battle with Dell on the PC front, one to do battle on the enterprise front—and focus the Compaq name on only one of the segments. But this would have been an expensive and risky alternative. Compaq could have aligned itself with one powerful emotionally connective idea—like HP's "Invent," for example. However, this was not a feasible option for a company trying to digest two enormous acquisitions, each with cultural and operational issues.

There are of course many more things Compaq could have or should have tried. The biggest lesson I learned from this was that while a business can be transformed with a stroke of a pen by way of a merger or acquisition, *brand* transformation, even on a modest scale, is a different matter. It requires internal cohesion, alignment between the business and brand strategies, brilliant branding signals, significant investment, and, most important, time and luck.

Compaq had started with a simple idea. This was relatively easy because when Compaq was launched, the PC business was simple, as was the product line. Battles were easy to fight and win. But when Compaq decided to expand into the systems arena, its game changed completely. It needed to build credibility it didn't have. It's extremely difficult to transfer brand capital from one space to another. In Compaq's case, it was competing with a whole new set of players on multiple dimensions. It needed to define who it wanted to compete with, who it wanted to talk to, and establish a unique point of difference on which to build its brand.

The Compaq brand had been a great one. But like many others in the brutally competitive, rapidly changing technology space of computers, Compaq was unable to transform itself fast enough to help the company compete in the marketplace. What differentiated the old Compaq from the new was the presence of a simple, different idea and a definite business strategy. Compaq was eventually bought by HP.

8

Step Five: Create Branding Signals Beyond the Name

In this chapter I'm going to talk to you about the next step in Brand-Simple: branding signals—the things beyond the name that convey to consumers what you stand for and why they should care about you. Great branding signals communicate immediately that what you do, sell, or provide is different in a relevant way.

We all know that the people behind the Apple brand are masterful at branding signals, but the brand never ceases to amaze me. Apple's got branding down to an art and a science. I think of myself as a pretty skeptical guy (as a New Yorker it takes a lot to impress me), but when I bought my iPod nano, I was amazed.

I knew the product would be cool, but in this case it was the packaging that amazed me. Apple begins the branding signals for its iPod nano on the outside and takes you on a deliberate and magical journey to the inside. (Apple's map of the customer journey must be indelibly imprinted on every Apple employee's mental desktop.)

The nano comes in a box about the size of a three-set CD. The box design is contemporary and minimal, yet visually warm and inviting. The surface material is smooth to the touch. The graphic elements on the box stand out in sharp contrast against the clean, gray matte finish; simple product picture, product name, and shiny silver Apple logo. The product itself, along with the accessories, is encased in another box, a box similar to one in which you might find a piece of jewelry. It flips open to reveal two compartments, each free of graphic elements—because the product is all that matters. Words aren't necessary. On the right side of the clean, white inner box is the nano—nothing else. The other compartment houses the instructional CD, the connection wire for your computer, and earplugs, which Apple calls earbuds. I wanted to play with my new iPod nano instantly. My reaction to the product was visceral. This is the Apple brand in a box.

Apple could have saved a fortune by using a blister pack to hold the iPod nano, but this would have diluted the essence of the Apple brand idea and the company knew this. Apple also could have saved quite a bit of money if its retail outlets were more like typical electronics retailers. But Apple is atypical. Apple stores are uncluttered, clean and white in design, much like its product packaging. They resemble modern museums. Products are accessible and meant to be played with. At a counter called the Genius Bar, friendly people with technological know-how answer your questions without making you feel dumb or uncool in any way. The customer shopping experience at Apple stores is a powerful branding signal in perfect alignment with its brand idea.

Apple is a brand that understands the importance of a customer journey and of a power signal. It knows where to invest its branding dollars and where to save them. This understanding is an integral part of the brand culture. It's what makes Apple hot and cool. It's what makes Apple hip to people from all walks of life. I like being part of the Apple community and so do all those people I see on the subway. Our funky white iPod earbuds connect to more than just our choice of music. They connect us to each other and to the brand.

The selection process for a brand name is proof of how important it is to start with a simple brand idea. It's almost impossible to name something without an absolutely clear understanding of its core meaning. The same holds true for other branding signals. The fundamental premise of this book is that when your brand idea is simple and clear, and different in a way that's relevant to people, the branding signals you create to express this idea will be intuitively right. They will have far greater impact in cementing the associations you want people to have about the brand in their mental files. The branding process will be simpler, almost instinctive, and gratifying. You'll find, as the strongest brands have, that your branding signals will be compelling and memorable. I've talked about how muddy ideas lead to muddy signals and befuddled consumers. You'll see how true this is in this next step.

For this step to be successful you should have no doubt about what you want your branding signals to say about your brand and to whom you want to communicate. You've identified your competition and established what you have to do to knock them off those mental desktops. You've made sure your employees understand your Brand-Simple idea and are good to go.

Before you begin thinking about specific branding signals, go back to that map of your customer journey. Confirm where your branding signals touch people. Then assess which of these signals have the greatest potential to influence perceptions—where and how can you most significantly generate brand-*ness*. You need to have a sense of where you should be investing in your brand more or less. For example, Dell doesn't have to invest as much in the packaging as Apple does. It isn't essential to Dell's position in the market. The ordering process or customer service is, and Dell has made the appropriate branding investments in these areas. In the cell phone category, packaging isn't a make-or-break branding investment, either. The technology to ensure fewer dropped calls is worthy of greater branding investment, as are product design and calling plans.

Even though its advertising is classic, American Express knows its customer service speaks volumes about what its brand represents, and the company invests accordingly in this branding signal. The fact that you can get a replacement card within twenty-four hours while on vacation in Bali is a genuine signal of its promise. The fact that American Express takes the hassle out of a disputed claim with a merchant indicates that membership does indeed come with privileges.

For your branding signals to have impact, you must examine your BrandSimple idea carefully. What does it say, and what should you be doing to get it across to people? Determine where and how others in the category are conveying branding signals. Should you do something similar to beat them, or send other types of signals altogether? Whatever you do, your branding signals must be consistent with your BrandSimple idea. Decide which signals will do the most good in getting your idea across. Then, put the money there.

Power Signals

As I've told you, all branding signals are not equal. Some branding signals—the power signals—are the signals that have the greatest ability to influence consumer perceptions of the brand. Once you're satisfied with your choice of name, you should focus on these branding signals next.

Virtually any form of branding expression—packaging, advertising, web sites, signage, product design or functionality, vehicles, retail environments, even refrigerator magnets—can be a power signal. It all depends on your brand, the dynamics of your brand category, and your BrandSimple idea.

Although a power signal can be tough to identify, start with another look at your customer journey. This will give you an indication of where you have the best opportunity to connect with people and get the greatest return on your branding investment. After this, I encourage clients to delve deeper into customer needs. Observe how people experience the brand. Not what they say they do, but what they actually do. For example, in my work with GMAC, it became clear that after first assessing whether people were physically okay after an automobile accident, people were concerned with what they were going to use for transportation while a car was being repaired. How were they going to get their kids to soccer practice, get to work, or pick up groceries? GMAC's insight into this aspect of the customer journey made it possible for them to address this issue and identify a branding signal that would help get people moving again—a core element of its brand promise.

Power signals communicate most effectively the associations that you want people to file in their mental folders about your brand. They're the branding signals that tell people to "save as." Power signals create brand-*ness*. The examples that follow will give you a sense of power signals at work.

The Power of People: FedEx

Once upon a time, you looked out the window of a New York City office building and gazed upon a gray landscape punctuated only by small spots of yellow. The taxicabs stood out against this monochromatic palette, of course. Today as you look out these windows you still see the gray and the yellow, but now you also see a generous sprinkling of distinctive white trucks each painted with what has become an iconic and very familiar logo. Whether the logos are purple and green, purple and orange, or purple and red, these trucks are unmistakable signals of the FedEx brand. As unmistakable as these white trucks have become, however, it's the people behind the brand that are the ultimate power signals of the company's revolutionary brand idea. The brand is, and always has been, driven by its people. And there has never been any confusion about the idea on which these people deliver—reliability.

When Fred Smith founded Federal Express in 1971, he invested in a business model that delivered on the idea of reliability, literally and figuratively: On-time delivery by 10:30 A.M. It was such a compelling, crystal clear idea that everyone in the organization knew what it meant, and what it meant to them relative to their roles. It wasn't vague as in "let's keep the customer happy." Rather it was "let's keep the customer happy by delivering by 10:30 A.M." There was no ambiguity. It was a line in the sand and an expectation well met. It was also about as simple as an idea can get, and central to everything the company did—and continues to do. The idea remains the driving force behind the brand. As competition in the industry changes and evolves, so too does FedEx, in order to keep its brand idea differentiated and relevant. In addition to adding an array of new business units and services over the years to maintain its category position, it made a significant change of another sort in the mid-1990s to guarantee that its simple, clear idea wouldn't become ambiguous to anyone inside or outside the company, anywhere in the world.

More than 20 years after the company had been founded it had, indeed, become much bigger. It had expanded in terms of both services and employees to better meet the needs of its customers. More than that, it had expanded its market to serve customers both domestically and on a global scale. While its business efforts had grown exponentially, the company realized that the name Federal Express as a branding signal didn't express as succinctly as it could the rapidly expanding brand offerings, nor the simple idea on which the brand had been founded. More than this, the name didn't capitalize on what had become a very positive fact of life for the company. FedEx had become the ubiquitous term everyone used for overnight delivery. In 1996, FedEx was formally adopted as the brand name.

The name and subsequent logo change, which was undertaken with help from Landor, accomplished a number of objectives. First, it moved the company away from the word "Federal," which sounded almost governmental in nature, not to mention U.S.-centric. A key objective was to signal the international scope of the brand's business. The name FedEx did this. Perhaps more important, however, was the evocative association the faster, sleeker, more efficient sounding FedEx name sent to people within the organization. While customers and everyone else were using the word to signify overnight delivery, it sent a powerful internal signal that FedEx was a company committed to continue leading the industry in getting things where they needed to be—reliably and on time. It refocused and clarified the brand idea in a way every employee could understand. FedEx is a fast, confident, super-efficient brand, and so are its employees. With its newly designed, turbo-charged logo as inspiration, it was a signal every employee could get—and get behind. It's a logo that telegraphs, instantly, the "world on time," a line that underscores the brand promise. As a service brand, FedEx relies on its people to ensure the promise of the brand is kept. Adopting the name FedEx gave it an almost intuitive way to signal to its fast-growing roster of employees that they were ultimately responsible for creating and managing the brand experience. They were the brand's power signals.

The name change added new vitality to the original brand idea and united all of the company's business units in delivering it. The fast, confident, super-efficient FedEx logo not only turned all of the brand's trucks and planes into instant icons representative of the brand's new energy, but served as motivation for every employee worldwide. Ask anyone in the FedEx organization what it means to "be the brand" and they'll tell you that it's doing whatever it takes. They know there is a line in the sand (and a clock on the wall). Adopting the name FedEx helped convey to everyone what it meant to deliver on the FedEx brand idea as Fred Smith had intended it to be delivered.

Step Five: Create Branding Signals beyond the Name

I talked to Gayle Christensen, marketing director for FedEx, about the challenge of branding in such a large company, especially as FedEx has taken on new business units and operating components. "First and foremost," she said, "it helps to have a CEO who understands the power of the brand. Fred Smith leads the charge. He's brilliant about sharing best practices and understands how important it is to operate as a cohesive organization, guided by a simple cultural philosophy, using a single voice. As we've gotten bigger over the years, 'whatever it takes' has been our mantra. While there have been challenges, bigger is much easier to manage when you have an idea that continues to be your brand DNA. Even as independent operating companies, FedEx Express, FedEx Ground, FedEx Freight, FedEx Kinko's, we all operate with the same objective.

"Remember that movie with Tom Hanks, *Castaway?*," Gayle asked during our conversation. "He was a FedEx systems engineer shipwrecked on an island after a FedEx plane crashes into the ocean. He's washed ashore along with remains of the wreckage, including a FedEx package. At the end of the movie, after years as a castaway on this island, the guy makes sure to deliver the FedEx package he's been safeguarding. Not one person who saw the movie questioned this behavior. Given that he was a FedEx employee, it seems people knew that delivering the package was ingrained in his soul. The only comments we got on our website after the release of the movie were not about FedEx as a company, but 'What was in the package?'! The system engineer's allegiance to his FedEx responsibility was never in doubt!"

Gayle explained to me that Robert Zemekis, the director of *Castaway,* knew that no other company could have played the role FedEx played in the movie. The behavior of the people associated with the FedEx brand, is that powerfully understood. In fact, Hollywood aside, FedEx couriers and drivers, the people who are the day-to-day face of the brand have actually been known to do whatever it takes to demonstrate their understanding of the brand commitment and have become legends in the company as a result. In one case, for example, a courier in Hawaii encountered a terrible storm while on his route along a beachside road. Opening the back of his truck to retrieve packages at a destination, one package flew out and into the crashing surf. He jumped into the water to pull out the package and delivered it, a bit wet (both the courier and the package), but intact.

As FedEx has expanded its operations and capabilities even further, it has continued to maintain focus on keeping its brand idea simple. To assure consistent behavior from business unit to business unit it has developed internal branding programs based on its "whatever it takes" mantra to ensure all employees understand what it means to work for FedEx. It has even established an internal employee awards program to honor those who do whatever it takes to meet customer needs in extraordinary ways. As Gayle told me, "You can't wear the FedEx brand unless you know what it means to be reliable."

Fred Smith started with 359 employees and 14 Dassault jets. FedEx delivered 186 packages to 25 U.S. cities on its first overnight flights. Today FedEx has a fleet second in size only to American Airlines. It serves more than 220 countries and territories, processes more than 3 million packages a day, and has close to 150,000 employees worldwide. There are more than 40,000 trucks on the road, which travel over 2.5 million miles per day. FedEx knows how to protect the value of its brand by investing in the people, the processes, and the transportation that fuels its success. FedEx employees are the brand's power signals. They know what it means to be the brand, and they deliver on it every day.

The Power of Product Placement: Gatorade

I don't get to watch as much football as I used to these days, but when I do, I'm always comforted by the familiar sights and sounds on the field of play. One of the most familiar is the Gatorade "dunking" of the winning coach at the end of a game. It's a sight as familiar to football fans as any other on game day, and we've come to watch for it. Its placement on the field is a power signal in more ways than one.

One of the most interesting things about this dunking of the coach is that it couldn't happen with any beverage other than Gatorade. Gatorade's placement on the field of play has attained

Can you see the arrow? Beyond the familiar bold typeface, one of the graphic elements that make the FedEx logo so effective and telegraphic is the strong, white arrow cleverly engineered into the negative space between the "E" and the "X." It's one of the reasons we can see the FedEx logo from blocks away, and what makes it so evocative of the FedEx brand. From here to there, the world on time, this confident arrow signals reliability.

iconic status for very good reason. It's a drink that was created specifically for athletes. It's authentic in every way. I talked to Cindy Alston, a Landor client, who is vice president of communications and equity development for Gatorade and has worked with the brand for almost fifteen years. To say she's passionate about her brand is an understatement. "Gatorade was developed by scientists at the University of Florida in 1965. The coaches realized that the players were becoming extremely dehydrated while playing under the hot Florida sun, which affected their ability to perform. Better hydration is a key to better performance, and water wasn't the answer. After extensive research, the scientists formulated a drink that was rich in carbohydrates and electrolytes. The Gators gave it a try, their health and performance improved, and a brand was born."

The Gatorade brand essence, Cindy told me, is based on improving athletic performance and having the science to prove it. The brand has loyal fans because it is what it says it is. Professional athletes use the stuff because the science behind it does improve performance, providing more energy through better hydration. It's a point of difference that no other beverage brand can claim with such authority. People watching games see the product on the field of play at high school, college, and professional football games, at baseball games, at basketball and soccer games. They say to themselves, "Hey, if it works for pro athletes, it will work for me."

"What makes Gatorade unique are its scientific underpinnings and the fact that it's used by professional athletes," Cindy said. "Do you know how many brands look for something they can stand for and have people relate to it? We've got it. It's our competitive advantage. When I was getting my MBA, I remember something my marketing professor told me, which is that good positioning is the art of sacrifice. We could try to represent more things to more people, but we'd lose our equity and our credibility."

Gatorade's simple, clear idea lends itself to some incredible branding signals. The bolt on the Gatorade bottles was imagery created to reflect the speed with which Gatorade is absorbed into your system. Gatorade has leveraged this symbol so significantly it has become similar to the Nike "swoosh" in its ability to bring to mind the Gatorade brand immediately. This icon was recently redesigned and now looks like what the Gatorade brand team calls the Sweaty Bolt. The new design signals even more quickly the product's ability to hydrate faster, enabling more energy and better performance.

Gatorade doesn't sit on the sidelines when it comes to updating what's inside the Gatorade bottle, Cindy told me. "We established the Gatorade Sports Science Institute in 1985 in order to be able to further the scientific underpinnings of the brand. The institute's mission is to find ways to improve hydration and nutritional practices among athletes through education and testing. We use the findings to help educate our employees to keep them 'on-brand' in everything they do."

If you go back to what Kevin Keller said about points of parity and points of difference, it's clear that Gatorade has taken its very obvious point of difference and leveraged it powerfully. Every good beverage brand has great advertising, great packaging, good distribution, and innovative promotions. So does Gatorade. Gatorade uses what no other beverage brand has to its advantage—the ability to hydrate better and improve performance on the real field of play, and it signals this in powerful ways. It makes investments to see that its packaging and its advertising signal its promise. That vivid orange cap is unmistakably Gatorade's. Ask anyone who watches sports of any kind. They'll tell you that the sight of Gatorade on the sidelines of the playing fields reinforces the Gatorade idea most powerfully. It's the familiar sight of athletes gulping the stuff and coaches getting dunked. Product placement is Gatorade's power signal.

The Power of an Icon: KFC

One of the most essential criteria in determining if something is worthy of power signal status is the speed at which it's recognized—how quickly people get what you want them to get. More than the brand attention deficit disorder I referred to, I'm talking speed of recognition when you're trying to get someone's attention as they're speeding down an interstate (one of the places KFC signals its brand) at sixty miles an hour.

Kentucky Fried Chicken was dealing with speed of a different sort a few years back when it took a look at its brand position. It concluded that to prosper it had to compete with fast food brands. It wanted to attract the younger, hipper audience attracted to fast food. Its original recipe was intact, but management felt the brand needed to change its identity—to move away from Colonel Sanders, its original power signal.

The first thing Kentucky Fried Chicken did was shorten the name to KFC, which sounded faster and did away with that verboten word, "fried." (People referred to the brand this way, so this was not a thorny issue.) The company also invested in new equipment that got the food out the door faster. The hungry customers couldn't actually see what was going on in the kitchen, and it wasn't something that had been an issue, so its effect was somewhat inconsequential to the brand.

Finally (and key to the story), the brand team looked at Colonel Sanders himself, and decided that his image on the buckets and signs could be reduced to the size of a postage stamp. In his place they put three bold red racing stripes to indicate speed.

It might have said fast, but the extreme change was one for the worse. Customers assumed that if the Colonel wasn't there, KFC couldn't possibly be producing that same delicious Original Recipe anymore. KFC began to lose market share immediately, so its team started talking to consumer groups and soon realized what had gone wrong. The name change to KFC was okay. As I said, people referred to it this way anyway. But people thought of KFC as a way of putting a home-cooked meal on the table without feeling guilty about the fact that it wasn't home-cooked at home. With the changes, they weren't sure it was home-cooked quality.

And, oh yes, one more thing. People wanted the Colonel back. His identity was the brand's power signal, representing all that was good about KFC. Colonel Sanders had a level of worldwide recognition equal to Mickey Mouse ears. People had total recall of the famous man with the beard. Nearly 99 percent of people asked said they loved the Colonel and associated him with the brand's heritage, authenticity, and famous secret recipe. The brand team realized it would have to be out of its mind to get rid of the Colonel, and that creating this kind of equity anew would take thirty years and millions of dollars.

The KFC bucket facelift brought the beloved Colonel front and center.

Armed with this knowledge, the KFC branding team decided to bring back the Colonel with some minor changes in the man who would now always represent KFC. The Colonel was gussied up a bit and given a nice warm smile. (Hey, anyone can benefit from a little makeover.)

KFC also found that besides the buckets in which the chicken came, another KFC power signal was pole-tops (the very tall signs along interstate highways that drivers can see from miles away). These signs got customers to stop, get off the highways, and visit KFC. The branding investment KFC makes in keeping Colonel Sanders front, center, and on top is now a top priority. The original KFC icon is effective, efficient, and right on target as a power signal. Guess who's smiling now?

The Power of First Impressions: Genworth

I mentioned Genworth earlier as an example of the type of challenging client assignments we take on at Landor. It's time to give you the bigger picture. Until 2004 Genworth was the insurance division of GE. Its employees were GE employees and proud of that fact. They were able to tell people they sold GE insurance products and services. Everyone understood what this meant. GE is one of the best-known brand names in the world. When GE decided to spin off its insurance division, the company formerly known as GE Financial was left brand-less. The largest initial public offering of 2004 left this insurance company both autonomous and anonymous. It still had all of its assets, including an incredible portfolio of insurance products and services, from long-term care, to immediate annuities, and term life insurance, as well as international leadership in mortgage insurance. It had thousands of employees who knew the intermediary insurance business inside and out. What it didn't have was the name that had been the anchor of its identity. While it wasn't technically in a start-up position, it had to start from scratch in establishing a brand of its own from which to move forward.

The now-independent GE Financial management team, including CEO Mike Frazier, came to Landor for help. It needed to get to market with a new brand and brand name—fast. And it had to build credibility and legitimacy with both its employees and its customers—fast.

More than this, it was very important from a business perspective that the loss of its original brand affiliation did not mean a loss of customers. The company had to convince Wall Street that this new entity could swim on its own. Bottom line, they told us, was that we need to let people know we're not a start-up but a strong and viable business.

The first step in creating the "new" brand was to establish a meaningful way to differentiate it from other global insurance firms—find a simple idea from which to launch everything else. Very few brands in the insurance category have a high degree of differentiation, so this seemed a challenge until we looked at the company's heritage. No other firm could lay claim to the reputation for excellent management and the credibility of having been an integral part of GE. GE was still a majority stakeholder, so it made sense to take advantage of all the powerful associations this implied, including the letters GE. Using these two letters as a starting point, the team went through a rigorous naming process. Genworth was chosen for two reasons. First, it made good use of the letters G and E. Second, the name emphasized the transfer of wealth from one generation to the next, as well as the company's long-standing reputation for protecting the assets—or worth—of generations. This was a relevant concept for an insurance brand in every respect. The tagline developed. The tagline developed was also a very powerful signal of the simple brand idea: "Built on GE Heritage." It clearly broke the illusion that Genworth was a start-up and emphasized the brand's deep roots.

Getting the simple idea to market—fast—was the second challenge the brand faced. The power of the right first impression was critical. Genworth made the right first impression by making two very bold moves, moves that signaled this was not your standard insurance company.

First, Genworth created advertising that signaled that it was a company that came from a great gene pool. In the ad, an adorable little boy is playing a very spirited game of tennis against a professional tennis player, and he's holding his own. This kid is good, and you're amazed at his skill. Then his parents enter the picture. These are no ordinary parents but Andre Agassi and Steffi Graf. The ad implied that while you may not be familiar with the name "Genworth" yet, it's a company with a great lineage. Great first impression.

Here's the second bold move Genworth took to make a powerful first impression. Imagine arriving at work one morning, getting into your voice mail system, and hearing this message: "Good morning. This is Donald Trump. I just wanted to tell you that you guys at Genworth are sensational and I think we make really great partners. I encourage you all to watch *The Apprentice* tomorrow night."

That's what all U.S. Genworth employees heard on the morning before Donald's hit NBC TV series aired the next night. Genworth, one of the world's largest insurance holding companies, had taken advantage of an opportunity to play a starring role when finalists were challenged to manage a Genworth-sponsored charity event. No insurance company had ever tried such a daring venture before. Genworth's industry recognition went through the roof following the episode, which was the series finale and generated the season's highest viewership. As Genworth financial chief marketing officer Buzz Richmond said to me when we spoke, "It was like catching lightning in a bottle. We couldn't have bought this amount of recognition. It enabled us to be seen as the hot, new, innovative, and forward-thinking brand we are. It established credibility, legitimacy, scale, and presence fast.

"We had established a point of difference for our brand, a new name, a new tagline," said Buzz, "but we realized that if there was ever a time to present ourselves as a really different and relevant kind of insurance company, it was now. The window for change was open. We didn't have any baggage associated with our name, and while we were certainly big enough to be regarded as a leader, we were small enough and new enough to be regarded as nimble. We wanted to be thought of as an innovative, energetic company."

Genworth's appearance on *The Apprentice* broke the mold in the way insurance companies go to market. It was an incredibly powerful reflection of Genworth's creative spirit and its ability to tap into contemporary life. Watching Genworth's CEO on *The Apprentice* alongside Donald Trump created a buzz in the industry and got everyone in the Genworth organization jazzed up, as Buzz said. It got people excited about their new "old" company and gave them confidence, not to mention greater motivation, to drive the new brand forward. If you're brand enough for Donald Trump, for goodness sake, you must be a leader. Donald doesn't play with anyone else.

Step Five: Create Branding Signals beyond the Name

Genworth went from having a fail-safe name to contemplating a blank slate. It wasn't a blank slate for long. Genworth looked to its past as inspiration for a meaningfully different idea on which to build its brand. And it looked to the present to make a very powerful first impression. It created branding signals that were bold because they needed to be, but smart because they were right for the brand. Its advertising as branding signal conveyed to people both inside and outside the brand organization that this was not a company from out of nowhere, but "Built on GE Heritage." As for *The Apprentice*, if you can show up on one of the hottest shows on television, you must be hot.

The key to success in the Genworth story was not missing a beat in going to market. Keeping the message utterly BrandSimple was critical. The simplest, most differentiating thing we could say was that this was an insurance company cut from a different cloth—GE cloth. GE immediately signaled world-class management and capability. Although the rest of the category may have been able to say, "trust us, we've been in business for years," it couldn't be signaled with the degree of trust signaled by the name GE. Genworth's first impression was a powerful branding signal within the category.

The Power of Advertising: U.S. Department of Transportation

When I was growing up, the notion of taking away a friend's car keys when he'd had a little bit too much to drink at a party didn't exist. Drinking and then getting into a car to drive was a societal norm—a deadly one—but intervening was not a recognized social behavior. I don't even want to begin to think about the drunk-driving fatalities that occurred as a result.

In 1983 the U.S. Department of Transportation approached the Ad Council. Since 1942, the Ad Council has been marshalling the volunteer forces of advertising and media companies to create timely and compelling messages about social issues in order to promote positive change. Its objective is to use the power of advertising signals to raise awareness of, and stimulate action against, problems that confront us all. The Department of Transportation wanted to address the problem of drinking and driving. In taking on this challenging subject, the Ad Council focused on the idea of intervention.

I spoke to Priscilla Natkins, executive vice president of client services at the Ad Council, about the powerful campaign that was created. "When you think about what young college kids did a generation ago, it was alarming," she said. "It never occurred to us to intervene when we saw someone too drunk to drive. This would have been totally uncool. It was unheard of. The objective of our assignment for the U.S. Department of Transportation was to change a societal norm, which is a very difficult thing to do. We had to change accepted behavior. We had to make taking away someone's keys, not letting them drive drunk, socially acceptable.

"The way we approached it was from a different angle. We knew we couldn't attack the problem head on, telling people not to drink. But telling friends it was socially acceptable, and in fact a positive behavior to intervene is how we did it. It's how the advertising campaign 'Friends Don't Let Friends Drive Drunk' was born. The strategic premise and the advertising campaign were extraordinarily simple, which made them extraordinarily successful.

"We created several dramatic ways to signal our message. One of these was the 'Innocent Victims' series of vignettes. In this series of advertisements a viewer is watching footage of real home movies. It might be of a little girl's fifth birthday party, or a runner crossing the finish line at a race, or a baby boy taking his first steps. You're caught by the disarmingly sweet nature of the films and then caught off-guard. All of a sudden the footage is interrupted by words superimposed over the final frame which state that this young person was killed by a drunk driver on a specific date. It closes with the simple line, 'Friends Don't Let Friends Drive Drunk.' What these ads were saying was that if you don't intervene and your friend gets on the road drunk, it's not just your friend who is endangered, but the lives of innocent people."

Priscilla told me that the "Innocent Victims" series of ads ran for almost eighteen years. By creating the Friends Don't Let Friends Drive Drunk campaign, the Department of Transportation and the Ad Council launched an effort that would change the way Americans think about drinking and driving. According to the Department of Transportation's website, 84 percent of Americans recall having seen or heard one of these public service announcements. Almost 80 percent report that they took action to prevent a friend or loved one from driving drunk, and 25 percent report they stopped drinking and driving as a result of the campaign. In addition, due to public awareness of this social issue, Designated Driver programs have become a key component of community-based impaired driving prevention efforts. In fact, hearing someone say "I'm the designated driver" at a social event or dinner has become a highly accepted and appreciated social norm.

I've been out of the business of directly developing advertising for some time, but I remember the principles of effective advertising very well. This advertising campaign is a powerful branding signal because it followed these simple principles.

Effective advertising must do four simple things. First, it needs to grab a viewer's attention. Over the last several years, doing this has gotten harder. Consumers have been inundated with messages, and they've been given the technology to click the remote button faster, not to mention delete ads entirely. The Ad Council's campaign for the Department of Transportation had the ability to grab your attention in every one of its executions.

Next, for advertising to be effective, it must communicate the right message to the right target. How many times has someone told you about an interesting TV spot, only then to tell you he couldn't remember who the advertiser was or what the ad was trying to get across? The ad was simply entertaining. Entertainment value is certainly important, especially these days, but if you can't link your message to your brand and have the viewer understand the point you're trying to make, you're wasting your money. This campaign effectively communicated the right message to the right audience—not the people who may not know or care that they've had too much to drink, but the people around them who can see the implications of not intervening.

In addition to grabbing your attention and communicating the right message to the right audience, effective advertising has to have the power to persuade you to take action. This is the hardest—and the most important—part. The Ad Council's campaign did this by demonstrating the tragic results of not taking action.

Finally, the best advertising has the ability to be effective over time. This one, as Priscilla said, lasted eighteen years. Although it's

Amanda Geiger bought these sunglasses to wear on spring break. She wore them only once before she was killed by a drunk driver.

Friends Don't Let Friends Drive Drunk.

U.S. Department of Transportation

Ad Council

The stories of accident victims provided the theme for this long-running effort from The Ad Council.

pure brand-building story, this advertising is an example of the incredible branding power advertising has to change your beliefs, in this case your belief about acceptable social practices. This advertising power signal has saved countless lives.

The Power of Word of Mouth: BlackBerry

After graduating from business school, I had a roommate, Jeff, who eventually ended up as a trader and player at Lehman Brothers. Given how busy we were over the years, I only saw him infrequently, usually when we could get a group of friends together for a poker game. Jeff was always impeccably dressed, so it came as somewhat of a shock to me when I saw him a few years back with a pocket protector tucked into his crisply pressed shirt holding some sort of communications device. This communications device—the BlackBerry—had become the elite power tool of Type-A personalities worldwide. And it had done so without any mass media. It had become the communications device of choice for movers and shakers by word of mouth. It had attained what is known as cult status.

I spoke to Paul Kalbfleish, director of marketing for BlackBerry, about how it had achieved this special niche position. "I came on board about five years ago," he told me, "and I spent some time trying to figure out what the brand was. It already existed in people's minds, because the experience of it was real and personal. These A-types were getting the functionality that kept them in the loop 24/7. It was a power tool that connected to a core emotional need they had—to be constantly in touch.

"First of all, it didn't have a typical techy name, like A520, or pocket e-mail, which made it unique from the get-go. The name BlackBerry caught everybody off guard, which helped generate buzz. The original shape was also unique. It looked kind of like the Hummer of mobile communications devices. It was both rugged and cool, without being too serious looking. The functionality, of course, was the key—it did what it said it would. It kept people connected.

"But the real story is about the way the BlackBerry established itself as a brand in people's minds. It spread person-to-person. The experience of this brand was so personally legitimate for these people

201

they actually defined its meaning. The users created the brand and what it stands for. We spent a lot of the early days seeding Wall Street with the product. We gave BlackBerries to investment bankers and other people of that ilk. It was the ultimate sampling tactic. What happened as these people started to use the devices is that they became badges of cachet. 'Hey, I've got one, you've got one. You must be in the same league with me.' Or, 'You don't have one, or you don't even know about these things—you're not in my league.' It was getting the Blackberry into the hands of people to whom this thing really connected on an emotional level that established its brand definition and its cult status."

Paul explained that BlackBerry was able to establish an internal definition of the brand with which to move forward by listening to what its key users said about the brand and what it meant to them. Over the past few years BlackBerry has broadened its appeal in the marketplace, but it has been very careful in its use of mass media as a branding signal. Not wanting to dilute the brand's functional status, the company is mindful of how to expand its initial base of dedicated users. It continues to rely on its advancements in technology, industrial design, and functionality as primary branding signals, as these are the types of signals most significant and meaningful to the brand's core users.

Research in Motion (RIM), founded in 1984, is the company that develops, manufactures, and markets BlackBerry products. It knows instinctively what's on brand and off in terms of its brand idea. Paul told me that over the past couple of years, RIM has been approached by licensing companies that want to put the BlackBerry name on everything from sunglasses to briefcases—anything of interest to the Type-A users of BlackBerries. All the offers were turned down. Even though it knew it could sell these things and generate revenue, RIM has remained very cautious about burning out the brand name as a result of off-brand branding signals—anything with the potential to water down the core meaning of the brand. "We respect the brand, and respect that it has achieved cult status by way of being true to the people who built the brand, the users," said Paul. "It's a tricky thing to say the customer owns the brand, but they do. The BlackBerry was created to do a specific job: keep our target connected. It's work to them, it's not a game."

BlackBerry: a cult brand turned category leader with a loyal customer following.

BlackBerry quickly became a cult brand for a very good reason. It was carefully seeded with a target that immediately understood its impact as a work tool and as a status signal, and immediately connected to it emotionally. BlackBerry let the people who use it talk about its authenticity. In doing so, it created the ultimately authentic power signal. The BlackBerry brand is authentic in its functionality and its industrial design. It delivers on its simple brand idea, which is to keep the movers and shakers connected 24/7 in a way that's highly practical and efficient, with a product designed to look cool yet rugged. It looks great with Armani suits, and it works like the power tool it is.

A great lesson to be learned from BlackBerry, and something I preach whenever I get the chance, is to stay in touch with your primary users. Listen to what they say to you in their letters, e-mails, and understand how they relate to and use your brand. Talk to customer service people in order to hear what they're hearing. Your customers are your best source of insight. And when you can count on their word of mouth, what one customer says to another, you've got one of the most effective branding power signals that exists. BlackBerry knows this.

The Power of Public Relations: Dove

Before I get to the power of public relations as a branding signal, let me explain very briefly what public relations is and why it can be a challenge, especially in branding.

Public relations is the art of getting the media to tell your story for you. The inherent challenge in any public relations effort is that sometimes your story isn't all that exciting or newsworthy (in spite of what you think). Perhaps, the greater challenge is that sometimes the story told isn't the story you *want* told. You can lose control of the content and, more important, the context of the tale you'd like the media to tell. The magic of successful public relations is getting the media to tell your story as well as, if not better than, you'd tell it yourself.

We've all been privy to positive public relations efforts—the movie that does gangbusters at the box office, the book that goes to the top of the bestseller list, or the naughty movie star who's given a second chance to make a good first impression. We've also seen what happens when a public relations story spins far out of control and how damaging it can be to the politician, the automaker, the movie, the movie star, the new pharmaceutical, or the newest diet guru in question. Smart public relations agencies know how to take a newsworthy story, how to control the way it's told, and how to control where it's showcased, be it in print media, broadcast media, on web sites or blogs, or any combination therein. Smart public relations agencies also ensure that these placements and the content are relevant to the people who read, watch, listen to, or log onto any given media source.

Although public relations can be a powerful tool for all types of brands, getting it to work as a branding signal for a packaged goods brand can be a little tricky. First of all, what can you say about a packaged goods brand that's really important, that has the genuine newsworthiness—the oomph—to get Oprah or CNN to give you air time? Then, can you ensure that the media will talk about your newsworthy idea in a way that's in sync with what consumers already feel about your brand, or will they distort or discredit your brand idea? Third, can you come up with enough substance—the tactics—to support the endeavor? To paraphrase Gertrude Stein, "Is there enough there, there?" to make the public relations effort meaningful?

Answer these questions in the affirmative, and you'll experience the success that Dove has experienced with public relations as its power signal.

Over fifty years ago, Dove soap was built on the simple idea that it was one-quarter cleansing cream. (I told you earlier in the book, I can see the original advertising signal in my mind every time I see any Dove product.) Its brand promise—not to dry your skin the way other soap does—was substantiated by dermatologists and a number of independent healthcare studies. It was also substantiated, passionately and honestly, by its users. When women used Dove brand, they raved about it. They wanted to talk about it and tell other people about it. Beginning in the late 1960s, testimonials became an integral part of Dove's branding strategy. Dove's simple brand idea—to make more women feel more beautiful every day—connected with women because they could trust it. It was authentic. The Dove product actually worked to help make women feel more beautiful. There was proof behind Dove's promise as a beauty brand.

Fast forward. In 2004, almost fifty years after introducing Dove, Unilever, the manufacturer of Dove products, fielded a global study to find out more about how women around the world feel about beauty. What they discovered was not only astounding in its simplicity and clarity, but a veritable observation of the obvious. Something women had been talking about for decades, but that no one had addressed head-on: The implications of a global society that narrowly defines beauty by the images seen in entertainment, advertising, and fashion magazines and the startling impact this has on women. One of the results of the study was the finding that only 2 percent of the thousands of women surveyed consider themselves beautiful. Women want a broader definition of beauty. It was an a-ha of global proportions and Dove decided to do something meaningful about it. The simple idea behind Dove has always been to make women feel more beautiful. Dove would take on the responsibility of broadening the stereotypical view of beauty.

Sparked by the results of the survey, the brand team at Dove launched The Campaign for Real Beauty, a major initiative designed to provoke discussion and encourage debate on the nature of beauty. The Campaign for Real Beauty asks women to give thought to society's definition of beauty, the constant search for perfection, and the way the media shapes consumer views. The Campaign for Real Beauty is a global effort intended to be a starting point to change cultural stereotypes about beauty, to inspire women to take better care of themselves and to feel more confident about who they are.

Stacie Bright, Director of Unilever Home and Personal Care, talked to me about the Campaign for Real Beauty and explained why only Dove could make it believable. "Dove has a simple mission," she told me, "to make more women feel beautiful every day. Dove has stood for real beauty for over fifty years. Everyone talks about beauty stereotypes, but no one was doing anything about it. Our research and global survey allowed us to get a better understanding of women's relationship with beauty. We brought in experts, including Dr. Nancy Etcoff, who works in collaboration with Massachusetts

General Hospital and Harvard University, and Dr. Susie Orbach of the London School of Economics. What we discovered was startling. Almost half of the survey respondents said that the media was responsible for creating unrealistic perceptions about beauty which led to lack of self-esteem and poor self-image. We knew we needed to take a stand and we wanted to put the focus on the critical self-esteem aspect. We wanted to be the ones responsible for promoting a broader definition of beauty to help women feel more confident."

Stacie and her team at Unilever developed the Campaign for Real Beauty with Ogilvy & Mather and Edelman Public Relations. She told me that the three pillars to the Campaign for Real Beauty are: to listen; to challenge and change stereotypes; and to "walk the talk." As part of the initial campaign, Ogilvy created television, print, and billboard advertising that feature women whose physical appearances differ from the stereotypical ideal. A number of the ads developed pose questions about the attributes of true beauty, whether "society will ever accept the notion that old can be beautiful," for example, or whether "true beauty only comes in size 6." Women are prompted to go to the website, www.campaignforrealbeauty.com, to vote and engage in conversation.

In terms of the public relations, Unilever recognized that it had an "oomph" of an idea that was not only newsworthy but wholly in line with the idea on which the Dove brand was built. Dove was a credible, trusted source. Advertising was a way to make people aware of the story. Public relations was used as the powerful branding signal with which to amplify and broaden the message.

Stacie worked with Edelman Public Relations to create the substance of the public relations efforts, the tactics to get people engaged and involved. Various communication vehicles were developed which invite women to join in the discussion about beauty and share their views with women around the world. The initiatives also include panel discussions held on the local level worldwide, as well as workshops led by leaders in the healthcare and beauty industries. Dove is also in partnership with the Woodhull Institute for Ethical leadership, a non-profit organization that offers professional development programs for women.

Lisa Sepulveda, who headed the Dove project at Edelman, explained that taking on an issue of this nature was not a matter of "one-offs," that is, an event here, an event there, but a long-standing and sustainable campaign built in phases. Among the latest initiatives is the creation of the Dove Self-Esteem Fund, established specifically to raise awareness of the link between beauty and body-related self-esteem. The Dove Self-Esteem Fund in the United States is working through Unilever to sponsor *Uniquely ME!,* a partnership program with the Girl Scouts of the USA that helps build self-confidence in girls from ages eight to fourteen. It covers topics that touch the lives of these young girls, including eating disorders and body image. The Dove Self-Esteem Fund also supports *Body Talk,* an educational program for schools in the United Kingdom and Canada.

If the goal of successful public relations is to get the media to tell your story the way you want it told, Dove is succeeding beyond expectations. Lisa told me that since its inception, the Campaign for Real Beauty has been the subject of over ninety national media stories, including segments and interviews on the *Today* show, *Good Morning, America,* the CBS *Morning Show, The View,* the *Oprah* show, and eight individual stories on CNN. On a local level, the campaign was featured in over thirty major broadcast and print stories in the Chicago area alone. Women want to talk about beauty and self-esteem, and they want to be heard. It's an emotional topic that connects on a visceral level.

The Edelman public relations team is fielding calls from educational facilities and teachers for help with curriculum, from book publishers, and from documentary filmmakers. They're also getting calls from women who want to volunteer to "further the cause." And, they're hearing from fathers of young girls thanking them for providing their daughters with good role models. The agency has put a task force into place just to field the calls coming in. As for brand performance, according to a 2004 A. C. Neilsen Report, one of every three households in the country uses a Dove product.

The key to the success of this public relations effort as a branding signal is also the key to all public relations success stories. What makes this one so special is that not too many packaged goods brands have been able to succeed in this area. To do so, Dove tapped into an incredibly newsworthy story—more newsworthy than even they could have imagined. Second, the newsworthy story was clearly in line with the brand's simple promise—to make more women feel beautiful every day—in this case, a broader, more realistic definition of beauty. Third, Dove developed the tactics that allowed it to "walk the talk" in a meaningful, credible, and sustainable way. From media coverage to documentary films, school curriculum to the Girl Scouts, the Dove brand has been able to get its story told just as it wants it told. That's public relations as a power signal.

The Power of a Typeface: Dean & DeLuca

For those of you who are not familiar with the streets of SoHo in downtown New York City, Dean & DeLuca is a gourmet landmark, an emporium of high-end treats from around the world. Its original owners, Joel Dean, Giorgia DeLuca, and Jack Ceglic, all food lovers, traveled the globe in search of the finest truffles, the most expensive caviar, and the most luscious chocolate. They opened the first store in the mid-1980s in SoHo, an area of New York populated by those who have both the taste and the wallet for the finest the world had to offer. (The store was named Dean & DeLuca because it had a more harmonious ring to it than it would have had with the third name.)

Jack, who is a designer, fashioned the interior of the store to resemble the food section of Europe's finest food establishments, fitted with white tile walls, Carrara marble floors, steel shelving, and exposed white columns. The store's design is understated and simple, almost under-designed.

Although the provisions and architecture certainly signal a delicious retail experience, it is the labels on the food that are perhaps Dean & DeLuca's most powerful branding signals. More specifically, the typeface on the labels. Jars and packages, truffles and jelly beans, caviar and coriander, bear a simple white label with the name Dean & DeLuca and in handwritten black Magic Marker a statement of what is inside. There are no ruffles and flourishes, no elaborate explanations, curlicues, or icons. Just a simple handwritten notation of the specific product contained within.

When Dean & DeLuca was set to expand to markets outside of New York City, they came to Landor, along with their investors, to discuss what it was that made the store so special and how it could be translated in other geographic regions. Richard Brandt, executive creative director at Landor, and his team examined the store elements to get an understanding of the special retail alchemy. They recognized that what made the store experience so engaging was that it was not about the store, itself, or even the fact that it was a contemporary New York institution, but that it was about the food and those labels. To translate the experience to other locations, the simple white, handwritten labels spoke volumes.

It was Jack Ceglic's own handwritten lettering—a unique typeface—that was key to the power of this branding signal. (Don't worry. Jack doesn't sit up all night writing labels. Richard and his team developed a way to digitize the writing—a small concession to modern technology and to the fact that the partners sold the business to a group of investors who could not write like Jack.)

The original partners, who were great retailers and brilliant at branding, wanted to convey that nothing was as important as the food they were selling. The minimalist labels do just that. A typeface can be a very powerful branding signal, especially when it says you may be about to eat the best chocolate money can buy.

The Power of the Experience

I had a fascinating conversation with Toni Belloni, a former executive at Procter & Gamble who is now CEO of the LVMH brand, the well-known purveyor of fashion and luxury goods. I asked Toni the difference between branding in the packaged goods category and branding in any industry where it's less about the actual product and more about the emotional experience of the brand.

"Branding, or signaling a packaged good, is a relatively linear process," he said. "There are very tangible components. You look at the market, you look at the target, put together a strategic plan, and you execute against this plan. The category stays somewhat static and you generally have a two-year framework within which to work. So your strategy and your signals hold for a period of time, the packaging, the advertising, the merchandising, or whatever they may be.

"When branding in the fashion industry or in any experiential industry, you need a strategy, certainly, but the execution process is completely different from a packaged goods model. It's not linear, at all. You have to coordinate all of your branding signals so as to express the experience as a whole. It may be an intangible quality you're trying to express, but it requires perfect orchestration to get your simple brand idea across.

"Let me give you an interesting analogy," he said. "Think about a surfer balancing on a wave. This surfer has to be responsive to several things at once: the height of the wave, the speed of the wave, the wind, and even the currents running beneath him. He has to be responsive to all of these forces simultaneously. He needs to make dozens of very quick, almost intuitive adjustments to keep his balance. The wave is constantly moving forward, changing shape, and the ocean floor is whirling below. His ability to react to minute changes determines success, or lack of success."

I liked what Toni was saying. When you're dealing with a fashion brand or any experiential brand, you need to keep your branding signals perfectly balanced and well orchestrated to create the seamless experience required to make an impression on the market. It isn't a matter of one branding signal, the clothing line, the merchandising, or the fabrics, but the blend of signals that make the brand powerful. It's like creating a theatrical experience.

In making his surfer analogy, Toni said, "Think about the surfer out there making all those intricate little changes in order to keep his balance. Then think about the consumers as standing on the shore watching the surfer ride the wave in. They don't see the spontaneous, reactive changes the surfer makes to stay balanced. All they see is the continuous, fluid motion of the ride. This is what an experiential brand must do. Not allow consumers to focus on the individual interactions with the brand but let them experience the brand as a whole."

The customer's journey with an experiential brand is obviously not linear at all. It's clear which brands understand this unique type of customer journey. Those that do deftly coordinate all of their branding signals to create a story. The Ralph Lauren brand tells a story of the American aristocracy. It's a tale of a gracious and classic style of life made real through the entirety of the Ralph Lauren experience. It's a consistent and evocative story: How the American aristocracy live, how they dress, how they play. The branding signals one

211

at a time don't make it come to life. It's the harmonious interplay of signals that make it authentic. The retail space, the quality of the fabric, the remarkable textures and colors, the styles, the refined tone of the advertising—together create an enticing brand experience.

In addition to fashion brands, those in the cosmetic industry understand the prerequisite to expressing the brand idea by way of an experiential net impression. The best know how to beautifully orchestrate their branding signals to convey an emotional benefit easily attainable by the consumer. It's why the category is so magical—and so profitable. The L'Oreal Group has been a worldwide leader in cosmetics for over a century. It has seventeen global brands within its organization, each with its own distinct personality. I spoke to Edgar Huber, president of L'Oreal about Lancôme, one of the brands in L'Oreal's luxury division. "Lancôme is the French word for beauty," Edgar told me, "and the simple idea behind the brand is what we refer to as 'true beauty.' The Lancôme rose, representative of this true beauty, is one of the most highly recognized brand symbols in the world. Everything we do relative to the brand is done with the objective of expressing the image of true beauty."

I talked to Edgar about Toni's reference to branding in the fashion world being a matter of balancing signals perfectly, the ability to make imperceptible adjustments to convey the brand as an experience, rather than a tangible product. "There are two reasons this is critical with a brand like Lancôme," Edgar said. "First, the idea of true beauty is constantly evolving. You have to stay modern and relevant to make sure you reflect its current meaning. There's a sensitive balance between where you've been and how to reinvent yourself without losing touch with the brand's original meaning. Second, the technology involved in the cosmetics industry is constantly evolving. You have to keep your technological research in alignment with the brand idea. We're constantly recruiting new consumers to the brand, so we must make sure we continuously create a contemporary, relevant experience."

Edgar told me that because Lancôme does not have direct influence over all of the brand's retail venues (specifically department stores), it's essential to ensure that all of the branding signals it does control are true to the brand's core. The packaging, the product research and development, how aestheticians are trained to talk to the customers, the public relations, and the advertising are among the variables Lancôme controls and orchestrates carefully to assure the Lancôme experience is what it should be. Lancôme is in the process of opening its own boutiques worldwide in order to better influence the way consumers interact with and perceive its brand. "We want our brand experience to be 100 percent Lancôme wherever our customers touch the brand," Edgar told me. "The brand idea is about true beauty and we want the emotional expression of this to be clearly identified in everything we do."

Branding in an experiential category is a matter of synchronizing branding signals perfectly in order to get across the intangible, emotional essence of the idea in a seamless way. As Toni said, it's not about any one individual interaction a customer has with the brand, but the experience the branding signals create as a whole that makes it memorable. Here are a few more examples of experiential brands that keep their branding signals perfectly balanced.

An Experience Reflected in a Store: Ann Taylor

You can count on most retailers to carry the current season's fashions just as you can count on them to stay relatively within their price niche, but few retailers remain consistently faithful to their simple brand idea, season in and season out. One such retailer is Ann Taylor, the ubiquitous carrier of classic yet current women's clothing. By staying true to providing high-quality, highly coordinated staples, it has managed, unlike its competition, to attract a broad age and income demographic.

Ann Taylor's appeal is to stylish, busy women, no matter the occasion. "The Ann Taylor brand is like the friend whose advice you can count on. She may not push you beyond your limits, but she often knows what's best for you," noted Joan Bogin, executive director at Landor.

The power behind Ann Taylor's appeal is its retail space and merchandising signals. Upon entering the store, you immediately decipher your "territory," whether you're seeking work wear or weekend casual. Once you've staked out your turf, you're invited to create a personalized look by mixing and matching among color-coordinated, well-cut separates that are classically designed but reflective of the season's trends. Every Ann Taylor store is based on a similar merchandising template. Each is warm and contemporary, aesthetically pleasing, and, most of all, simple to navigate. A busy woman can run into Ann Taylor on a lunch break and come out with a perfectly put together outfit appropriate to whatever occasion she had in mind. The petite section is always in the same place, as are the dressier items, the shoes, and the accessories. This branding signal as retail space conveys that the Ann Taylor brand knows well the challenges busy women face and makes it easier for them to find just what they're looking for.

There are few missteps at an Ann Taylor store, either in its design or in the way it ensures the customer always feels appropriately outfitted. By defining and understanding its relationship with the customer and by staying focused on its brand promise of simple mix-and-match fashion, Ann Taylor has buffered itself against the wild swings in fashion don'ts, the roller-coaster of dress-down, dress-up trends, and provided customers with the one thing many fashion brands can't deliver: self-assurance.

Going back to what Toni said, the success of Ann Taylor is due to its ability to balance all of its branding signals. In much the same way that any woman can go into an Ann Taylor store and put an outfit together, Ann Taylor puts the experience together. The caliber of the fashions, the way they're merchandised, how the windows draw one inside, the Ann Taylor website are all part of the signal balancing act. In fact, the website is structured in much the same way the physical retail space is structured. It offers recommendations for outfit-specific occasions, shows how to mix and match, and provides fashion tips.

Ann Taylor knows what it wants its brand to look like to its customers standing on the shore watching the surfer come to shore (or standing outside the store window looking in). It understands that fashion is not a linear customer journey but a careful balancing act among all branding signals. When it comes to fashion, Ann Taylor coordinates its signals in classic style. The idea behind the brand comes to life most significantly in the stores. Ann Taylor has obviously defined the simple idea and the experience it wants to communicate: We make it pleasant and simple to find what you need to look stylish and beautifully coordinated.

The Experience of a Category Makeover: Sephora

Some female-inspired Seinfeld-like observations on the subject of beauty and cosmetics: Ever wonder why you arrive home from buying makeup in a department store with more than you went in to buy? Ever wonder why you always have to ask the price of something from those commanding ladies behind the glass-enclosed counters? And what's with all that passive-aggressive perfume spritzing as you walk through the aisles? Ever wonder why when you buy makeup in the drugstore the color of the makeup inside the package never matches the color shown on the outside?

Until recently, there were, generally speaking, two ways for women to experience the world of cosmetics. One was the high-end department store, where everything is behind glass-enclosed counters separating you from the products, and for which you do have to ask the price. And then there was the mass-market way, where cosmetic packaging is hung on wall racks and you play a color guessing game. Both customer journeys are without much thought to customers' needs.

Sephora retail stores introduced a third, category-transforming way in which women could experience cosmetics and beauty as they should be experienced. David Suliteanu, president and CEO of Sephora, sums it up like this: "What would happen if you opened up the cosmetics floor and let women play with the products?" Sephora did just that. It broke with the two industry conventions: prestige brands sold at individual brand counters staffed by commissioned representatives in department stores and mass-market brands sold in hard plastic packages with no service component at all. Sephora changed the business model, the category, and the customer journey in one beautiful move. I asked David about the name "Sephora." "It's biblical in origin," he told me, "without any preattached associations. It was up to us to communicate the associations we wanted women to have about us."

"Our simple brand idea is accessibility," David told me. "Everything is accessible, emotionally and physically. The products are accessible, the testers are open and meant to be played with. The service is accessible. Our personnel are there to assist the customer. They don't work on commission and there is zero brand affiliation. Our approach to service is knowledge intensive, not pressurized in any way. If the customer just wants to play, she can play. It she wants to buy, we do everything we can to see that what she buys is just what she wants. Most of the time her basket is filled with products from multiple brands. And our prices are accessible. No customer has to feel the embarrassment of asking a salesperson for the price. Everything is priced where she can see it. We want to make the whole beauty experience both enjoyable and accessible."

I asked David about the challenge of experiential brands, coordinating all the branding signals to create an overall expression. "It was our primary intention to do this, to create a holistic experience for the customer," he said. "Our product lines, the people who work for us, the open design of the store, the service we provide are all coordinated to create the Sephora experience.

"Our product mix is unique in the category. Because the larger cosmetic companies didn't initially want to sell to us, we were forced to discover smaller, more innovative and contemporary brands. It's an important part of the Sephora customer experience. Women know they'll find familiar names here, but also brands they can't find anywhere else—all in one place. The traditional counters at department stores long ago started to follow our accessible approach. We don't think it's the same experience, but I guess when others start to emulate you, you're onto something!"

Sephora is growing rapidly and has nearly a thousand stores worldwide. Its market share has increased exponentially, especially in the United States, and without a lot of traditional marketing. It seems word of mouth and public relations does a fine job endorsing the Sephora name. "From the PR side, we are always in the pages of fashion and beauty publications. It's because what we carry is unique, what we do is innovative. We're seen as a creative force in the industry," David said.

It's obvious that the associations women have about Sephora are exactly what the company had in mind when it developed its business strategy and its brand. The Sephora customer journey is a beautiful coordination of sight and touch and feel. Sephora did an

Sephora revolutionized the customer experience by bringing the products out to play.

extreme makeover of the beauty industry, and customers are happy with the results.

An Experience of a Higher Nature: Virgin Airlines

I mentioned Richard Brandt a few stories back. As an executive creative director at Landor, Richard flies a lot. And he flies Virgin airlines whenever he can. In discussing this book with him, I asked him about the Virgin brand. I struck a very positive chord.

"The only time I like to fly for business is when I fly Virgin airlines. I don't consider this flying in the conventional sense, because it's not. It's not conventional at all. Virgin airlines has done what only the very best brands can do. It's transcended the category."

"Most airlines are okay to good," Richard said. "Virgin has surpassed okay to good. It's not so much about the funky interiors or groovy lounges, but the fact that it has identified the truly miserable parts of flying and fixed them. It's found a way, a hundred ways, to eradicate the tedium of flying. The service is first class from pick up to drop off. On the London side, you're checked in, inside your limo, then your bags are checked, and you're taken right to the fast-lane security check and, from there, to the V.I.P. lounge. It's not a matter of one power signal, but a whole delightful mix of signals coming together into one incredible experience." From what Richard described, Virgin's branding signals communicate attention to detail at 37,000 feet.

When I talked earlier about looking at your enemy brand as a way to take a different position in the market, I used Virgin as an example, with good reason. It saw the enemy as ordinary, mundane, a sin in the mind of Virgin's CEO, Richard Branson. "Let's not be ordinary," Branson declared. "Let's be anything but ordinary." Virgin is, and the signals come together as a way of proving his intention.

Richard (the Landor executive creative director, not the airline's founder), continued with a description of Virgin's on-board branding signals. "The seat is spectacular—more comfortable than the chairs I have at home. The interior is done in shades of magenta and red, with a rhinestone-studded bulkhead. It's very Austin Powers. You eat when you want to eat—it's about meals on demand. The food service is meant to accommodate passengers, not the flight crew."

I asked Richard about typically mundane and compulsory things like safety videos. "Virgin's is not mundane at all. It's intriguing and it's funny," he said. "You *want* to watch it. Which is what you're supposed to do. It conveys all the pertinent information, but instead of using actors who look close to robotic, it's in the form of a cartoon. The characters include a rhinestone cowboy who tells you to take off your shoes when sliding down the chute onto the rubber safety raft, which he demonstrates by showing off his high-heeled boots. Other characters include a hippie kind of dude with a peace sign, a girl with a tank top blowing bubbles with her bubble gum, and a very Super-fly kind of guy. This video is fully approved by the Federal Aviation Administration because it tells you everything you need to know. I think the FAA probably looks forward to the updates.

"When you're ready to sleep, the flight attendants make up your bed which is a flatter, better bed than other airlines offer. It's not like an ordinary airline experience. You can actually sleep."

Virgin airlines has a simple idea—make air travel anything but ordinary—and it doesn't miss a trick in coordinating its branding signals to make good on its idea. The Virgin experience is genuinely and uniquely Virgin's. It's got a clear understanding of the literal and figurative journeys its customers take, and it delivers on both. Yeah, baby.

A Final Word on Branding Signals

A brand can transform the way people see the world. It can change perceptions, preferences, and priorities. A power signal is that expression (or expressions) of your brand that defines and shapes how people see and experience your brand. Beyond the name, successful branding means being able to identify points along the customer journey at which to create powerful, meaningful interactions. More so, it means being able to make these interactions uniquely yours. Doing this takes creativity and focus. Creativity without focus may be interesting, but it's not motivating.

The creation of powerful branding signals requires business-driven thinking and creativity. To create a genuinely powerful power signal, you must clearly understand your business strategy and see that it aligns perfectly with your brand driver—the essence of the idea that drives your brand. You must determine at which points along the customer journey you can most strongly influence customer perception of the brand. It is at these points that you create power signals—the interactions that inspire the associations you want consumers to have about your brand. The associations that get filed in the mental folders labeled with your brand's name.

A brand is in the mind of the consumer. The right branding signals will see that your brand is "saved as" just as you want it to be.

9

Ten Mental Files to "Save As"

When I was teaching, I used to end each semester by giving the class a top-ten list. It distilled, from everything we had talked about over the past months, the ten essential things it would be important to take away from the course. If you take away nothing but these ten key points, you're still better off than you were before you got here. Here is my BrandSimple top ten list:

1. *Understand that brand and branding are different concepts.* The "ing" makes a huge difference in meaning. A brand exists in your mind. It's a collection of associations or feelings people have about a particular product, service, or an organization. Branding is the tangible process of creating the signals that generate these associations.

2. *Establish a differentiated meaning for your brand that the consumers you want to reach care about—find relevant—before you try to begin branding.* Differentiation and relevance—not awareness—make a brand strong and keep it strong. You can't build awareness without having something to build it on. The most successful brands know this.

3. *Know exactly who you want to talk to—that is, know your audience.* Also, know exactly who you want to beat—who your competition is—and make sure the difference between you and the other guy is crystal clear.

4. *To find a different and relevant brand idea, look for the obvious.* The best answers are usually right under your nose.

Good brand people never stop looking for insights, and they know to look in the most obvious places. They read letters from customers, go to call centers, speak to retailers, hang out in supermarket aisles. The key is to find something meaningful that no one has noticed before.

5. *Make sure your brand idea aligns with your business strategy.* What exactly are you selling? Is your brand idea in sync? You can deliver what your brand idea promises to deliver by validating the brand experience at optimal points of customer contact.

6. *Capture the essence of your brand idea in a brand driver—a simple statement of what your brand stands for.* Make sure it's as succinct, as focused, and as compelling as possible. It has to be able to drive your branding signals, brand actions, and brand behavior—intuitively. It's your brand recipe and it has to be simple to follow and remember by heart.

7. *Draw a map of the customer's journey with your brand.* Take everyone in your organization on this journey to give them an understanding of the points of interaction that have the greatest potential to impact people's perceptions of the brand. Doing so also allows them to see how their role in the organization influences customers' perception through the branding signals they bring into being.

8. *Pick your battles.* After you've established which points of customer interaction have the greatest potential to drive consumer perception of your brand idea, invest your branding dollars in these interactions. These are your power branding signals.

9. *Remember, only the paranoid survive.* Make sure you keep your brand difference differentiated, and make sure it's a difference people care about. Always pay attention to your core customers. Don't lose the center.

10. *Remember that brand building is a marathon event.* Success is not a one-time thing. Make sure you have the nerve and the verve for the long haul. Good brands last and there's a reason they do.

10

A Final Simple Thought

For a brand to be successful it must stand for something different, and this difference must be relevant to its users. Most important, this difference and relevance must be simple to understand. The most successful brands today are based on ideas that are not just different and relevant, but simple.

A brand's idea must be simple in order for its branding to be powerful and compelling. The people who are responsible for the branding must be able to understand the brand idea, get it, and deliver on it intuitively. They must be able to make the branding signals memorable, authentic and proprietary to the brand. A brand idea that is simple makes this possible.

A brand must execute and deliver powerful and compelling branding signals because the world is more complex, it's noisier and more complicated than ever before. Consumers are overwhelmed. Information pours over us. Change is relentless. Life is moving fast. There is almost infinite access to data that we're not always sure what to do with. And, "the world," as Thomas Friedman said, "is flat." From China, to India, to Korea, brands compete on a genuinely global scale. More than this, as consumers, we experience brands in all sorts of new ways, across multiple points of interaction. Branding signals must be able to cut through all of this in order to connect, and connect on a gut level. For a brand to succeed today, its branding signals must be breakthrough.

Some brand organizations fail to recognize that they must stand for something different and relevant. Many more brand organizations fail to recognize that this difference and relevance must be simple to understand. I hope this book makes it clear that both steps are essential to breakthrough branding. And that breakthrough branding is essential to being a successful brand. I believed this was important when I began my career more than twenty-five years ago. I believe it is even more important now.

The title of this book, *BrandSimple,* is its brand driver and its brand idea. The book, itself, is the power signal.

If you'd like to find out more about any of the stories in this book, to read more stories, or to share your thoughts on *BrandSimple,* please go to another of my branding signals, www.brandsimple.com.

A Few of the Terms You Need to Know

We're in the business of communication, which means that we'd better know how to communicate clearly with each other and with our clients. To that end, I'd like to end the book on the same simple note on which I started. Here are simple definitions of a few of the key terms I've talked about. I would be less than truthful if I stated that these are all the terms you need to know to be fully articulate on the subject of brands. However, the terms I've included provide a good baseline.

Products	Brands
A product occupies functional territory. It does something.	A brand exists in your head. It stands for something.
A product is based on something tangible. It's bigger, faster, longer lasting.	A brand is based on associations. It makes you feel something.
A product expands choice. "Where do you want to stop for lunch?"	A brand simplifies choice. "Let's go to Subway."
One product can be identical to another. "It comes with earphones."	A brand differentiates. I want the one with white earbuds."

You don't have products in your head, you have brands in your head. Think of the inside of your head as a mental desktop and brands as mental file folders. Click on a brand file, and all the images and expressions associated with the brand are set free. You feel something that will make it easier to determine which brand to choose.

Brand Idea

The simple, differentiated, and relevant meaning you establish for your brand. A brand idea is what a brand stands for in people's minds.

Business Strategy

The plan you have to sell a product or service. How your company makes money.

Brand Strategy

The plan you have to use your brand idea to deliver on your business strategy. A brand strategy necessitates understanding what branding signals will best reinforce your brand idea.

Branding

The process of creating and managing the associations that generate images and feelings about a brand. Associations are transmitted by way of signals. Branding is the process of creating signals that communicate to consumers how your brand is different and relevant.

Branding Signals

The actual expressions of a brand that generate feelings and opinions about it and create the experience of the brand. Anything that is an expression of the idea the brand is trying to convey is a branding signal.

- The name of the brand, colors, taglines, music, and all marketing communications;
- Package design, product functionality, and product design;
- Retail environments, online experiences, websites, customer care;
- The behavior of the people who work for the brand;
- The service a brand provides is a signal;
- Anything that makes you feel something about a brand.

Index